Fun with the Family™ Kentucky

Praise for the *Fun with the Family™* series

"Bound to lead you and your kids to fun-filled days,
those times that help compose the
memories of childhood."

—Dorothy Jordon, *Family Travel Times*

Help Us Keep This Guide Up to Date

Every effort has been made by the author and editors to make this guide as accurate and useful as possible. However, many changes can occur after a guide is published—establishments close, phone numbers change, hiking trails are rerouted, facilities come under new management, etc.

We would love to hear from you concerning your experiences with this guide and how you feel it could be improved and be kept up to date. While we may not be able to respond to all comments and suggestions, we'll take them to heart, and we'll make certain to share them with the author. Please send your comments and suggestions to the following address:

The Globe Pequot Press
Reader Response/Editorial Department
P.O. Box 480
Guilford, CT 06437
Or you may e-mail us at: editorial@GlobePequot.com

Thanks for your input, and happy travels!

INSIDERS' GUIDE®

FUN WITH THE FAMILY™ SERIES

fun WITH the Family™

KENTUCKY

HUNDREDS OF IDEAS FOR DAY TRIPS WITH THE KIDS

TERESA DAY

THIRD EDITION

INSIDERS' GUIDE®

GUILFORD, CONNECTICUT
AN IMPRINT OF THE GLOBE PEQUOT PRESS

The prices, rates, and hours listed in this guidebook were confirmed at press time. We recommend, however, that you call establishments to obtain current information before traveling.

To buy books in quantity for corporate use or incentives, call **(800) 962–0973** or e-mail **premiums@GlobePequot.com.**

Text design by Nancy Freeborn and Linda R. Loiewski
Maps by Rusty Nelson © Morris Book Publishing, LLC
Spot photography throughout © Photodisc and © RubberBall Productions

ISSN 1542-1783
ISBN 978-0-7627-4548-7

Manufactured in the United States of America
Third Edition/First Printing

To Michael, Anthony, and Esta . . . intrepid travelers, all.

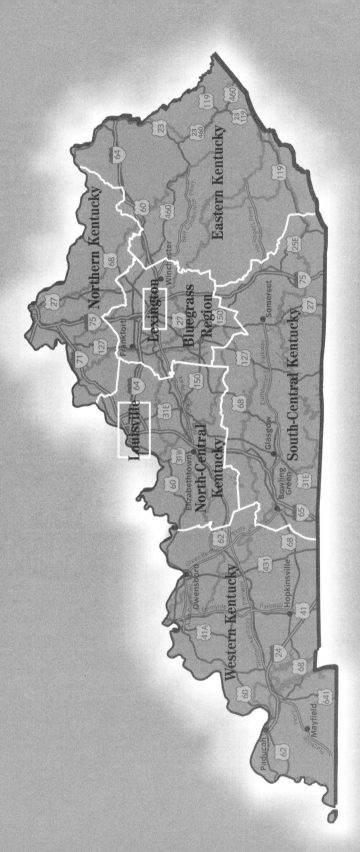

KENTUCKY

Contents

Acknowledgments

Special thanks to Laura Crawford for helping prepare this information. Thanks also to the many friends and colleagues who shared their experiences and suggestions.

Introduction

Kentucky is a wonderful playground for families. With beautiful scenery and abundant recreation areas, a history full of fascinating events and characters, rich cultural traditions, friendly people, and dozens (probably hundreds) of amazing, quirky, and just plain strange attractions, Kentucky can provide your family with enough fun and discovery to last several generations. This book points out some of them, from places my children and I have returned to time and time again to others that I just learned about in the course of doing research.

One of the very best things the state offers families is an excellent system of state parks. If you want to get away, even for a day, you just can't go wrong with a state park. Kentucky has seventeen "resort parks"—one-stop vacation spots with lodging, food, recreation, and special activities—plus thirty-three other "recreational parks" and historic sites, all with many free and affordable activities. When my children were very young, sometimes we'd just drive to a park and visit the playground or have a picnic, and it would be a great day.

This book divides the state into eight areas, two of them cities—there's enough to do in Louisville and Lexington alone for many day trips. Because ideas of "fun" vary widely, I've tried to include a variety of attractions—outdoor, historical, cultural, and recreational. Age appropriateness, too, varies from child to child. I've indicated general guidelines, but the best guideline is your knowledge of your children's interests and abilities.

Price ranges are based on the following guide. Lodging rates are for double occupancy for one night (excluding any taxes or other fees); rates may vary seasonally.

Lodging

$	up to $50
$$	$51 to $75
$$$	$76 to $99
$$$$	$100 and up

Restaurants

$	most entrees under $10
$$	most $10 to $15
$$$	most $16 to $20
$$$$	most over $20

Attractions

free	no charge
$	up to $5 per person
$$	$6 to $10 per person
$$$	$11 to $20 per person
$$$$	over $20 per person

State and local travel departments are great sources for information, and I urge you to use them in planning your trips and while on the road. The local visitor center is usually our first stop. We ask a lot of questions and take an armload of brochures. In addition to the local tourism bureaus mentioned in each chapter, you can get information from the state tourism department by calling (800) 225–8747 or visiting www.kentuckytourism.com.

For state park information, call (800) 255–PARK, or visit www.kystateparks.com. You can make reservations online at http://parks.ky.gov up to a year in advance. Summer and fall weekends tend to fill up the fastest. At press time, the state parks system was offering special Family Adventure Quests, trivia quizzes and scavenger hunts in which families could earn prizes and state park gift certificates; check at the Web site to see if this program is continuing.

Kentucky is a spread-out state—it's more than 400 miles across from west to east—and there are lots of rural and mountainous areas without interstate access. Getting to your destination sometimes means a lengthy trip in the car, so plan accordingly! Take along a small cooler with water and snacks, and pack some survival gear—puzzles, books, drawing paper, and crayons or markers. Make a trip to the library to see if there are any books or CDs relating to what you're going to see. (You'll find lots on such famous Kentuckians as Abraham Lincoln, Daniel Boone, and John James Audubon, as well as on many others whose history you can explore in the state.)

Particularly as your children get older, they'll probably bring their own entertainment, such as video games and iPods, but we try to use at least some of the time in the car to talk, listen to songs or stories together, or make up silly games. This is a great opportunity to get to know your children away from everyday distractions.

Kentucky has an amazing variety of attractions—historic, outdoors, recreational, artistic—and I encourage you to try a little bit of everything when you travel. Traveling together is a great way for parents and grandparents to share their interests with their children and grandchildren (and it's a great way to find out what the kids like), but it's also a wonderful opportunity to learn and explore *together*. So what if you're not an expert on art or classical music? Go to a museum or concert anyway—you may surprise yourself by finding it interesting. Never had much desire to sleep in a tent? Give camping a try; you and your children will discover a whole new world, and maybe new things about yourself, under the stars.

Another suggestion I would make is to avoid the temptation to overschedule, particularly with younger children. A leisurely pace and a flexible attitude will make the trip more enjoyable than getting to see every exhibit at the museum or go on every ride at the amusement park. That advice goes for the traveling part, too—try to allow time for lots of stops. Most of us adults get antsy cooped up in a car for hours, and most children simply can't do it. So leave time to stop at the scenic overlook or intriguing site you see along the way.

As you travel you're sure to find even more things to see and do than are listed in this book; I'd love to hear about them. Make traveling with your children an adventure, and you're sure to make wonderful memories.

My family and I have had a lot of fun in Kentucky, and I hope you and your family will, too.

Attractions Key

The following is a key to the icons found throughout the text.

SWIMMING		FOOD	
BOATING / BOAT TOUR		LODGING	
HISTORIC SITE		CAMPING	
HIKING / WALKING		MUSEUM	
FISHING		PERFORMING ARTS	
BIKING		SPORTS/ATHLETICS	
AMUSEMENT PARK		PICNICKING	
HORSEBACK RIDING		PLAYGROUND	
SKIING/WINTER SPORTS		SHOPPING	
PARK		PLANTS /GARDENS /NATURE TRAILS	
ANIMAL VIEWING		FARM	

Louisville

L ouisville is a good kid-size city—big enough to have a lot to see and do, but not so big that it seems intimidating. People are friendly, and there's an optimistic outlook—it seems like there's always something "new" in the works. In recent years, the new project in Louisville has been exciting redevelopment along the river-front, which has added a new waterfront park, baseball stadium, and state-of-the-art skateboarding park.

Louisville sits along the Ohio River. The city was founded in 1778, when George Rogers Clark arrived with a group of settlers. Clark planned to use the location as a base for his "Northwest Campaign" against the British, but some of the settlers stayed behind. Today Louisville is Kentucky's largest metropolitan area, with about a

Teresa's
TopPicks for Louisville

1. Louisville Zoological Gardens, (502) 459–2181

2. Louisville Science Center, (502) 561–6100

3. The Speed Art Museum and Art Sparks, (502) 634–2700

4. Stage One Children's Theatre, (502) 589–5946

5. Louisville Slugger Museum, (502) 588–7228

6. Muhammad Ali Center, (502) 584–9254

7. Louisville Bats Baseball, (502) 212–BATS

8. Waterfront Park, (502) 574–3768

9. Six Flags Kentucky Kingdom, (502) 366–2231

10. Gheens Science Hall and Rauch Planetarium, (502) 852–6664

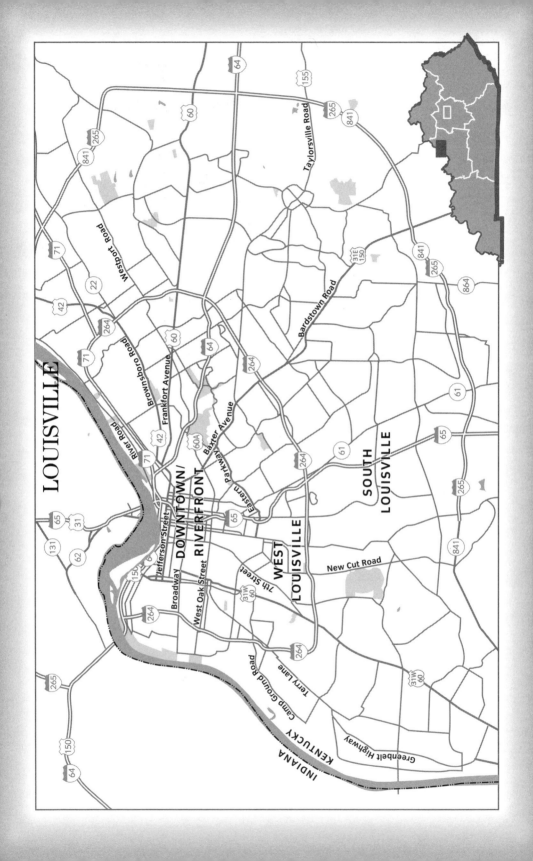

million residents. Distinctive neighborhoods, great parks, and a comfortable pace make it a good place to live (I know; I grew up here). Those same qualities make it a good place to visit.

Another asset for visiting families is the diverse mix of attractions. There's a little bit of a lot of different things going on in Louisville, so whether your interest is sports, the arts, outdoor activities, history, horses, or just taking in the scenery, Louisville can fill the bill.

To help you in getting around, keep in mind that Interstate 64 east-west, Interstate 71 north-south, and Interstate 65 north-south pass through Louisville. Interstate 264 (Watterson Expressway) loops through the city from east to west (with exits to most major thoroughfares), and Interstate 265 (Gene Snyder Freeway) connects the southwestern and northeastern parts of Jefferson County. There are one-way streets in the downtown area, so if you haven't been here before, expect to spend some time circling the block to get where you really want to go. If you get lost, just remember that friendly part: Louisvillians will be happy to give you directions.

Downtown/Riverfront

Waterfront Park (all ages)
129 East River Road; (502) 574–3768, www.louisvillewaterfront.com. Free.

An eighty-five acre recreation and event area with playgrounds (including separate ones for toddlers), scenic pools and fountains, and several miles of bikeways and walking paths, Waterfront Park can be a place to relax before or after seeing other downtown attractions, or a destination in itself. On a typical weekend you might find an antique car show in the parking lot, a benefit concert on the Great Lawn in the amphitheater, and a bevy of kite fliers and Frisbee players in between. Especially popular with youngsters is the huge Adventure Playground, which includes a water play area. The park also includes docks for pleasure boats. In the final phase of development, an abandoned bridge will be converted into a walkway across the Ohio River. All areas are handicapped-accessible.

Wheel Fun Rentals (all ages)
135 East River Road in Waterfront Park; (502) 589–BIKE, www.wheelfunrentals.com. Hours vary seasonally; summer hours are Tuesday through Sunday from 10:00 A.M. to dusk. $–$$$

If you go to Waterfront Park, you will undoubtedly see people riding around jauntily in four-wheel, foot-pedaled vehicles. Be prepared for someone in your crew to plead, "Can we ride one of those, puh-leese?" If you say yes, you can rent one from the folks at Wheel Fun Rentals. They operate out of a little kiosk at the east end of the park and offer the aforementioned "quadcycles," plus tandems, mountain bikes, kids' bikes, and beach cruisers. Expect some sticker shock (up to $24 per hour for the largest quad) and sore thighs. It's harder to pedal than you think, especially if you're the only one who can reach the pedals. Yet, if gigantic smiles and whoops of glee are any measure, most riders seem to find the trip worth the expenditure of cash and muscle.

Muhammad Ali Center (ages 4 and up)

144 North Sixth Street; (502) 584–9254, www.alicenter.org. Open Monday through Saturday from 9:30 A.M. to 5:00 P.M., Sunday from noon to 5:00 P.M. Closed major holidays and Kentucky Derby Day (first Saturday in May). Adults $$, children 6–12 $, ages 5 and under free. Parking is available in a garage under the center.

The goal of this museum/educational center is to inspire greatness within every child through the life and ideals of the athlete known as "The Greatest," boxer Muhammad Ali, a Louisville native. Exhibits not only explore Ali's life and career but also focus on his values—respect, confidence, conviction, dedication, spirituality, and giving. The result is an innovative and moving combination of activities, some focused on Ali and boxing (you can watch a film about his life, view boxing artifacts, and try your hand at shadow boxing in a mock training ring), others designed to elicit self-discovery (interactive exhibits in the Walk with Ali guide visitors in identifying their strengths and setting life goals). Artwork, poems, and written messages from children around the world also are on exhibit. The Web site includes a "Cultural Buzz" section especially for children, with activities ranging from mask-painting to quizzes relating to diversity and equal rights.

Louisville Bats Baseball (all ages)

401 East Main Street; (502) 212–BATS, www.batsbaseball.com. Season opens early April and runs through early September. Game times vary. $–$$, parking ($) available next to the stadium. Tours given Monday through Friday from 9:00 A.M. to 4:00 P.M.; call to arrange. $

The Louisville Bats, a Cincinnati Reds affiliate team, take on other AAA competitors in Louisville Slugger Field, a 13,000-seat stadium near the riverfront. There's not a bad seat in the house—especially if you're a youngster. You're close to the action, so bring your glove. In addition to watching the game, kids can ride the merry-go-round, hang out at the jungle gyms, get their faces painted, and be entertained by an assortment of costumed characters including Jake the Diamond Dog, Birdzerk, and Buddy Bat. Picnic areas abound, whether you bring your own snacks or buy hot dogs, sodas, and pizza slices on site. Kids twelve and under can join the Knothole Gang ($) and get a free T-shirt, e-mail newsletters, a discount on admission to Sunday games, and an invitation to a meet-and-greet the players event. And if the whole family would like a behind-the-scenes look, schedule a Louisville Slugger Field tour, which includes the dugout, the clubhouse, a luxury suite, the press box, and the operations room; call for reservations at least one week before you would like to tour.

Louisville Extreme Park (all ages)

Witherspoon and Clay Streets, near Louisville Slugger Field; (502) 456–8100, www .louisvilleextremepark.org. Open daily, twenty-four hours. Free. No rentals available.

If you want to convince your kids that you're still cool, lead an expedition to Extreme Sports Park (just don't call it "gnarly" or you'll blow it). Louisville's state-of-the-art "X-park" features 40,000 square feet of bowls, pipes, ramps, and rails, and is already drawing rave reviews from extreme bikers, bladers, and skateboarders around the country. Areas are color-coded by difficulty level, but for most of us, just watching these stunts will be extreme enough. The park's long-range plan calls for the addition of indoor skate areas.

Stage One Children's Theatre (ages 4 and up)

501 West Main Street; (800) 989–5946 or (502) 589–5946, www.stageone.org. The season runs fall through spring. Public performances are usually on Saturdays (times vary) at the Kentucky Center for the Arts, 5 Riverfront Plaza. $$$

Louisville's oldest theater company caters to the youngest patrons. Stage One, a professional company, brings adventure yarns, classic fairy tales, fantasy stories, and thought-provoking contemporary dramas to life onstage. Plays are geared to a variety of age groups, from participatory drama for ages four to seven to plays for young teens that deal with complex moral and ethical issues. A recent season included *The Legend of Sleepy Hollow, Dr. Seuss's Green Eggs and Ham, Hansel and Gretel, Jemima Boone,* and *Dream,* a drama about Dr. Martin Luther King Jr. High quality and highly entertaining, Stage One is an excellent place to introduce your children to live theater.

The Kentucky Center (all ages)

5 Riverfront Plaza (Fifth and Main Streets); (502) 562–0100 for show schedule, (502) 562–0187 for tour reservations, (502) 584–7777 for tickets, www.kentuckycenter.org. Performance tickets $$$–$$$$, tours $.

At the heart of Louisville's performing arts scene since its star-studded opening in 1983, the Kentucky Center is host to performances ranging from touring Broadway shows to concerts and speeches. A tour of the center's three performing halls and some behind-the-scenes areas can be scheduled in advance (call at least a week before you want to visit) and is geared to the age group of participants. You can check out the fascinating twentieth-century paintings and sculptures found inside and outdoors anytime, free.

Amazing
Kentucky Fact

Superstar actor Tom Cruise, originally Thomas Cruise Mapother IV, went to high school at St. Xavier High School in Louisville.

Actors Theatre of Louisville (ages 6 and up)
316 West Main Street; (502) 584–1265 or (800) 4ATL–TIX, www.actorstheatre.org. $$$–$$$$

Most of the productions by this nationally acclaimed theater company are geared to adult audiences, with a few notable exceptions. Older children may enjoy ATL's spine-tingling version of *Dracula* performed throughout the month of October. Even five- and six-year-olds will enjoy the annual production of Charles Dickens's *A Christmas Carol.* For these two holiday productions, order tickets well in advance since many performances sell out.

Louisville Orchestra (ages 3 and up)
300 West Main Street; (502) 587–8681, www.louisvilleorchestra.org. Dates and location depend upon concert series. $$–$$$$

In addition to its venerable Masterworks series for general audiences, which is performed at the Kentucky Center, Louisville's excellent orchestra offers special performance series for young music lovers. There are several Saturday OrKIDStra performances between September and May at the Brown Theatre. In July, the orchestra performs its Roarchestra series at the Louisville Zoo. These concerts combine music with lively activities; past performances have featured everything from whistling to a petting zoo. Older children might also enjoy the Nightlites performances, which feature light classical music and are performed at The Louisville Palace theater on Fourth Avenue.

More for **Sports Fans**

University of Louisville football games are played at Cardinal Stadium, a 42,000-seat stadium near the campus in South Louisville. The **U of L basketball** team (coached by Rick Pitino, former University of Kentucky and Boston Celtics coach) plays at Freedom Hall at the Kentucky Fair and Exposition Center. For ticket info about both, call (502) 852–5863.

Belvedere/Riverfront Plaza (all ages)

Riverfront between Fourth and Sixth Streets. Free.

This eight-acre plaza is a good place to view the river. You'll see motorboats, huge barges, and a giant clock across the river in southern Indiana. The clock at the Colgate-Palmolive Plant is the second largest in the world. The Belvedere often is the site of concerts and special events.

Belle of Louisville/Spirit of Jefferson (all ages)

401 West River Road (end of Fourth Street); (502) 574–2992, www.belleoflouisville.org. $$$, children $$.

A bevy of river cruise types and times are offered aboard the *Belle,* an authentic 1914 sternwheeler with whimsical calliope, and the newer *Spirit,* built in 1962 to look like a vintage riverboat. Most sightseeing cruises last a couple of hours and include a narrated presentation about Louisville history and river lore. The *Belle of Louisville* operates from Memorial Day through Labor Day, with additional special cruises in September and October. Although the *Belle* has some indoor seating, keep in mind that the old gal does not have air-conditioning, and a two-hour cruise on a steamy steamboat might be difficult for young children. The more updated (and air-conditioned) *Spirit of Jefferson* cruises year-round. Both boats have onboard concessions and restrooms.

Louisville Science Center and IMAX Theatre (all ages)

727 West Main Street; (502) 561–6100 or (800) 591–2203, www.louisvillescience.org. Open year-round Monday to Thursday from 9:30 A.M. to 5:00 P.M., Friday and Saturday from 9:30 A.M. to 9:00 P.M., Sunday from noon to 6:00 P.M. $$, check into the museum/IMAX combo ticket.

Here's more than 40,000 square feet of science and natural history exploration and fun, housed in a beautiful old cast-iron-front nineteenth-century warehouse building. Permanent exhibits include the highly interactive The World Within Us, which lets children see how they will look in thirty years, exercise with a skeleton, and explore body systems at work; The World Around Us, which focuses on natural sciences; and The World We Create, which challenges youngsters to build and invent. There's also a space gallery with a replica of an Apollo space capsule, bubble activities, Kentucky's largest indoor climbing wall, and the action-packed IMAX Theatre. If your children are seven or under, be sure to reserve a forty-five-minute session in Kid-Zone (no additional charge, but ticket required). KidZone is the playroom of your dreams—a huge water play area, dramatic and dress-up play areas, and creative building areas—with no way for your child to escape. (Your kids will love it too.) Don't be late for your session, though, or you may find yourself looking through a locked door with a very sad child.

A Little **Too Much Adventure**

Older children and adults love the IMAX film experience for its big, loud, "in your face" action. But before you take younger children, consider whether it might all seem a little too real for comfort. A friend took her nearly three-year-old son to see an IMAX film about elephants, thinking he would love it because he was obsessed with elephants. But when the huge beasts came thundering forward on the screen he was terrified—and for several years he refused to go to movies of any kind.

Louisville Slugger Museum (all ages)
800 West Main Street; (502) 588–7228 or (877) 775–8443, www.sluggermuseum.org. Open Monday to Saturday from 9:00 A.M. to 5:00 P.M., Sunday from noon to 5:00 P.M. Last tour begins at 4:00 P.M., so get there by 3:30 P.M. $$, children 6 to 12 $, children 5 and under free.

Any youngster who watches or plays baseball has heard of Louisville Slugger bats, and here's a chance to see how they're made. By the way, although the company started in Louisville in 1884, for a while "Louisville" Sluggers were actually made in southern Indiana. In the 1990s, the Hillerich & Bradsby Company came back to Louisville in a BIG way. How big? Well, there's a 120-foot-tall, 68,000-pound bat leaning against the building that houses this combination museum/manufacturing facility. Plus there's a giant baseball glove holding a ball carved out of a fifteen-ton piece of limestone. Inside, exhibits honor the game's big stars and big plays. The ninety-minute tour begins with a moving film, *The Heart of the Game,* and includes visiting the "Ballfield," where you can sit in a dugout and step up to a virtual plate to get a sense of what it feels like to have a ball heading your way at 90 miles per hour. There are also recordings of the calls of actual famous plays, and bats used by big leaguers such as Babe Ruth and Hank Aaron are on display. A walk through a white ash "forest" leads to the bat-making factory. Go during the week to see it all: There's no bat production on Sundays and holidays or on Saturdays from December to March. At the start of the tour, you can order a miniature bat with your child's (or your) name engraved on it; it will be waiting for you at the end of the tour.

Amazing
Kentucky Fact

The song "Happy Birthday to You" was written by Louisvillians Patty and Mildred Hill. It was originally called "Good Morning to You."

Glassworks (ages 6 and up)

815 West Market Street; (502) 584–4510, www.louisvilleglassworks.com. Self-guided tours Monday to Friday from 10:00 A.M. to 4:00 P.M., guided tours Saturday at 10:00 A.M., 11:00 A.M., 1:00 P.M., and 2:00 P.M. Opens at 11:00 A.M. in winter. Guided tours $$, self-guided tours $.

Learn how three kinds of glass are made at this beautiful combination gallery and workshop. The tour begins with a short video, *Transformed by Light,* then takes you through the three departments—the Frameworks area, where glass is melted and sculpted; the Architectural Glass area, where stained glass is made; and the Hot Shop, where glass is hand blown. If you aren't too nervous at the thought of your children in a confined location with lots of fragile, expensive glass, take a few minutes to visit the gift shop. And be sure to check out the special do-it-yourself events, offered at various times of the year, at which you and your children can blow your own sun disk or holiday ornament ($$$$).

Falls of the Ohio Interpretive Center and Park (all ages)

201 West Riverside Drive, Clarksville, IN; (812) 280–9970 (if calling from Louisville, area code not needed), www.fallsoftheohio.org. Open year-round, Monday to Saturday from 9:00 A.M. to 5:00 P.M., Sunday from 1:00 to 5:00 P.M. $. Take the Second Street Bridge from downtown Louisville.

Yes, technically, this attraction is in Indiana, but it would be a shame to be this close and not take advantage of the opportunity to go back in time 360 million years. Back then, the Louisville area was at the bottom of an inland sea; when the water receded, it left behind the fossils of hundreds of different plants and animals. This is, in fact, the world's largest exposed fossil bed from the Devonian period. The best time to visit is August through October, when the river is at its lowest level. The Interpretive Center offers a stirring laser disc presentation and an eclectic assortment of exhibits related to the history of the Falls of the Ohio, most notably a life-size diorama depicting area inhabitants through the ages (with the main attraction being a 20-foot mammoth skeleton replica). There's also a Lewis and Clark exhibit and hands-on activities such as building a bridge with Styrofoam blocks and making fossil rubbings.

Cathedral of the Assumption (ages 7 and up)

433 South Fifth Street; (502) 583–3100 or (502) 582–2971, www.cathedralofthe assumption.org. Open Monday to Saturday from 10:30 A.M. to 4:30 P.M. Free.

Children and adults will be in awe looking at the 8,000 twenty-four-karat gold-leaf stars on the ceiling, the ornate columns, and vaulted ceilings of this beautiful Catholic cathedral, one of the oldest in the United States in continuous use. But the Cathedral of the Assumption offers much more than a history lesson in church architecture. It has become a vibrant center celebrating spirituality and interfaith understanding. Visit the Spiritual Art Gallery, which exhibits art from diverse spiritual perspectives across cultures, and the Inspiration Gift Shop, where you're as likely to find a Buddha statue as a crucifix. Or attend one of the many concerts or lectures offered.

Trolley **Hoppin'**

The Toonerville II Trolley is a fun and **free** way to get around downtown Louisville. Trolleys run from the riverfront to Broadway approximately every twelve minutes between 9:00 A.M. and 6:30 P.M. Monday to Saturday, with stops at major hotels and other attractions (call 502–585–1234 for route information). These reproduction trolley buses honor Louisville's historic trolley system and are named for the comic strip trolley made famous in the early 1900s by Louisvillian Fontaine Fox Jr.

Frazier International History Museum (ages 8 and up)

Corner of Ninth and Main Streets; (866) 886–7103 or (502) 412–2280, www.frazier museum.org. Open Monday to Saturday from 9:00 A.M. to 5:00 P.M., Sunday from 1:00 to 5:00 P.M. $$, children under 5 $.

A look at history, artistry, and social and technological development through weaponry, this 2004 addition to Louisville features an impressive collection of artifacts ranging from George Washington's long rifle and Geronimo's bow and arrows to a full suit of armor belonging to Henry VIII. Exhibits combine the collection of Louisvillian Owsley Brown Frazier with a museum-within-a-museum of artifacts on loan from Britain's Royal Armouries (an unprecedented arrangement that required an act of British Parliament). Three floors encompassing some 74,000 square feet of exhibit and activity space include reenactment areas, life-size tableaux, and costumed interpreters along with cases and cases of rare and representative rifles, pistols, swords, daggers, lances, pikes, and other weapons and items relating to American, Kentucky, and Louisville history.

South Louisville

Leave the downtown area via Third Street. You'll pass beautiful Victorian mansions in Old Louisville and find yourself at the University of Louisville campus, location of two popular family attractions.

The Speed Art Museum and Art Sparks (all ages)

2035 South Third Street; (502) 634–2700, www.speedmuseum.org. Open Tuesday, Wednesday, and Friday from 10:30 A.M. to 4:00 P.M., Thursday from 10:30 A.M. to 8:00 P.M., Saturday from 10:30 A.M. to 5:00 P.M., Sunday from noon to 5:00 P.M. Closed Monday. Permanent exhibits free; Art Sparks Interactive Gallery $.

This is a great place for children and parents to enjoy art and explore their own creativity together. No stuffy museum atmosphere here! Throughout the museum you'll see Trading Cards with suggested activities to go along with works of art, especially for Family Tours, which usually are on Saturdays and offer guided experiences geared to children. Family First Days, held one Saturday a month, feature a variety of hands-on activities and sometimes special tour guides such as artists, musicians, dancers, or magicians. And then there's Art Sparks, a special area just for children and parents. Activities range from high-tech explorations such as Kiddy Face—a touch-screen computer program that allows children to explore shapes and colors by manipulating images of works in the collection—to quiet reading space inside a copper tepee. A hands-on art room allows young artists to create their own masterpieces, from masks to self-portraits, and there's an area especially for the five-and-under set, called Planet Preschool. The museum's collections are diverse—everything from antiquities and African and Native American art to a complete room from an English Tudor mansion to "old masters" and contemporary works—and many family activities are designed to enhance the enjoyment and understanding of the exhibits.

Gheens Science Hall and Rauch Planetarium (all ages)

108 West Brandeis Avenue, on the University of Louisville campus; (502) 852–6664, www.louisville.edu/planetarium. Closed Sunday. Afternoon and evening traditional programs Monday to Saturday. Several laser shows each Friday night. Hands-on astronomy shows the first Saturday of each month. Adults $$, children $.

Some very cool laser and rock music shows and a lively schedule of traditional and educational programs are offered at this updated planetarium. Its Spitz projection system fills the "sky" with more than 4,000 stars, planets, and other celestial objects, while the 15,000-watt sound system fills your ears with music. Saturday morning shows are geared to ages three to eight and use animal characters, puzzles, and games to introduce astronomy. Monthly "Skies over Louisville" shows offer practical guides to local stargazing. "The Tonight Show," the first Saturday of each month, combines a planetarium show with viewing through telescopes (weather permitting). The Friday night laser shows (hourly shows from 8:00 to 11:00 P.M.), for older children and adults, combine star programs with hot music. *NOTE:* Children under age five not admitted to evening laser shows.

Amazing
Kentucky Fact

Only New York City has more cast-iron storefronts than Louisville's Main Street.

Amazing
Kentucky Fact

Derby Pie, created by the Kerns Family of Louisville, is the world's only trademarked pie. You can try this delectable concoction of chocolate, sugar, and nuts (the actual recipe is secret) at many local restaurants. If the menu doesn't say Derby Pie, but something similar, like Famous Horserace Pie or Winners Circle Pie, they're serving an impostor.

Kentucky Derby Museum/Churchill Downs (all ages)

704 Central Avenue; (502) 637–7079, www.derbymuseum.org. March 15 to November 30, Monday to Saturday from 8:00 A.M. to 5:00 P.M., Sunday from noon to 5:00 P.M. Opens at 9:00 A.M. Monday to Saturday December through mid-March. Closed Christmas Day and Kentucky Oaks and Derby Days (first Friday and Saturday in May). Backside tours begin at 7:00 A.M. Monday to Saturday and at 12:30 P.M. on Sunday. $$, children 4 and under free.

Louisville's most famous event is the Kentucky Derby horse race, always run the first Saturday in May and held since 1875. But you can experience the heritage and excitement of the race every day at this museum adjacent to Churchill Downs race track. Youngsters will enjoy climbing aboard a scale model "racehorse" for a jockey's-eye view and meeting the resident Thoroughbred and his pony friend out back. Many exhibits are interactive, and the 360-degree video presentation that takes you from foal to finish line is impressive. As for the real race, Derby Day, when some 160,000 throng the historic track, is probably not the best time to take young children to the races. Many who go this day don't even see a horse; it's all for the party. Choose another day in the spring (May through July) or fall race meets (November) for a more relaxed time with better seating. Ask about the special children's activities and Junior Jockey Club. For more information about the races, call Churchill Downs at (502) 636–4400, or visit www.churchilldowns.com.

Kentucky Derby Festival (all ages)

Early April through first Saturday in May. Locations around town; (502) 584–6383, www.kdf.org. Many events free.

The Kentucky Derby isn't just a horse race—it's nearly a month of festivities all over Louisville. There are free concerts, an outdoor "chuckwagon" for food, contests, big fireworks, a hot air balloon race and several people races, and on and on. For many, the festival is even more enjoyable than the race. Some of the major events of interest to families are as follows.

Thunder over Louisville takes place in mid–late April at the riverfront. The world's largest fireworks show, this is twenty-eight minutes of intense and incredible pyrotechnics. People watch from Waterfront Park, Bats Stadium, even from boats on the Ohio River. The **Hot Air Balloon Race** takes place in late April. Balloons take off from Kentucky Fair and Exposition Center. The **Great Steamboat Race** is held the Wednesday before the derby. Boat tickets are available, or join the party on shore at the riverfront. The **Pegasus Parade** occurs on the Thursday before the derby. The parade runs along Broadway in downtown Louisville.

Iroquois Park (all ages)

Taylor Boulevard and Southern Parkway; (502) 456–8100. Park open from 6:00 A.M. to midnight daily. Park admission free.

This lushly forested 739-acre park is perhaps best known for Iroquois Hill, traversed by hiking trails that lead to scenic overlooks at the top. The park's outdoor amphitheater is the stage for concerts and plays in the summer months. In July folk music fills the amphitheater.

Little Loomhouse (ages 8 and up)

328 Kenwood Hill Road (near Iroquois Park); (502) 367–4792, www.littleloomhouse.org. Open Tuesday to Thursday and the third Saturday of each month from 10:00 A.M. to 3:30 P.M. $

Have your children ever made woven pot holders or interlaced strips of colored paper to make "woven" pictures? If so, they'll enjoy seeing the master weaving on big looms at these three rustic board-and-batten cabins atop a hill in south Louisville. The Little Loomhouse is the legacy of master weaver Lou Tate, who dedicated her life to preserving the traditional craft of hand-weaving. During the tour you'll see hand-spinners and weavers at work, as well as their beautiful finished coverlets and crafts.

Louisville Zoological Gardens (all ages)

1100 Trevilian Way; (502) 459–2181, www.louisvillezoo.org. Open daily from 10:00 A.M. to 5:00 P.M. April through Labor Day, closes at 4:00 P.M. September through March. In summer, the zoo may stay open later some days. $$, children 2 and under free. Easily accessible from I–264 (Watterson Expressway); take exit 14 and follow the black-and-white signs.

Spacious, attractive, and always adding something new, the zoo has been a perennial favorite of my children since they were preschoolers. Home to more than 1,300 animals, from roaming peacocks to polar bears and penguins, the environments are naturalistic and innovatively designed. For example, the four-acre

Gorilla Forest leads you through a dense forested area, then puts you right in the middle of a circular habitat. You're eye to eye with a troop of lowland gorillas, separated only by glass. Younger children especially will enjoy the African Village petting zoo. My family has always liked the polar bear exhibit. And the HerpAquarium. And the antique carousel. And . . . The list goes on and on. A visit involves a lot of walking, so wear comfortable shoes and think strategy: Gauge your group's stamina, and make plans to turn around before everyone is pooped. (Even if you think your toddler has outgrown the stroller, you may want to bring it.) The best times to go are March through June and September through November, when it's not too hot or cold and the animals are most active. The zoo sponsors many enjoyable special events, including the World's Largest Halloween Party, Breakfast with Santa, Summer Camps and Safaris, and Louisville "Roarchestra" concerts. The new Glacier Run Splash Park, open in summer months, is a great place to cool off and take a break during your visit. This area, with slides, small boats, a geyser, and other water play is included in zoo admission, and there are special activities for toddlers. The seals and sea lions exhibit is in the center of Glacier Run, and an overhead chute allows the zoo's polar bears to move from one side of the exhibit to the other.

Louisville Nature Center/Beargrass Creek State Nature Preserve
(all ages)

3745 Illinois Avenue (across from the Louisville Zoo); (502) 458–1328, www.louisville naturecenter.org. Open from 9:00 A.M. to 5:00 P.M. Tuesday to Saturday. Free.

With over 180 species of trees, shrubs, and flowering plants, and 150 species of resident and migratory birds, Beargrass Creek State Nature Preserve calls out to the overwhelmed urban dweller in need of a sanctuary. The Louisville Nature Center serves as a gateway to this secluded getaway and sponsors many classes and camps throughout the year. Kids love the "bird blind," a small building with one-way glass and audio equipment from which visitors can view birds in their natural habitat. When heading for the trails, be sure to grab a map from the Nature Center, or bring a bag of popcorn to mark your trail—one family we know wandered around in circles for an hour.

Amazing
Kentucky Fact

Louisville's Cherokee, Iroquois, and Shawnee Parks are considered among the finest in the United States and were designed by Frederick Law Olmsted, father of American landscape architecture and designer of New York's Central Park.

Six Flags Kentucky Kingdom (all ages)

Watterson Expressway (I–264) adjacent to the fairgrounds and across from Louisville International Airport; (502) 366–2231, www.sixflags .com. Open from 11:00 A.M. to 10:00 P.M. in summer, weekends only in spring and fall. Splashwater Kingdom is open from 11:00 A.M. to 7:00 P.M. seasonally. $$$$, children 48 inches or less $$$, children under 3 and adults 65 and over free.

If your family thrives on amusement parks, you'll find plenty of stomach-churning action at this medium-size "kingdom." The roster includes the Deluge, a water coaster; a suspended looping coaster called T2; two wicked wooden coasters called the Twisted Twins; and the monstrous 4,155-foot Chang, on which riders stand. Many of the super-thrill rides have minimum height requirements of 48 to 56 inches, but there's plenty for shorter or less adventurous fun-seekers to do as well. Looney Tunes Movie Town has rides named for cartoon characters. The Splashwater Kingdom Water Park has, in addition to the Deluge coaster, a six-story water funnel, water slides, and a huge wave pool. A limited number of Flash Passes ($$) are available each day; these allow you to reserve a ride time on some of the most popular rides. If you plan to visit more than once a season, check into the season pass (less expensive than two admissions and offers unlimited admission during a season). Be sure to pack sunscreen. And measure your child's height before going. You don't want to stand in line two hours for a ride only to find out he or she's an inch or two shy.

Cherokee Park (all ages)

Between Eastern Parkway and Lexington and Cherokee Roads; (502) 456–8100. Park open from 6:00 A.M. to midnight daily. Free.

Louisvillians' favorite greenspace, Cherokee Park, with its trails and paths, rock bridges and steps, and towering trees, is a vision of natural beauty—and a place to have a lot of fun. The centerpiece of the park is a 2 ⁹⁄₁₀-mile scenic loop in which auto traffic is routed one way and the other half of the road is reserved for pedestrians. On a beautiful day, the loop is a sea of runners, walkers, bike riders, and in-line skaters. At the top of one hill is Hogan's Fountain, with picnic areas, playgrounds, and a fountain where kids can cool off in summer (bring water shoes or flip-flops). In summer months, many families hold reunions and parties here. The other major hill (Hill Number One to some, Dog Hill to others) has long been a gathering spot for dogs and their people, as well as a favorite kite-flying area. Take a few minutes to drive through Cherokee Park, and you'll see one reason Louisvillians love their city.

Farmington (ages 8 and up)

3033 Bardstown Road; (502) 452–9920, www.historicfarmington.org (Web site includes virtual tour). Open Tuesday to Saturday from 10:00 A.M. to 4:30 P.M., Sunday from 1:30 to 4:30 P.M. $, children under 6 free. Guided tours on the hour (half hour on Sunday).

Abraham Lincoln slept here. He really did. In fact, he stayed here for six weeks, visiting his good friend Judge John Speed, the original owner of this early nineteenth-century home. It was once the center of a 522-acre hemp plantation; today it's tucked amid subdivisions and the city's expressway. Take the guided tour and you'll learn lots of interesting tidbits about the Speeds and their eleven children (even what the youngsters thought of Lincoln's table manners). The house itself is something of a curiosity, with two octagonal rooms, a "hidden staircase," and some mystery doors. Some of the rooms include children's items such as dolls, toys–even an antique baby walker. At no charge you can take a self-guided tour of the grounds. Farmington holds special events at which kids can try their hand at nineteenth-century games, and the gift shop includes inexpensive games and booklets about the life of children in early America.

Stoneware Stops

Louisville has two historic stoneware companies where you can not only shop for delightful hand-painted dishes but also take a tour and see how they're made. Children will enjoy these tours because both companies make much more than dishes—everything from mugs to birdhouses. It's also interesting to see how something can come out of playing with dirt. These tours are best for ages six and up.

Hadley Pottery, 1570 Story Avenue (near American Printing House for the Blind), (502) 584–2171, has been making its whimsical hand-painted stoneware since the 1940s. On free tours Monday through Friday at 2:00 P.M. you'll learn about the special single-firing process. There's no air-conditioning, so tours may not be offered on extremely hot days.

Louisville Stoneware, 731 Brent Street (off East Broadway near Barret), (502) 582–1900, is even older—the company started in 1815. Free tours are offered at 10:30 A.M. and 1:30 P.M. Monday to Saturday, where you'll see the process from raw clay to finished product. There's also a paint-your-own pottery area where your children can decorate a piece of pottery for a fee. Be sure your child understands that the piece won't be ready for a few days. And if you're not going to be in town that long, you'll need to arrange for it to be shipped to you. There's also a small museum of pottery making.

Amazing
Kentucky Fact

Thomas Edison introduced his incandescent lightbulb at Louisville's
Southern Exposition in 1883.

Thomas Edison House (ages 5 and up)
729–31 East Washington Street; (502) 585–5247, www.edisonhouse.org. Open Tuesday to Saturday from 10:00 A.M. to 2:00 P.M. $, children under 6 free.

Thomas Edison's Louisville story is a good demonstration that success isn't always instant. When Edison lived in Louisville, in 1866 and 1867, he worked as a Western Union telegraph operator and tinkered with inventions in his spare time. He supposedly got fired when acid from one of his experiments ate through the floor and dripped onto his boss's desk on the floor below. A number of Edison's inventions are on display here, including a Dictaphone, an early movie camera, and a large collection of lightbulbs. Edison lived in the front room of this house for only a couple of years, but exhibits cover his life's work, from the inventions that really caught on—such as the phonograph and lightbulb—to those you may not have heard of, such as the "Power Nap," Edison's answer to finding more hours in the day. You can also listen to early recordings and try your hand at sending a message in Morse code via telegraph.

American Printing House for the Blind (ages 9 and up)
1839 Frankfort Avenue; (800) 223–1839 or (502) 895–2405, www.aph.org. Factory tours offered Monday to Thursday, except holidays, at 10:00 A.M. and 2:00 P.M. Museum hours are 8:30 A.M. to 4:30 P.M. Monday to Friday and 10:00 A.M. to 3:00 P.M. Saturday. Free; donations appreciated.

Did you know that the first braille book was printed in France in 1786? It's one of the items on display in this museum devoted to the history of visual aids. There's also a Bible belonging to Helen Keller, tactile maps and globes, and various other devices that have been used to help vision-impaired people. Your children will enjoy trying to read and write braille, they'll get a sense of some of the challenges of being visually impaired, and they'll learn about the history of one of the oldest and largest braille printing companies. Guided tours of the manufacturing facility show how braille and talking books are made; you're urged to watch your children carefully during the tour, though, since this is a working factory.

More **Historic Houses**

- **Brennan House,** 631 South Fifth Street; (502) 540–5145. Victorian mansion and doctor's office.

- **Conrad/Caldwell House,** 1402 St. James Court; (502) 636–5023. Elegant Romanesque Revival house in Old Louisville.

- **Whitehall,** 3110 Lexington Road; (502) 897–2944. Antebellum-style house with formal Florentine garden.

Locust Grove Historic Site (ages 6 and up)

561 Blankenbaker Lane; (502) 897–9845, www.locustgrove.org. House tour offered Monday to Saturday from 10:00 A.M. to 4:30 P.M., Sunday from 1:00 to 4:30 P.M.; last tour at 3:30 P.M. $, children 6 to 12 half price.

Locust Grove was the last home of General George Rogers Clark, the founder of Louisville. An introductory video explains Clark's and the home's historic significance, and guided tours highlight the features of this stately Georgian-style home. The fifty-five-acre setting also offers room to run.

West Louisville

Portland Museum (all ages)

2308 Portland Avenue; (502) 776–7678. Open Tuesday to Friday from 10:00 A.M. to 4:30 P.M. $. From downtown, take I–64 west. Exit onto Twenty-second Street, and turn right onto Portland Avenue.

Louisville's west-end Portland neighborhood was once a separate city, settled in 1814 by French immigrants. This interesting little museum delivers Portland history and river history via a sound-and-light show featuring animatronic figures representing such characters as naturalist John James Audubon and Mary Miller, the first female riverboat pilot. There are also videos of the 1937 flood, the worst in Louisville history, as well as videos made by and featuring children.

Louisville Outskirts

Riverside, the Farnsley-Moremen Landing (all ages)

7410 Moorman Road; (502) 935–6809, www.riverside-landing.org. Open Tuesday to Saturday from 10:00 A.M. to 4:30 P.M., Sunday from 1:00 to 4:30 P.M. Tours every hour on the half hour beginning at 10:30 A.M. Last tour 3:30 P.M. $, children 5 and under free. To get there, take I–65 south to I–265 west; go 10 miles to flashing yellow light. Make a left on Lower River Road. Turn right at the sign for Riverside.

Located in far southwestern Jefferson County, this historic house and property offer a view of farm life along the Ohio River during the nineteenth century, when the river was the center of commerce and travel. Besides the spectacularly restored brick house, Riverside includes a nineteenth-century detached kitchen, a kitchen garden where vegetables and herbs of the original era are grown, and an active boat ramp. In late spring or early autumn you may see an ongoing excavation in progress as archaeologists are digging for the remains of former outbuildings. Riverboat cruises on the *Spirit of Jefferson* leave from the landing July through October, but not every day, so call (502) 574–2992 before you promise anyone a boat ride.

Henry's Ark (all ages)

7801 Rose Island Road; (502) 228–0746. Open 10:00 A.M. to 6:00 P.M. Tuesday to Sunday; hours may vary seasonally. Free; donations appreciated. Off Route 42 near Jefferson–Oldham County line.

No, your eyes aren't deceiving you; that is an emu in the parking lot. Henry's Ark began as a family menagerie, gradually evolved into a refuge for displaced and neglected animals, and along the way became a popular tourist destination. Over 25,000 visitors each year come to see the zebras, bison, camels, elk, Watusi cattle, goats, water buffalo, reindeer, and ostrich in this unusual setting. But Henry's Ark offers more than just a close-up look at exotic animals—its very existence reminds us of what an independent spirit and creative vision can accomplish. Bring carrots and other veggies to feed the animals (no bread or cereal, please), but pay attention to all posted notices: Ark staff rely on their visitors to be responsible, and the animals can be very assertive when hungry.

E. P. "Tom" Sawyer State Park (all ages)

3000 Freys Hill Road; (502) 429–3280. Free. Take the Gene Snyder Freeway (I–265) northeast to the westbound Westport Road exit, and follow the signs.

Located at the far east end of Louisville, E. P. "Tom" Sawyer State Park may be Kentucky's most urban park. Along with the usual picnic shelters, pool, and playgrounds, this park includes a bicycle motocross track and model airplane field. If you're lucky, members of the Tom Sawyer Model Aircraft Association will be flying their radio-controlled planes during your visit. Designated "fitness" and "nature" trails keep joggers and amblers apart. In September, the park is the site of many activities of the Corn Island Storytelling Festival, a major showcase of the art of storytelling.

Renaissance Fun Park (all ages)

201 Park Place Drive, off U.S. Route 60 (Shelbyville Road), just inside I–265; (502) 253–9700, www.funatthepark.com. Hours vary widely by season, so check the Web site or call.

You can drop $30 or more fast at this amusement center, but there are times when miniature golf, go-karts, and bumper cars are just what everyone has in mind. The park emphasizes clean fun, so there are no violent video games in the clubhouse, and smoking and alcohol are prohibited. There's a special playground for smaller kids and a picnic area. Indoor attractions include lasertag.

Other Things to See and Do

Cave Hill Cemetery, 701 Baxter Avenue; (502) 451–5630. Scenic 300-acre arboretum with lakes, walking paths, and graves of Colonel Harland Sanders and explorer George Rogers Clark. Particularly stunning when dogwoods bloom in the spring.

Filson Club Historical Society Museum, 1310 South Third Street; (502) 635–5083. Includes tree stump carved by Daniel Boone to record the fact that he killed a "bar."

Joseph A. Calloway Archaeological Museum, Norton Hall, Southern Baptist Theological Seminary, 2825 Lexington Road; (502) 897–4039. Features an Egyptian mummy, rare Bibles, a copy of the Rosetta stone, and a room dedicated to Billy Graham.

Louisville Horse Trams Inc., (502) 581–0100. Horse-drawn carriage rides through downtown Louisville.

National Society of the Sons of the American Revolution Museum, 1000 South Fourth Street; (502) 589–1776. Historical artifacts, including a replica of George Washington's study and an original thirteen-star flag.

Where to Eat

Baxter Station, 1201 Payne Street; (502) 584–1635. A mixture of international and regional cuisine with a corner bistro feel. Kids will love the model train, which loops the dining room. $$

City Cafe, 505 West Broadway; (502) 589–1797. Very popular downtown lunch place famous for its affordable box lunches. $

Ditto's Grill, 1114 Bardstown Road; (502) 581–9129. Casual restaurant serving burgers, pizzas, and burritos, plus kid-approved side dishes such as cheesy broccoli. Fun atmosphere. $$

El Mundo, 2345 Frankfort Avenue; (502) 899–9930. Mexican with a twist. Outdoor dining and a kid-friendly menu. $$

Kaelin's Kitchen, 1801 Newburg Road; (502) 451–1801. Kaelin's claims to have originated the cheeseburger in 1934, though they are not the only ones to make this claim. Try one anyway and hear their

AnnualEvents in Louisville

- **Edison Birthday Celebration,** early February, Thomas Edison House; (502) 585–5247

- **Kentucky Derby Festival,** early April through first weekend in May; (502) 584–6383, www.kdf.org

- **Cherokee Triangle Art Fair,** late April, Cherokee Park area

- **Kentucky Shakespeare Festival,** outdoor drama, June and July, Central Park, 1114 South Third Street; (502) 637–4933, www.kyshakes.org

- **Waterfront Independence Festival,** July 4; (502) 574–3768

- **Louisville Blues-n-Jazz Festival,** mid-July, Water Tower on River Road; (502) 584–6383

- **National City Kentucky Music Weekend,** July, Iroquois Park Amphitheatre; (502) 348–5237

- **Kentucky State Fair,** ten days in mid-August, Kentucky Fair and Exposition Center off I–264; (502) 367–5005, www.kystatefair.org

- **Rock the Water Tower,** early September, Water Tower on River Road; (502) 584–6383

- **Farm Fest,** mid-September, Farnsley-Moremen Landing; (502) 935–6809

- **Corn Island Storytelling Festival,** late September, E. P. "Tom" Sawyer State Park and Long Run Park; (502) 245–0643

- **Adam Matthews Balloon Festival,** late September, Plantside Drive; (800) 499–2253, www.balloonglow.com

- **St. James Court Art Show,** early October, St. James Court, Old Louisville; arts, crafts, and food; (502) 635–1842

- **World's Largest Halloween Party,** weekends in October, Louisville Zoo; trick-or-treating and fall activities; (502) 459–2181

- **Riverside Heritage Festival,** mid-October, Farnsley-Moremen Landing; (502) 935–6809

story. Kaelin's used to have a sign out front that read IF YOU CAN'T STOP, JUST WAVE. Now it has a sign that reads YOU'VE WAVED LONG ENOUGH, COME ON IN. $

Kingfish, 3021 River Road; (502) 895–0544. A city favorite since 1948, featuring riverboat decor and all kinds of fried, broiled, and baked seafood. $

Lynn's Paradise Cafe, 984 Barret Avenue; (502) 583–3447. A Louisville institution serving three meals a day of creative "nouvelle comfort food" in a cartoonish atmosphere. The fun starts when you pull into the parking lot and see the oversized animal sculptures and giant perking coffee pot. Lynn's tends to pack up quickly, so

plan your arrival accordingly. If you go on New Year's Day for brunch, you may be surprised to see all the patrons in their pajamas. The portions are huge, so plan to share. $$

Nancy's Bagel Grounds, 2101 Frankfort Avenue; (502) 895–8323. A variety of delicious homemade bagels, soups, and sandwiches. $

Twig and Leaf, 2122 Bardstown Road; (502) 451–8944. Inexpensive neighborhood diner where neither wait staff nor patrons will be perturbed by noise, activity, or even the accidental dropping of food on the floor. $

Accommodating Thoughts

As Kentucky hotel rates go, Louisville's tend to be pricey. That's not surprising, since it's the biggest city, but it does mean that you'll want to make an effort to look for a way not to pay "rack rate." Think discount! And ask for one: It can make a real difference. For example, for one hotel I checked, the AAA discount knocked $50 off the regular rate. Here are some strategies:

- Ask if there's a better rate, a family rate, or a weekend rate. If you're coming in for a specific reason or event, mention that.

- Visit the Louisville Convention and Visitors Bureau Web site (www.gotolouisville.com), or call the bureau at (888) LOUISVILLE to check out special seasonal or tour packages. Hotels in all price ranges and categories offer them. Some packages combine your room with attraction tickets and other freebies.

- Schedule your visit at times other than the busiest—you're not going to find any bargains Kentucky Derby Week.

- Even if you think a hotel or bed-and-breakfast looks too expensive, compare rates. Sometimes you'll be surprised. And remember that closer proximity to where you want to be, better amenities, and more space can make a slightly higher-priced accommodation a better value overall.

Amazing
Kentucky Fact

E. P. "Tom" Sawyer, for whom the Louisville park is named, is the father of TV journalist Diane Sawyer.

Where to Stay

Baymont Inn and Suites, 9400 Blairwood Road; (502) 339–2494. Off I-64 east of Louisville. Outdoor pool, free continental breakfast. $$-$$$

The Brown Hotel, 335 West Broadway; (502) 583–1234 or (888) 888–5252. Very elegant renovated 1825 hotel, but with larger rooms than many historic hotels. Access to pool and health club, good restaurants. Try a "Hot Brown," a sandwich invented here. Convenient to downtown attractions. Offers family packages. $$$$

Executive West, 830 Phillips Lane, next to fairgrounds and Kentucky Kingdom; (800) 626–2708. Pool, fitness center, restaurants; offers packages. $$$

Holiday Inn Downtown, 120 West Broadway; (502) 584–8591. Convenient to downtown attractions. Indoor pool, restaurants. $$$-$$$

Holiday Inn Hurstbourne, 1325 Hurstbourne Parkway, at I-64; (502) 426–2600. Indoor pool, sauna, sundeck, game room. $$$-$$$$

Pinecrest Cottage and Gardens B&B, 2806 Newburg Road; (502) 454–3800. An alternative to a hotel, this privately owned lodging offers space and privacy. Guesthouse on six-and-a-half acres with lovely gardens, indoor pool, swings, trampoline, and kids' playhouse. Guesthouse features one bedroom, sleeper sofa, stocked eat-in kitchen, and fireplace. $$$$

For More Information

Greater Louisville Convention and Visitors Bureau, located in the Kentucky International Convention Center, Third and Market Streets; (800) 626–5646 or (502) 584–2121, www.gotolouisville.com. Open Monday to Saturday from 8:30 A.M. to 5:00 P.M., Sunday from 11:00 A.M. to 4:00 P.M.

North-Central Kentucky

From Louisville, you can drive in any direction and quickly trade the city atmosphere for open countryside. The north-central Kentucky region surrounding Louisville features small towns with museums and quaint shops, major historic attractions such as Abraham Lincoln's birthplace and the famous mansion My Old Kentucky Home, farm tours, and some lovely parks and natural areas. To the west and south, small hills or "knobs" dot the landscape. To the east the terrain begins to take on the graceful rolling silhouette of the Bluegrass. These attractions are easy day trips from Louisville if you want to use the city as a base. But you don't have to: Plenty of comfortable, affordable hotels are available in the smaller cities surrounding

Teresa's
TopPicks for North-Central Kentucky

1. Bernheim Arboretum and Research Forest, (502) 955–8512

2. Kentucky Railway Museum and excursions, (502) 549–5470

3. Fort Duffield, (502) 922–4574

4. Abraham Lincoln Birthplace National Historic Site, (270) 358–3137

5. My Old Kentucky Home State Park, (502) 348–3502

6. Civil War Museum, (502) 349–0291

7. Gallrein Farms, (502) 633–4849

8. Yew Dell Gardens, (502) 241–4788

9. The Schmidt Museum of Coca-Cola Memorabilia, (270) 234–1100

10. Rough River Dam State Resort Park, (270) 257–2311

NORTH-CENTRAL KENTUCKY

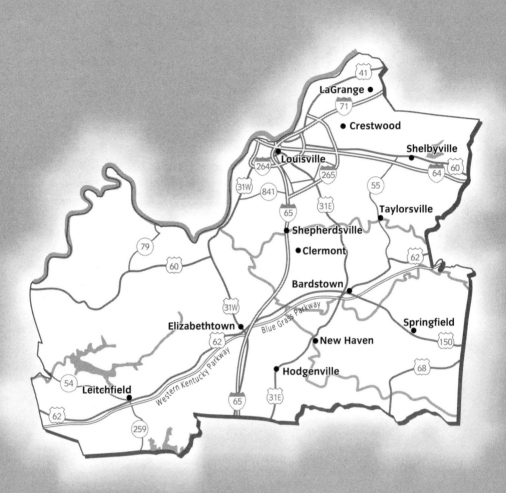

Louisville, with special concentration in the Elizabethtown, Bardstown, and Shepherdsville areas. Interstates 65 south and 64 east and Western Kentucky parkway—and combinations thereof—will get you into the general area; then take the scenic state and county highways to reach the attractions. Attractions are arranged starting south of Louisville and ending in the northeast area of this region to position you to continue your travels in northern Kentucky.

Shepherdsville Area

Kart Kountry (all ages)

At exit 117 off I–65 south, Shepherdsville; (502) 543–9588, www.gokartkountry.com. Open daily from 10:00 A.M. to midnight during peak summer months. Hours vary during other seasons, depending on weather; call for hours. Go-kart ride fees are by the lap: $ (but you can drop $$$$ really fast).

For go-kart enthusiasts, it doesn't get much better than this: The track is 1½ miles long. (Kart Kountry is the longest track in the United States.) You pay by the lap, but there are discounted multilap packages that can be divided among drivers. To drive a go-kart, you have to be at least seven years old and 4 feet tall, but younger, shorter children can ride in a double-seater kart with an adult at the wheel. In addition to go-karts, there are batting cages, bumper boats, minigolf, and an indoor arcade. Snack food is available.

Slowpoke Farm (all ages)

8910 Cedar Grove Road, Shepherdsville; (502) 921–9632, www.slowpokefarm.com. No set hours; open when the Bleemels are home, usually daily in summer, though it may be closed around lunchtime. Take exit 116 off I–65, turn left, and go about 9½ miles. Look for the farm sign.

You've got to love a place called Slowpoke Farm. Belonging to the Bleemel family for five generations, Slowpoke Farm is a working cattle, soybean, and tobacco farm that sells seasonal produce and flowers. In recent years the family has started hosting workshops, lunches, and festivals. If your family would like to poke around, call ahead to schedule a lunch or a hayride. Also call to check the schedule of special events, including Mother's Day Brunch on the Farm, Annual Gourd Day on the Farm, and Car Show on the Farm. Or just stop by and see what's in season in the produce shop.

Junction Jamboree (all ages)

Highway 434, Lebanon Junction; (800) 518–OPRY, www.countrycookinband.com. Concerts are Saturday at 7:30 P.M. Adults $$, children $, children under 6 free. Get off I–65 at exit 105, and go west on Highway 61 to Highway 434.

If you like country music, you'll enjoy this family-oriented music hall. The house band, Bill Aiken and the Country Cookin' Band, is joined by an array of local, regional, and sometimes nationally known country, gospel, bluegrass, and comedy guest artists. Doors open at 6:00 P.M. Burgers, sandwiches, and snacks are available at the Junction Grill.

Other Things to See and Do

Shepherdsville Music Show, Highway 44, Shepherdsville; (502) 543–6551. Friday night bluegrass shows and Saturday night country music shows.

World's Most Awesome Flea Market, I–65, exit 116, Shepherdsville; (502) 543–7899. Weekends only.

Where to Eat

Country Cupboard Restaurant, 636 Buckman Street, Shepherdsville; (502) 543–2780. Country cooking with generous portions and a family atmosphere. $

Where to Stay

Best Western Shepherdsville, 211 South Lakeview Drive (I–65, exit 117), Shepherdsville; (502) 543–7097. Outdoor pool, Denny's '50s-style diner restaurant. $$

Holiday Inn Express, I–65, exit 121, Hillview; (502) 955–4985. Outdoor pool, free continental breakfast. $$

KOA Louisville South, 2433 Highway 44 east, Shepherdsville; (502) 543–2041. Primitive and full-hookup camping, pool, game room, minigolf, playgrounds, nature trail leading to prehistoric Indian rock shelters. $

For More Information

Shepherdsville/Bullitt County Tourism, 395 Paroquet Springs Drive, near I–65, exit 117, Shepherdsville; (502) 543–8687 or (800) 526–2068, www.travelbullitt .org. Open Monday to Friday from 8:00 A.M. to 5:00 P.M.

Clermont

Bernheim Arboretum and Research Forest (all ages)
Off Highway 245; (502) 955–8512, www.bernheim.org. Park open daily from 7:00 A.M. to sunset, visitor center open from 9:00 A.M. to 5:00 P.M. Free admission on weekdays; $5 per vehicle on weekends and holidays. Take exit 112 off I–65, and follow signs.

Thank you, Isaac W. Bernheim. Back in 1929, this German immigrant, wanting to return something to Kentuckians for the success he enjoyed here as a whiskey distiller, set aside acreage for the Bernheim Research Forest. Generations of Kentuckians have enjoyed his thoughtfulness. A tried-and-true Kentucky getaway spot (I remember coming here on a school field trip), Bernheim Forest just seems to get better as it ages and very much lives up to its slogan, "Connecting People to Nature." The 12,000 acres include some 35 miles of hiking trails, several lakes (one for fishing), manicured gardens, playgrounds, tree trails where the species are identified, and picnic areas. Children will enjoy the Nature Center, where they can see birds of prey and visit the deer pen. This is a great place to go for an impromptu picnic or hike (pick up a Scavenger Hunt list at the Nature Center), but you also may want to call ahead and plan a trip around the many special activities and classes for all ages. Every Saturday at 11:30 A.M., the "Young Explorers" meet by the silo behind the Nature Center. This hour-long program for children ages five and up usually focuses on plants or animals. There's usually a hike or animal program for kids on Sunday afternoon.

Elizabethtown Area

The Schmidt Museum of Coca-Cola Memorabilia (all ages)
109 Buffalo Creek Drive, Elizabethtown; (270) 234–1100. Open Monday to Saturday 10:00 A.M. to 6:00 P.M., Sunday from 1:00 to 5:00 P.M. $

There's no mistaking what this museum is about. A giant hand emerges from the front of the building holding a bottle of Coca-Cola. And inside is just about anything you can think of emblazoned with the Coke logo (and probably a few things you would never think of). The Schmidt family, who used to own the Coca-Cola bottling plant in Elizabethtown, amassed the largest private collection of Coke memorabilia. Items on display include delivery trucks, signs, toys, bottles, Santa items, the only known complete collection of serving trays, and various other items used to promote Coke from its earliest days. You can have a snack or sandwich at the '50s-style soda fountain (washed down with you-know-what), and there's a large gift shop.

Historic Downtown Walking Tour (all ages)
Leaves from the Hardin County Courthouse, downtown Elizabethtown; (270) 737–8932. Open June through September on Thursdays at 7:00 P.M. Free.

This forty-five-minute tour is part history lesson, part theater. Costumed characters relating to local history, such as Sara Bush Johnston Lincoln (Abe's stepmother), the hatchet-carrying prohibitionist Carry Nation, and even George Armstrong Custer greet you and tell you their stories as you pass twenty-five historic sites and buildings. The costumes, singing, and banjo playing will appeal to children, even if the younger ones don't understand all that's being said.

Freeman Lake Park (all ages)
North U.S. Highway 31W, Elizabethtown; (270) 769–3916. Park open daily year-round. Historic buildings open Memorial Day to Labor Day, Tuesday to Saturday from 10:00 A.M. to 6:00 P.M., Sunday from 1:00 to 6:00 P.M. Free.

In addition to hiking trails, picnic areas, fishing, docks, and rowboat and pedal boat rentals, this park features several historical structures, so you can get a lot of mileage out of a stop here. The One-Room School House, built in Summit, Kentucky, in 1892 and moved to this location in 1978, has original desks and materials, complete with a lesson plan on the chalkboard. Lincoln Heritage House consists of two pioneer cabins built from 1789 to 1805 with the help of Lincoln's father, Thomas Lincoln, a skilled carpenter. Too tiny to actually enter, the Sara Bush Johnston Lincoln Memorial is a replica of Lincoln's stepmother's Elizabethtown cabin.

Swope's Cars of Yesteryears Museum (all ages)

1100 North Dixie Highway (US 31W), Elizabethtown; (270) 765–2181, www.swope museum.com. Open Monday to Friday from 10:00 A.M. to 5:00 P.M. Free.

Children must be accompanied by adults at this museum of vintage and rare automobiles. No problem. There are cool cars for all ages here: Children will love the old cars, like the cute 1910 Hupmobile and the 1920 Brush, as well as the more recent, cartoonish '61 Metropolitan, while Dad and Grandpa (and/or Mom and Grandma) can salivate over the '69 Camaro, the pink '55 Dodge Custom Royal Lancer, and the '53 Jaguar XK 120. The collection's twenty cars are in pristine condition.

The Greenbelt (all ages)

Network of trails around Elizabethtown. Pick up a brochure at the Elizabethtown Tourism and Convention Bureau. Free.

This network of trails and parks was created by a private foundation and the city of Elizabethtown. It currently includes more than 13 miles of trails, ranging from short and easy to long and moderately challenging, that go through town and around Freeman Lake, Buffalo Lake, Fisherman's Lake, and other streams in between.

The **Food Run**

The little town of Glendale, about 8 miles south of Elizabethtown on Highway 22 (from Elizabethtown, take I–65 to exit 86), is chock full of antiques and gift shops. That may or may not appeal to your family, but everyone will enjoy eating at **The Whistle Stop** (270–369–8586). The restaurant's name reflects the town's role as a bustling passenger train stop in the 1800s, and it's a great place to stop for good food at moderate prices in a casual atmosphere. Be sure to try the homemade pies.

Amazing
Kentucky Fact

The door to the vault in the United States Bullion Depository at Fort Knox weighs more than twenty tons and is made of concrete and steel. No one person has the entire combination to the lock.

Patton Museum of Cavalry and Armor (all ages)

Keyes Park near the main entrance to Fort Knox Military Reservation; (502) 624–3812, www.generalpatton.org. Open daily year-round, except major holidays. Hours are 9:00 A.M. to 4:30 P.M. weekdays, 10:00 A.M. to 4:30 P.M. weekends. Open until 6:00 P.M. in summer. Free. To get to Fort Knox from Elizabethtown, take US 31W to Chaffee Avenue.

From big tanks to toy-sized soldiers (used in dioramas illustrating military strategies), this museum traces the history of armored vehicles from World War I through Desert Storm and Desert Shield. The children will love climbing into a tank; for adults, there are many informative and interesting items relating to famous World War II general George S. Patton.

Fort Duffield (all ages)

Salt River Drive, off US 31W, West Point; (502) 922–4574. Open daily from 9:00 A.M. to dusk. Take US 31W north from Elizabethtown. If coming from Louisville, a quicker way is to take Interstate 265 (Gene Snyder Freeway) to US 31W south; the park is a little over 7 miles from the exit. Free; donations suggested.

Older children interested in Civil War history will like this preserved Civil War site the most, but all ages can enjoy the open spaces and scenic river views. Fort Duffield was a Union fortification built on orders from General William Tecumseh Sherman to help protect supply routes along the Ohio River. The remote hilltop location (and the fact that for many years this was part of Fort Knox Military Reservation) meant that the earthen-wall fortifications remained little disturbed over the decades. They're reputedly some of the best remaining in the state. In recent years a group of local volunteers has made the fort a labor of love, building Civil War–replica cabins and an amphitheater for living history demonstrations. When you visit, you may see people working on the park dressed in Civil War uniforms. To get to the earthen fort, you have to hike about ¼ mile. On living history weekends (Memorial Day and Labor Day weekends) a shuttle bus is available; small donation suggested. The park also has picnic areas and 10 miles of advanced-level mountain bike paths.

Other Things to See and Do

Brown-Pusey Community House, 128 North Main Street, Elizabethtown; (270) 765–2515. Restored Federal-style stagecoach building.

Emma Reno Connor Black History Gallery, 602 Hawkins Drive, Elizabethtown; (270) 769–5204. Photos and articles on local African-American history. By appointment.

Hardin County History Museum, 201 West Dixie Highway (US 31W), Elizabethtown; (270) 737–4126. Artifacts and documents tell the story of Hardin County from pioneer times to the present day.

Otter Creek Park, Highway 1638, off US 31W, Brandenburg; (502) 574–4583 or www.ottercreekpark.org. Hiking trails, nature center, pool overlooking the Ohio River.

Where to Eat

Back Home, 251 West Dixie Highway (US 31W), Elizabethtown; (270) 769–2800. Home cooking and regional specialties. $

Stone Hearth, 1001 North Mulberry Street, Elizabethtown; (270) 765–4898. Good fried chicken and fresh salad and soup bar. $

Where to Stay

Comfort Inn, 2009 North Mulberry Street, Elizabethtown; (800) 4–CHOICE or (270) 765–4166. Outdoor pool. $$$

Days Inn, 2010 North Mulberry Street, Elizabethtown; (270) 769–5522 or (800) 329–7466. Outdoor pool, laundry, twenty-four-hour restaurant, free continental breakfast. $$

Elizabethtown KOA, U.S. Highway 62, near I–65, exit 94, Elizabethtown; (270) 737–7600. Seventy sites, full hookups, playgrounds, miniature golf. $

Hampton Inn, 1035 Executive Drive, Elizabethtown; (I–65, exit 94); (270) 765–6663. Indoor pool, exercise room, free breakfast. $$$

Otter Creek Park, Highway 1638, off US 31W, Brandenburg; (502) 574–4583. Two- and four-bedroom cabins overlooking the Ohio River; $$–$$$. Camping with hookups, bathhouses also available. $

For More Information

Elizabethtown Tourism and Convention Bureau, 1030 North Mulberry Street, Elizabethtown (near I–65, exit 94); (800) 437–0092 or www.touretown.com. Open Monday to Friday from 8:00 A.M. to 5:00 P.M. Open until 6:00 P.M. weekdays and Saturday from 10:00 A.M. to 2:00 P.M. in summer.

Radcliff/Fort Knox Convention and Tourism Commission, P.O. Box 845, Radcliff 40159; (800) 334–7540.

West Point Tourism, City Hall, 509 Elm Street, West Point; (502) 922–4260.

At **Fort Knox**

- View the **United States Bullion Depository,** where America's gold has been stored since 1969. (Exterior viewing only.) **Free.**

- Make a splash at the **Fort Knox Water Park,** with its slides and outdoor pool. Open to civilians. (502) 624–1253. $

- Just drive around to see the barracks and other buildings; if your children have never been on a military base, they'll find it interesting.

NOTE: Since fall 2001, security on the base has been tight. To enter you must present identification, your car registration, and proof of auto insurance.

Leitchfield

Rough River Dam State Resort Park (all ages)
Highway 79, between Leitchfield and Hardinsburg; (270) 257–2311 or (800) 325–1713, www.kystateparks.com. Admission and many facilities **free.** From I–65 south at Elizabethtown, get on Western Kentucky Parkway and look for the park exit sign. Lodge rooms $$–$$$, cabins $$$–$$$$, camping $. Dining room $.

You're not exactly "roughing it" when you spend a day, a weekend, or longer here. This state park, which boasts a 5,000-acre manmade lake, offers fishing and lake sightseeing (boat rentals available), minigolf, tennis, playgrounds, picnic areas, and a couple of easy nature trails. The lodge features overnight accommodations and a dining room. Cottages and camping are also available. There's a swimming pool for lodge and cabin guests. In July, the park is host to one of Kentucky's premier traditional music events—the Official Kentucky Championship Oldtime Fiddling Contest. Fiddle players compete for top bragging rights, as do harmonica, banjo, and mandolin players. Camp and join in the jam sessions and main performances (www.kentuckyfiddler.com).

Hodgenville

Abraham Lincoln Birthplace National Historic Site (all ages)
US 31E and Highway 61, 2995 Lincoln Farm Road; (270) 358–3137, www.nps.gov/abli. Opens at 8:00 A.M. daily year-round, closes at 6:45 P.M. Memorial Day through Labor Day and at 4:45 P.M. rest of year. Closed Thanksgiving, Christmas, and New Year's Day. **Free.**

Lincolnmania

Does someone in your family look like Abraham Lincoln or Mary Todd Lincoln? If so, head to Hodgenville the second weekend in October and enter the Lincoln lookalike contests, all part of the fun at the annual **Lincoln Days Celebration** (270–358–3411). There are rail-splitting contests and pioneer games, too.

Northeastern Kentucky is the Bluegrass State's "Land of Lincoln," and his birthplace shrine, located on one hundred acres of land that was part of the Lincoln family farm, is a good place to begin your all-Abe adventure. This is one of the most visited shrines in the United States, and it's an imposing sight: The building rises like a granite temple atop fifty-six massive steps (one for each year of Lincoln's life). Make the climb, and inside you'll find a one-room log cabin similar to the one in which Lincoln was born in this area on February 12, 1809. It all symbolizes the humble beginnings that led to great things. Be sure to stop at the visitor center, which includes an audiovisual presentation about Lincoln's childhood and Lincoln family artifacts. My daughter also enjoyed the park's hiking trail and the walk down to Sinking Spring.

Lincoln Museum (ages 4 and up)
66 Lincoln Square; (270) 358–3163, www.lincolnmuseum-ky.org. Open Monday to Saturday from 8:30 A.M. to 4:30 P.M., Sunday from 12:30 to 4:30 P.M. $

Located on the town square in Hodgenville, this museum houses memorabilia relating to Lincoln and his life, including newspaper articles, campaign posters, and drawings. Wax figures re-create important events in Lincoln's life.

Happy Birthday, **Abe**

From 2008 to 2010, America will celebrate the two hundredth anniversary of the birth of Abraham Lincoln, and many sites in Kentucky will hold special events in honor of the occasion. Hodgenville has already begun sprucing up the town to host up to a million visitors who will come for the official opening ceremonies of the celebration on February 12, 2008, at the Abraham Lincoln Birthplace National Historic Site and afterward. Visit the Hodgenville Lincoln Bicentennial Web site at www.lincolnbirthplace.com and the Kentucky Lincoln Bicentennial Commission Web site at www.kylincoln.org for more information about places in Kentucky related to Lincoln and a calendar of bicentennial events.

Lincoln's Boyhood Home (all ages)

Knob Creek Farm, US 31W, northeast of Hodgenville; (270) 358–3137. Grounds open daily from 9:00 A.M. to 4:30 P.M. Free.

As an adult, Abraham Lincoln said his earliest memories were of the "Knob Creek place," and this is it—the farm where the Lincolns lived from 1811 to 1816, the place where young Abe played, learned to read the Bible, and, by some accounts, nearly drowned in the creek that runs through the farm. LaRue County presented the 228-acre farm to the National Park Service in 2002. The cabins, which are not related to the Lincolns, are closed, but visitors are welcome to drop by and stroll the grounds.

Lincoln Jamboree (ages 6 and up)

2579 Lincoln Farm Road; (270) 358–3545. Saturday at 8:00 P.M. year-round. $$

I've never heard anything about Lincoln singing, so this family-oriented country music show honors Abe in name only. The folks here do a lot of singing: Local, regional, and some national acts have been giving weekly shows here since 1954. The on-site Joel Ray's Restaurant serves cafeteria-style food ($).

Where to Eat

Joel Ray's Restaurant, 2579 Lincoln Farm Road; (270) 358–3545. Cafeteria-style breakfast, lunch, and dinner. Adjacent to Lincoln Jamboree. $

Paula's Hot Biscuit, 311 West Water Street; (270) 358–2237. Breakfast and lunch. $

Ruthie's Lincoln Freeze, 700 South Lincoln Boulevard; (270) 358–4987. Burgers and plate lunches plus ice cream. $

For More Information

LaRue County Chamber of Commerce, 58 Lincoln Square; (270) 358–3411 or www.laruecountychamber.org.

Amazing
Kentucky Fact

Stephen Foster, who wrote "My Old Kentucky Home," never had a Kentucky home. He lived in Pittsburgh, Pennsylvania. His distant cousins, the Rowans, owned Federal Hill, and local legend claims that Foster stopped to visit them on his way to New Orleans.

New Haven

Kentucky Railway Museum (all ages)

136 South Main Street, exit 10 off Bluegrass Parkway, 15 miles south of Bardstown on US 31E; (502) 549–5470 or (800) 272–0152. Museum open March through December, 10:00 A.M. to 5:00 P.M. Monday through Saturday, noon to 5:00 P.M. Sunday. Excursions run at 2:00 P.M. Tuesday through Friday, 11:00 A.M. and 2:00 P.M. Saturday, and 1:00 and 3:30 P.M. Sunday. Museum $; train tickets adults $$$, children $$; locomotor car rides adults $$$$, children $$$.

From this restored depot you can take a 22-mile, one-hour scenic excursion on authentic vintage coaches powered either by a diesel locomotive or a restored Louisville and Nashville steam locomotive. In summer there are daily departures from New Haven and weekend departures from both New Haven and the community of Boston to the north. Both are round-trip excursions through scenic Rolling Fork River Valley. Throughout the year there are a variety of special excursions with children in mind, including the Easter Bunny Express, Train Robbery excursions, Haunted Trail and Friendly Ghost excursions in October, and the Santa Express. One of the most popular special events is a visit by Thomas the Tank Engine, a life-size version of the popular fictional engine, in July. The depot at New Haven also includes a railroad museum. Your children will probably make a beeline for the model train center, which includes several working trains running through miniature landscapes built with precision and absolute attention to detail. If you have younger children, you might want to bring something for them to stand on or you will be holding them the entire time so they can see.

Scenic **Route**

From Hodgenville, take US 31E 30 miles to Bardstown, along the Old Kentucky Turnpike Scenic Byway, formerly the main road from Louisville to Nashville.

Bardstown

My Old Kentucky Home State Park (all ages)

U.S. Highway 150; (502) 348–3502. Open daily 9:00 A.M. to 5:00 P.M., except for Thanksgiving Day, Christmas week, and December 31. $

You've already had the twenty-five-cent tour of this lovely Georgian-style house—it's the house featured on the Kentucky state quarter. Pay a little more and you can go inside, visit the gardens, and learn how it supposedly inspired composer Stephen Foster to write the state song. (If you don't know the words to Kentucky's state song, "My Old Kentucky Home," before you visit Bardstown, you will when you leave!) Kentucky's most famous historic house is named Federal Hill, and it dates to 1818. For tours, the Old South atmosphere is re-created complete with tour guides dressed as Southern belles. Children especially enjoy the costumes and hearing about life for the children in the house. The park also includes picnic areas, a playground, and an amphitheater where *Stephen Foster: The Musical* is performed seasonally.

Old Bardstown Village, Civil War Museum, Women in the Civil War Museum, Mid-America War Memorial Museum, and Wildlife Natural History Museum (ages 5 and up)

302 and 310 East Broadway; (502) 349–0291. Open March through mid-December Monday to Saturday from 10:00 A.M. to 5:00 P.M., Sunday from noon to 5:00 P.M.; open weekends only in January and February. Individual attraction admission $; combo ticket for all five (best deal) $$$ adults, $ children.

Five attractions in one complex take you from pioneer times through the present day. **Old Bardstown Village** is a collection of replica pioneer cabins, including a forge, as well as Native American items. (*NOTE:* The village may not be open if it's raining.) The star attraction is the **Civil War Museum,** which several Civil War publications have named as one of the finest in the United States. The museum focuses on the war's western theater, the battles in Kentucky and points west, and includes numerous interesting and rare artifacts, from cannons, uniforms, and flags to hardtack, the food soldiers often lived on. The newest attraction in the complex is the **Women in the Civil War Museum,** housed in a separate 1840 building. You might be surprised to learn that 400 women fought in the Civil War. It was also the first war in which women

Bardstown's **Boat Man**

Why is there a monument shaped like a steamboat in Bardstown's town square? Because Bardstown was the last home of inventor John Fitch, who received the first patent for a steamboat in 1791.

served as nurses—prior to the Civil War, that was considered men's work. The museum includes costumes, photographs, and other items, and exhibits explain women's roles as wives, soldiers, nurses, and spies. The **Mid-America War Memorial Museum** includes items relating to American conflicts from the Revolutionary War to Desert Storm. Minerals, fossils, and preserved animals are among the items on display at the **Wildlife Natural History Museum.**

Abbey of Gethsemani (ages 10 and up)

Highway 247, off US 31E at Trappist; (502) 549–4406. Open Monday to Saturday from 9:00 A.M. to 5:00 P.M. Free.

This community of Trappist monks has lived in Kentucky since the 1850s. And though the cheeses, fudge, fruitcake, and other products they make are known worldwide, only recently has the monastery opened a visitor center. Although no tours of the abbey are offered, there is a film about what it's like to live the life of a monk, and you can visit the abbey church and gift shop and explore the grounds—in all, a peaceful and lovely place to visit, offering a glimpse into a life seldom seen.

A Day **Family Adventure**

Interstate 65, which runs north-south through this region, is such a busy and crowded interstate that it's sometimes nerve-racking to drive. On the other hand, the east-west parkways through this region, Bluegrass Parkway and Western Kentucky Parkway, can be nerve-racking for just the opposite reason. Both seem somewhat desolate, and there are few gas stations and restaurants along the exits, except for major city areas such as Elizabethtown and Bardstown. Late one Sunday night, I forgot this. The low-gas light had been on for a while, but when we reached Elizabethtown, the traffic was so bad that I didn't want to have to pass the parkway exit, get gas, then turn around and find the parkway entrance. "I'll just wait and get gas on Bluegrass Parkway," I said. Soon everyone in the car realized what a mistake this had been. The first exit had no reentry to the parkway. The next had no gas station in sight. And so on. From the back seat: "Mom, what will we do?" "Are we going to have to spend the night out here?" By the time I saw a sign that read BARDSTOWN 9 MILES, the gas gauge showed "E." We reset the trip odometer and watched the miles tick away, breathing a sigh of relief as each one passed. We did make it to an open station in Bardstown, but I'll never do that (at least on Bluegrass Parkway, late at night) again.

Other Things to See and Do

Around-the-Town Carriages, 223 North Third Street; (502) 348–0331. Horse-drawn carriage tours of downtown area.

Distillery tours. There are several in the "Bourbon Capital of Kentucky." Ask at the tourist and convention bureau (see For More Information).

St. Joseph Proto Cathedral, 310 West Stephen Foster Avenue; (502) 348–3126. First Catholic Church west of the Alleghenies; includes beautiful European paintings.

Where to Eat

Hurst Discount Drugs Soda Fountain, 102 North Third Street, Courthouse Square; (502) 348–9261. Sandwiches, soups, and ice cream treats at an old-fashioned soda fountain. $

Kreso's Family Restaurant, 219 North Third Street; (502) 348–9594. Soups, sandwiches, and entrees, some with an Eastern European flair. Carryout also available. Lunch $$, dinner $$$

Kurtz Restaurant, 418 East Stephen Foster Avenue; (502) 348–8964. Soup/sandwich/pie special for lunch, regional specialties for dinner. Famous for its fried chicken. Lunch $, dinner $$

Old Talbott Tavern, 107 West Stephen Foster Avenue; (502) 348–3494. Southern specialties in an inn operating since 1779. Kids menu. Lunch $, dinner $$

Where to Stay

Days Inn, US 31 and Bluegrass Parkway; (502) 348–9253 or (866) 348–6900. Nine-hole golf, fitness room, game room, outdoor pool. $$

Hampton Inn Bardstown, 985 Chambers Boulevard, off Highway 245; (502) 349–0100 or (800) 426–7866. Indoor pool. $$$

Jailer's Inn, 111 West Stephen Foster Avenue; (800) 948–5551 or (502) 348–5551, www.jailersinn.com. Five rooms decorated with antiques; "cell room" features jail motif. $$–$$$$

My Old Kentucky Home State Park Campground, US 150; (502) 348–3502. Thirty-nine sites with utility hookups available. On-site grocery, central service building with showers and toilets, laundry, and picnic area. Eighteen-hole golf course and tennis courts. Pets allowed if restrained. Open April through October; no reservations accepted. $

For More Information

Bardstown-Nelson County Tourist and Convention Bureau, Nelson County Courthouse, 113 East Stephen Foster Avenue; (502) 348–4877 or (800) 638–4877, www.visitbardstown.com.

Outdoor Drama in North-Central Kentucky

If your children are old enough to sit still for a couple of hours, they might enjoy theater "under the stars."

- **Stephen Foster: The Musical.** J. Dan Talbott Amphitheatre, My Old Kentucky Home State Park, Bardstown; (800) 626–1563 or (502) 348–5971, www.stephenfoster.com. June through mid-August. Tuesday through Friday at 8:30 P.M., Saturday at 2:00 and 8:30 P.M. Musical (more than fifty songs) about the composer's life. Adults $$$, children seven to twelve $$, children six and under free.

- **Pine Knob Theatre,** Pine Knob, 14 miles south of Rough River Dam State Resort Park; (270) 879–8190 or www.pineknob.com. Early June through late September. Friday and Saturday at 8:00 P.M. Four or five shows per season, looking at the past (1800s to 1950s) in song and dance. Old-fashioned store and '50s-style diner near theater. $$$

Springfield

Lincoln Homestead State Park (all ages)

5079 Lincoln Park Road; (859) 336–7461. Park open year-round; buildings and golf course open May 1 to September 30. Admission to buildings and golf course $; otherwise free.

Though Lincoln's birth is commemorated in Hodgenville, this park pays tribute to the lives of his parents. Two cabins relate to Lincoln history. The Berry House is the original house where Abe's mother, Nancy, lived and where (legend has it) Abe's father, Thomas, proposed to her. It is furnished with period pieces. The other, the Lincoln Cabin, is a reproduction of the home and blacksmith shop where Thomas Lincoln lived and contains furniture he made. Picnic areas and a playground are near the cabins. There's also a small lake for fishing.

Beech Fork Covered Bridge (all ages)

Highway 458 off Highway 55, north of Springfield. Free.

This 204-foot-long span is one of only thirteen covered bridges remaining in Kentucky (there were once several hundred). The bridge is closed to traffic, which means you can leisurely explore the inside and its interesting burr truss construction.

Washington County Courthouse (all ages)
Main and Cross Streets. Free.

The wedding records of Abe's parents, Thomas and Nancy Lincoln, are among the historic documents on display on the walls of this courthouse. The building itself is historic: The oldest courthouse in continuous use in Kentucky, it dates to 1816.

Where to Eat

Cecconi's Family Restaurant, 117 West Main Street; (859) 336–5136. Burgers, plate lunches, and homemade pies. $

offers plenty of opportunity for animal lovers to make friends with the resident llamas, horses, dogs, and cats. $$$–$$$$

Where to Stay

Glenmar Plantation Bed and Breakfast, 2444 Valley Hill Road; (800) 828–3330 or (859) 284–7791. This one-hundred-acre working farm with house (built in 1785) and lovely gardens welcomes children and

For More Information

Springfield/Washington County Chamber of Commerce, 112 Cross Main Street; (859) 336–3810, www.springfield kentuckychamber.com.

Taylorsville

Taylorsville Lake State Park (all ages)
1320 Park Road (off Highway 248); (502) 477–8713, campground (502) 477–0086. Park open daily year-round, campground seasonal. Admission free; camping $, boat rental $$–$$$.

This state park's 3,050-acre lake is the closest major lake to Louisville (about a forty-five-minute drive). With playgrounds and picnic areas, it makes an easy day getaway. Or you can camp and stay longer. There are 16 miles of hiking trails, plus a marina with boat slips and rentals. Horseback riding is allowed on some trails, but you must bring your own horse. The campground includes some horse campsites.

Amazing
Kentucky Fact

Kentucky has about 90,000 farms—more than forty-six other states.

AnnualEvents in North-Central Kentucky

- **Dulcibrrr Weekend,** February, Rough River Dam State Resort Park, Leitchfield; (270) 257–2311

- **Kentucky Gourd Festival,** May, Taylorsville; (877) 765–8594

- **Living History Reenactments,** Memorial Day and Labor Day weekends, Fort Duffield, West Point; (502) 922–4574

- **Shelby County Fair and Horse Show,** mid-to-late June, Shelbyville; (502) 633–6388

- **Official Kentucky Old-Time Fiddlers Championship,** July, Rough River Dam State Resort Park, Leitchfield; (800) 325–1713

- **Ice Cream Festival,** mid-July, Leitchfield; (270) 259–3165

- **Oldham County Fair,** late July, Oldham; (800) 813–9953

- **LaRue County Fair,** late July or early August, Hodgenville; (270) 358–3411

- **Shelbyville Horse Show Jubilee,** early August, Shelbyville; (502) 633–5029

- **Buttermilk Days Festival,** August, Bardstown; (800) 638–4877

- **Native American Festival,** August, Westport; (800) 813–9953

- **Kentucky Heartland Festival,** late August, Elizabethtown; (270) 765–4334

- **Lincoln Days Celebration,** mid-October, Hodgenville; (270) 358–3411

- **Glendale Crossing Festival,** late October, Glendale; (270) 369–6188

U.S. Corps of Engineers Taylorsville Dam Visitor Center (all ages)

Highway 2239, off Highway 55; (502) 477–8882. Open daily. Free.

Get a good view of the 1,280-foot-long dam over the Salt River that created Taylorsville Lake. Visitors can also take hiking trails to view wildlife and to see pioneer cabins and an early schoolhouse.

The Berry Farm (all ages)

1168 Wilsonville Road; (502) 477–2334. Open daily. Gourds available all year; other produce seasonal.

This is a "u-pick-it" place for strawberries in spring; blueberries, blackberries, tomatoes, and grapes in summer; apples, pumpkins, and cushaws (big, green-striped squashes used in pies) in fall; and gourds for drying, painting, and craftmaking year-round.

Where to Eat

Lynda's Grill, 108 Jefferson Street; (502) 477–2857. Plate lunches and sandwiches. $

The Tea Cup, 37 East Main Street; (502) 477–0287. Hearty breakfast, sandwiches and soups for lunch. $

Shelbyville

Gallrein Farms (all ages)

1029 Vigo Road, off Highway 43; (502) 633–4849 or (502) 633–0724, www.gallreinfarms .com. Open daily April through October 31, Monday to Saturday from 9:00 A.M. to 6:00 P.M., Sunday from 1:00 to 5:00 P.M. Admission free; charges for some seasonal activities $.

Spring through fall, you'll find something interesting to see and do at this very family-friendly working farm. There's a small petting zoo with donkeys, goats, and rabbits. Children can also feed the ducks and geese at the pond and watch bees making honey in an observation hive. In fall, there are hayrides to the pumpkin patch. Produce available varies by season but includes raspberries, blackberries, sweet corn, and pumpkins.

Other Things to See and Do

Science Hill, 525 Washington Street. Shops housed in historic buildings.

Shelby County Flea Market, off I–64 at exit 28, Simpsonville; (502) 722–8883. Weekends only.

Standardbred Horse Farms. Arrange tours through tourism office: (502) 633–6388.

Where to Eat

Claudia Sanders Dinner House, 3202 Shelbyville Road; (502) 633–5600. Open Tuesday to Sunday from 11:00 A.M. to 9:00 P.M. Housed in the former home of Colonel Sanders of Kentucky Fried Chicken fame and named for his wife, this restaurant serves traditional cooking with family-style service and homemade breads and desserts. $$$

Firefresh Barbecue, 81 Jeannie Drive, (502) 647–7675. Hickory-smoked ribs, pork, and chicken as well as honey-glazed ham, with good sides and hand-dipped ice cream. "Sparky Plates" for kids. $

Where to Stay

Best Western Shelbyville Lodge, I–64, exit 32B, 115 Isaac Shelby Drive; (502) 633–4400. Outdoor pool, complimentary breakfast, pets allowed. $$

Holiday Inn Express, 110 Clubhouse Drive; (502) 677–0109. Indoor pool, free continental breakfast. $$

For More Information

Shelbyville/Shelby County Tourism Commission, 316 West Main Street; (502) 633–6388 or (800) 680–6388, www.shelbyvilleky.com.

LaGrange/Crestwood

Oldham County History Center (all ages)

106 North Second Avenue, LaGrange; (502) 222–0826. Open Tuesday, Wednesday, Thursday, and Saturday from 10:00 A.M. to 4:00 P.M., Friday from 10:00 A.M. to 8:00 P.M., and Sunday from 1:00 to 4:00 P.M. **Free.**

This interpretive history museum traces the history of Oldham County through permanent and changing exhibitions. Of most interest to children is the replica of the railroad that ran through Oldham County on its journey between Louisville and Cincinnati. Be sure to see the outdoor sculpture while enjoying the Heritage Walk.

Yew Dell Gardens (all ages)

6220 Old LaGrange Road, Crestwood; (502) 241–4788, www.yewdellgardens.org. Open Monday to Saturday from 10:00 A.M. to 4:00 P.M. Guided tours are offered at noon and 1:00 P.M. Tuesday and at 10:00 and 11:00 A.M. Saturday. Closed Saturday December through March. Closed major holidays. Adults $$, children 12 and under **free.**

With its woodlands and formal gardens, topiaries, and small stone castle, this looks like an enchanted place out of fairy tales. In addition to being a charming and peaceful place to leisurely explore, Yew Dell Gardens is a place for children and adults alike to learn about trees, plants, flowers, and the art of gardening. The garden preserves the life work of Theodore Klein—nurseryman and gardener supreme—and his wife, Martha Lee, who over sixty years created these wonderful spaces. Klein also developed new varieties of plants. After his death in 1998, a group of local volunteers raised funds to save the property from development. Yew Dell is one of the preservation projects of the national Garden Conservancy. In addition to the self-guided and guided tours, the gardens hold special events throughout the year. The Old-Fashioned Family Picnic is in June, and the annual plant sale is in April; both include special children's activities.

In **LaGrange**

Cute shops are found along LaGrange's small-town Main Street, including one of the region's most beloved toy stores, **The Treasured Child** (115 East Main Street; 502–225–9646), and **Christmas in Kentucky** (203 East Washington Street; 502–222–7421), where the holiday spirit reigns year-round. Don't be surprised when a freight train rumbles through town, just feet from where you're standing.

Where to Eat

Frascelli's New York Deli, 6247 Crestwood Station, Crestwood; (502) 243–9005. Terrific New York–style pizza, subs, and sandwiches. $

Red Pepper Deli-Cafe, 103 East Main, LaGrange; (502) 225–0770. Huge, creative sandwiches served in an artsy cafe atmosphere. $

Where to Stay

Holiday Inn Express, Interstate 71, exit 22, 1001 Paige Place, LaGrange; (502) 222–5678. Indoor pool. $$

Super 8 Motel, I–71, exit 22, 1420 East Crystal Drive, LaGrange; (800) 800–8000. Continental breakfast, outdoor pool. $

Northern Kentucky

The northern Kentucky region offers both rural and urban entertainment. Northeast of Louisville, small towns hug the Ohio River. Historic sites, state parks, and many interesting community festivals are some of the things to enjoy in this part of the state. Then you reach Boone, Campbell, and Kenton counties (home to the cities of Burlington, Florence, Covington, Newport, Fort Mitchell, Fort Thomas, Highland Heights, Alexandria, and Wilder, among others). In this busy metro area, one of the state's largest, you'll find plenty of hotels, restaurants, and major attractions, such as the Newport Aquarium, Newport on the Levee with shops and movie theaters, and the German neighborhood of MainStrasse Village. Cincinnati is

Teresa's
TopPicks for Northern Kentucky

1. Newport Aquarium, (859) 491–FINS

2. Behringer-Crawford Museum, (859) 491–4003

3. Big Bone Lick State Park, (859) 384–3522

4. Dinsmore Homestead, (859) 586–6117

5. Farm fun (Sunrock: 859–781–5502; Noah's Ark: 859–635–0803; Farmer Bill's: 859–823–1058)

6. Kentucky Gateway Museum Center, (606) 564–5865

7. National Underground Railroad Museum, (606) 564–4413

8. General Butler State Resort Park, (866) 462–8853

9. Vent Haven Museum of Ventriloquism, (859) 341–0461

10. Carnegie Visual and Performing Arts Center, (859) 491–2030

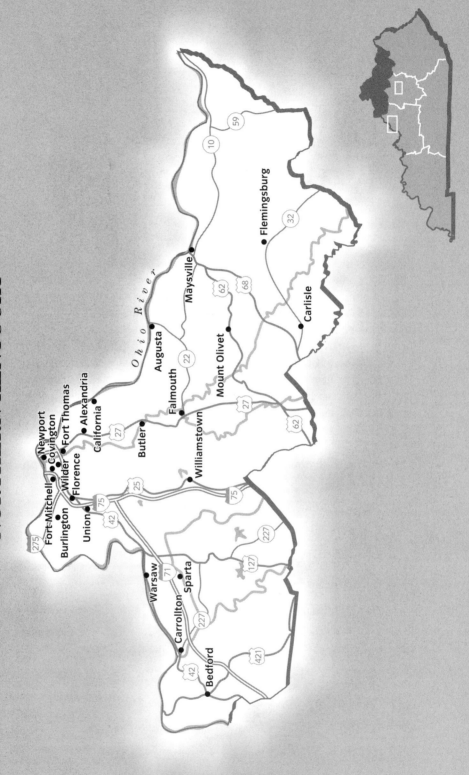

NORTHERN KENTUCKY

Newport
Covington
Fort Thomas
Fort-Mitchell
Wilder
Florence
Burlington
Union
Alexandria
California
Butler
Augusta
Falmouth
Williamstown
Mount Olivet
Maysville
Flemingsburg
Carlisle
Warsaw
Sparta
Carrollton
Bedford

Ohio River

59
10
32
68
62
22
27
62
27
25
75
42
75
227
127
71
227
421
42
275

just across the Ohio River; in fact, northern Kentucky is a good place to stay if you're visiting downtown Cincinnati attractions such as the Cincinnati Zoo or attending a Reds baseball game. This is big-city driving, so be prepared for heavy traffic and some confusing one-way streets. There are many interesting neighborhoods. Heading east to Maysville, then south into the upper Bluegrass region, your journey becomes rural again, with covered bridges, pioneer cabins, and farm fun.

The major roads in this region are Interstate 71, between Louisville and the Cincinnati area, and Interstate 75, which runs north-south, connecting northern Kentucky and the Lexington/Bluegrass region. Interstates 275 and 471 are connecting routes that you use to get around the metro area. To see many of the area attractions—or for a more scenic approach wherever you're heading—you can get off the interstates and take the back roads.

Bedford

Bray Orchards (all ages)
U.S. Highway 42, between Sligo and Bedford; (502) 255–3607. Open daily mid-May through mid-December, from 8:30 A.M. to 7:00 P.M. Admission free (charge for purchases and some activities).

The Pyle family's farm market offers all kinds of homegrown seasonal goodies, from strawberries in late May to pumpkins and apples in the fall, with sweet corn, beans, peaches, blueberries, and apples in between, plus jams, jellies, and honey. Always in season, however, is the farm's own rich and delicious homemade ice cream. Many of the fruit flavors are made using the farm's own produce. It's available by the pint and quart as well as by the cone, so bring a cooler. Every weekend in October, there are hayrides out to the pumpkin patch, and youngsters can play in the straw, wander through the corn maze, and enjoy the tricycle race track.

Apple Days

The community of Bedford celebrates the apple harvest the second week of September with the **Trimble County Apple Festival.** Events include a children's art workshop along with food, music, crafts, and antiques booths. (502) 255–7196.

Carrollton

General Butler State Resort Park (all ages)
Highway 227 North, off I–71; (502) 732–4384 or (866) 462–8853,
www.butlerkentucky.com. Follow the signs from I–71, exit 44. Admission and many
activities **free**. Butler-Turpin House tour $. Lodge rooms $$, cabins $$–$$$$, camp-
ground $. Restaurant $.

If you're trying to please a family with varied interests—or want to dabble in a lot of
different recreational activities—this state park is a good choice, because there's

Lots of Special Reasons to
Visit Carrollton

- **Kilts and bagpipes.** Clans gather at General Butler State Resort Park
  the second weekend in May for dancing and athletics at Kentucky
  Scottish Weekend. (800) 325–0078 or www.kyscottishweekend.org.

- **Music with a point.** Bring a blanket, or camp over for a weekend of
  blues at the Blues to the Point Festival at Carrollton's riverside Point
  Park in early September. Children twelve and under admitted **free**
  with paying adult. (888) 831–3280.

- **Mud, Sweat, and Gears.** Several big mountain bike competitions are
  held annually at General Butler State Resort Park, including a bike
  triathlon and Mud, Sweat, and Gears race in summer. (502) 484–2998
  or www.bikebutler.com.

- **Good scares.** The Family Halloween Weekend at General Butler State
  Resort Park the weekend before Halloween features pumpkin-carving
  contests, ghost stories, hayrides, and "haunted" train rides. (502)
  732–4384.

- **Trees, teas, and treats.** December events abound, including a Festi-
  val of Trees, Children's Winter Wonderfest, and holiday teas at the
  Butler-Turpin House at General Butler State Resort Park. (502)
  732–4384.

- **Tiny tracks.** Several toy train shows and swap meets are held
  throughout the year at General Butler State Resort Park. (502)
  732–4384.

everything from miniature golf to a historic house tour. Whether you come in just for the day or are staying over in the lodge, cabins, or campground, you can rent pedal boats, canoes, and rowboats at the thirty-acre lake, walk two short (¼- and ½-mile) and easy hiking trails, tour the 1819 Butler-Turpin House, play miniature golf, or take on the nine-hole regulation golf course. There's a swimming pool for overnight guests. There are several playgrounds at the park, including a special one for children ages two to six. Picnic facilities are available, and there's a good restaurant in the lodge. The park has one of the best and busiest events schedules of any state park, so call ahead to see if something special is going on. (See sidebar on page 50 for a few of the events.)

The Little Kentucky Flyer Railroad (all ages)
Within General Butler State Resort Park; (502) 743–5414. Open Saturday and Sunday afternoons late spring through October, weather permitting. $

If you visit General Butler State Resort Park on a weekend in late spring through fall, be sure to take a ride on the Little Kentucky Flyer Railroad. This little train and its ⅓-mile route have been a part of the park for more than fifty years, but it was about out of steam when train enthusiast Chris Pate bought and restored it in the 1990s. He's the one wearing the engineer's cap.

Old Stone Jail (ages 8 and up)
Courthouse Square; (800) 325–4290. Available for viewing Monday to Friday. Free.

Pick up keys at the county judge's office in the courthouse (440 Main Street) if you want to see the inside of this jail, used from 1880 to 1969. The first floor has been restored to show the old cells.

Masterson House (ages 5 and up)
304 Ninth Street; (502) 732–5786. Open by appointment. $

This house overlooking the Ohio River was built in 1790 and is one of the oldest buildings still standing along the river west of the Alleghenies. Your children will notice the basement, which includes the kitchen and servants' quarters, and the family cemetery in front of the house.

Amazing
Kentucky Fact

There used to be a downhill ski resort at General Butler State Resort Park. Kentucky winters, however, proved too warm for the resort to make snow.

Scenic **Picnic**

Point Park in Carrollton is a good place for a picnic. The park overlooks the point where the Ohio and Kentucky Rivers meet.

Where to Eat

Cooper's Restaurant, 1420 Gillock Road; (502) 732–4990. Sandwiches and carryout. $

Welch's Riverside Restaurant, 505 Main Street; (502) 732–9118. Buffet and burgers with a great view of the Ohio. $

Hampton Inn, 7 Slumber Lane (Highway 227); (502) 732–0700. Indoor pool, free continental breakfast. $$$

Holiday Inn Express, Highway 227; (502) 732–6661. Outdoor pool, free continental breakfast. $–$$

Where to Stay

Best Western, 10 Slumber Lane (Highway 227); (502) 732–8444. Outdoor pools, pets allowed. $$

Days Inn, I–71 and Highway 227 (exit 44); (502) 732–9301. Outdoor pool, free continental breakfast, pets allowed. $–$$

For More Information

Carrollton/Carroll County Tourism and Convention Commission, 515 Highland Avenue; (502) 732–7036 or (800) 325–4290, www.carrollcountyky.com.

Warsaw/Sparta

Markland Locks and Dam (all ages)

Off US 42 on the Ohio River, 3½ miles west of Warsaw; (859) 567–7661. Open daily dawn to dusk. Free.

One of twenty lock and dam complexes built on the Ohio River by the U.S. Army Corps of Engineers, Markland offers an excellent view of both the river and the locking process, with displays that explain how it works. The whole point is to maintain a water level suitable for river traffic. Bring a picnic (there are tables, a shelter, and restroom facilities), and wait for a barge or boat to come along so you can see the locking process in action.

Kentucky Speedway (ages 8 and up)

Highway 35, Route 1, Sparta; (888) 652–RACE for ticket information or (859) 567–3400 to schedule a track tour, www.kentuckyspeedway.com. Race and events dates vary. Race admission $$$$, track tour $. Camping for weekend $$ (general admission), $$$$ (reserved).

Older children might enjoy NASCAR racing at this 66,000-seat, 1½-mile track, which opened in summer 2000. The track includes a restaurant and concessions; many families also come early and tailgate in the parking lot. Keep in mind that races can last up to four hours and that many are held at night and end very late. On nonevent days you can tour the complex, including taking a ride around the race oval and its banked turns; reservations are required.

Union

Big Bone Lick State Park (all ages)

3380 Beaver Road, off Highway 338, south of Union; (859) 384–3522. Open daily from dawn to dusk. Museum open daily from 9:00 A.M. to 5:00 P.M. in summer; closed Monday and Tuesday the rest of the year. Admission and many activities free.

Some 12,000 years ago, at the end of the last Ice Age, this was a place where giant bison, sloths, mastodon, and oxen came to lick salt, got stuck in the boggy soil, and died. Today it's a place where the buffalo roam. The combination of old bones and new bison makes for a great family outing. Your children will enjoy the Discovery Trail, an easy 1-mile loop (paved, so you can take a stroller or wheelchair) that meanders through the swampland and past the last remaining salt-sulphur spring. Along the way are diorama displays with models of prehistoric animals. But the best part awaits at the end: the park's bison herd. If you visit in late spring or summer you'll likely see some calves. There's also a seasonal indoor museum with plenty of real bones, including a huge mastodon tooth that you can touch, and changing exhibits about local history. You're not allowed to take any found fossils from the park, but children may have fun looking anyway, and the museum shop sells some as souvenirs. The

Rabbit **Hash**

Take Highways 18 and 536 between Big Bone Lick and Burlington for a scenic drive that offers river views and passes right by a shopping spot popular since 1831. **Rabbit Hash General Store** looks as if it has been around at least that long. Step inside and admire the old wooden display cases, and pick up a soft drink or a bottled version of old-time sarsaparilla. The store carries some crafts, along with snacks and general foodstuffs, and is open from 10:00 A.M. to 7:00 P.M. daily. (859) 586–7744.

park also includes playgrounds, picnic areas, basketball and tennis courts, and a campground with a swimming pool. But don't expect to get a restful night's sleep—those bison can be loud! The **Salt Festival** in mid-October includes demonstrations of pioneer activities and crafts.

Boone County Arboretum at Central Park (all ages)

6028 Camp Ernst Road (Highway 237), Union; (859) 384–4999, www.bcarboretum.org. Open daily year-round from dawn to dusk. Free.

Nature meets high tech at this arboretum, the result of a massive county and volunteer planting effort in the late 1990s. If you see people walking around with handheld computers, here's why: The more than 1,100 kinds of trees and 1,700 kinds of shrubs planted are electronically catalogued using a global positioning system. Using the computers, arboretum staff can easily locate any plant for care and growth tracking. At the arboretum Web site before they visit, visitors can find specific plants or learn what's blooming. For most of us, however, it's good enough just to walk the 2½ miles of paved paths to see butterfly gardens, woodland areas, and ornamental plantings. Central Park, 121 acres in all, also includes a large playground.

Big Bone Gardens (all ages)

Across from Big Bone Lick State Park; (859) 384–1949. Open Saturday and Sunday mid-April through mid-July. Free.

You can look at a variety of demonstration gardens at this privately owned nursery. There are water gardens, herb gardens, and a children's favorite, the Gnome Garden, filled with decorative statuary.

Northern Kentucky Metro Area

As you head northeast from Big Bone Lick and Rabbit Hash, you will enter one of Kentucky's largest metropolitan areas, which is also the southernmost part of the Cincinnati, Ohio, metro area. The "Southern Side of Cincinnati," as the area calls itself, is a collection of distinct communities and neighborhoods that make up three large counties: Boone, Kenton, and Campbell. Some parts, such as Burlington to the west, seem almost rural (until a big jet from Cincinnati International Airport goes overhead); the riverfront areas of Covington and Newport seem like the neighborhoods in a big city (which they are). I–71/75 is the major north-south artery. I–275 cuts across the metro area from west to east, and I–471 connects certain portions of the northeastern part of the area. We've actually had better luck getting around off the interstates, although it takes longer. The Northern Kentucky Convention and Visitors Bureau dispenses information about all the communities in the metro area and can provide a map. It's a good idea to request one in advance through the Web site at www .staynky.com, or stop at the Florence Welcome Center at exit 177 off I–75. The folks

Amazing Kentucky Fact

Over 239 million tons of commodities (everything from coal to grains) are transported by barge along the Ohio River each year. For comparison, about 30 million tons are transported on the Great Lakes system.

at the main office in Rivercenter are extremely helpful, but getting there can be a hassle with little ones in tow, since you have to park (and pay) in an underground garage complex and find your way to the office inside.

In this section, attractions are listed in the individual communities in which they are located, and communities are listed from west to east. Lodging in any of the areas would be fairly convenient to all the attractions.

Burlington/Florence

Dinsmore Homestead (all ages)
5656 Burlington Pike (Highway 18), 6½ miles west of Burlington; (859) 586–6117, www .dinsmorefarm.org. Open from April 1 through December 15, Wednesday, Saturday, and Sunday, from 1:00 to 5:00 P.M. Tours on the hour. $

Take a tour of this 1842 house and numerous outbuildings, and you'll learn about family life in Kentucky before and after the Civil War. Five generations of the Dinsmore family lived here, and the house is decorated with a bounty of original possessions, including clothing, furnishings, the elk head bagged by family friend Theodore Roosevelt, and letters. Costumed interpreters add to the illusion with demonstrations of nineteenth-century farm activities and home arts such as cooking and basketmaking. The homestead frequently sponsors wonderful summer educational programs for elementary-school children—everything from archaeology to writing workshops—and there are programs for older children and adults, too. Julia Dinsmore, a daughter of original owners James and Martha Dinsmore, lived here for fifty-four years and wrote many poems and sonnets extensively about her experience; you can buy a book of her poems in the gift shop. The Dinsmore Harvest Festival, on the last weekend of September, features demonstrations of pioneer crafts from cider making to silhouette cutting, plus a petting zoo, children's activities, art displays, and live music.

Boone County Cliffs State Nature Preserve (ages 8 and up)

Middle Creek Road off Highway 18 west of Burlington; (502) 573–2886, www.nature preserves.ky.gov. Open daily from dawn to dusk. No restroom facilities. No picnicking or pets allowed. Free.

It's kind of surprising to find so much nature so close to an urban area, but here's another good hiking place. Interesting 20- to 40-foot cliffs, abundant wildflowers (especially in spring), and plenty of birds are what you'll see. (*NOTE:* Some areas are fairly steep.) Trail maps may not be available on-site, so call the state nature preserve commission in advance.

Where to Eat

Karlo's Bistro Italia, I–75, exit 182, Florence; (859) 282–8282. Made-to-order pasta and Italian favorites, reasonably priced with generous portions. Lunch $, dinner $$

Little Place Restaurant, 2971 Washington Street (Highway 18), Burlington; (859) 586–9421. Family run for thirty years and a favorite with locals; serves Southern fried chicken and other old-fashioned cooking, chili, Kentucky Silk Pie. Breakfast and lunch only. Cash only; no credit cards or checks. $

Matsuya Japanese Restaurant, 7149 Manderlay Drive, Florence; (859) 746–1199. Extensive menu of authentic Japanese sushi and noodle dishes (the restaurant opened to accommodate Japanese families at Toyota's North American headquarters in nearby Erlanger). $–$$

Ming Garden, 4953 Houston Road, Florence; (859) 268–2688. Exceptional buffet with Chinese favorites. $

Where to Stay

Courtyard Cincinnati Airport, 3990 Olympic Boulevard, Erlanger; (859) 647–9900. Indoor pool, restaurant, continental breakfast. $$$$

Hampton Inn Cincinnati Airport South, 7393 Turfway Road, Florence; (859) 283–1600. Outdoor pool, free continental breakfast. $$$–$$$$

Wildwood Inn Tropical Dome and Theme Suites, 7809 US 42, Florence; (800) 758–2335 or www.wildwood-inn.com. Stay in a "tree house," aboard a pirate ship, in a cave, or in an Aztec village—just a few of the themed suites for families. Regular rooms overlooking a large pool area with playground and games also are available. $$$–$$$$

For More Information

Florence Welcome Center, Exit 177 off I–75, Florence; (859) 384–3130. Open daily from 8:00 A.M. to 6:00 P.M. The easiest and most convenient place to get brochures and maps about the northern Kentucky area. The staff is also very helpful on the phone.

Northern Kentucky Convention and Visitors Bureau, 50 East River Center Boulevard, Suite 100, Covington; (800) STAY–NKY or (859) 261–4677 (hotel reservations and packages); general info (800) 447–8489 or www.staynky.com.

Fort Mitchell

Vent Haven Museum of Ventriloquism (ages 6 and up)
33 West Maple Avenue; (859) 341–0461. May 1 to September 30, by appointment only. $

So why are there more than 500 "dummies" in Fort Mitchell, Kentucky? This unusual collection is the legacy of a local businessman and amateur ventriloquist, W. S. Berger, who collected ventriloquist "figures" (the term preferred by serious ventriloquists) from the 1930s until his death in 1973. He left a trust fund to maintain and expand the collection. Along with the merely curious, this little museum attracts professional and amateur ventriloquists from around the United States. In addition to the figures there are such novelties as a talking cane, a talking painting, and a grandfather clock that turns into a ventriloquist figure. Some children and adults will be fascinated by the rows and rows of staring figures; others might find the experience a bit eerie.

Morning Star Pottery Painting Studio (ages 5 and up)
Fort Mitchell Station, 2220 Grandview; (859) 581–3900. Open Wednesday to Friday from 1:00 to 9:00 P.M., and Saturday from 10:00 A.M. to 7:00 P.M. Hourly studio fee ($$ for adults, $ for children), plus price of piece.

The brightly painted walls and multicolored star ornaments hanging from the ceiling make an inviting atmosphere for parents and children to express their creativity together at this paint-your-own pottery place. Choose a bisque item—the inexpensive tiles and plates are good choices for younger children, with everything from piggy banks to large bowls for the more experienced painter—and start with an hour's studio time. When your masterpiece is finished, the staff will fire it for you and have it ready to take home and display in a week or two. If your creative inclinations are diverse, note that there are several crafty stores in the Fort Mitchell Station complex. Morning Star shares space with Knitwits, a contemporary yarn store, and a scrapbooking store is nearby.

Covington/Kenton County

MainStrasse Village (all ages)
Between Fifth and Eighth Streets north and south, Philadelphia and Main Streets west and east, Covington; (859) 491–0458; twenty-four-hour events line (513) 357–MAIN, www.mainstrasse.org. Shop hours vary daily. Public sculpture always on view free. To get there from I–75/71, take Covington Fifth Street exit (exit 192). Free parking is available in the Fifth Street lot.

The historic buildings with their Old World look and the quaint shops and restaurants found along Covington's Main Street and surrounding streets are a reminder of north-

MainStrasse Village **Celebrations**

- **Maifest,** the weekend after Mother's Day
- **Goetta Festival** (celebrating a local food), June
- **Oktoberfest,** the weekend after Labor Day
- **Halloween party,** in late October
- **Santa Claus arrives** in the village in early December—on horse-back!—with apples and nuts for the children. The village offers **Lunch with Saint Nick** for children, usually the second and third Sundays in December, with **vintage carousel rides** the second and third weekends in December.

ern Kentucky's nineteenth-century German heritage. Public sculptures have a fairy-tale motif. Read the Grimm brothers' story of the "Goose Girl" about the princess whose identity is stolen before you come, then see the bronze fountain created by Greek sculptor Elefcherious Karkadoulias. The familiar tale of "The Pied Piper of Hamelin" comes to life on the hour at the **Carroll Chimes Bell Tower** in Goebel Park (Fifth and Philadelphia Streets). This Gothic tower includes a forty-three-bell carillon that plays while wooden figures called jacquemarts act out the story of the Pied Piper of Hamelin on the tower's second level. Among the shops in the neighborhood is **The Magic Shop,** 526 Philadelphia Street (859–491–1313), which features a variety of tricks and novelties (remember the whoopee cushion?). Stop by **Lucy Blue Pizza,** 611 Main Street (859–581–3555), for slices, salads, and soups, or have a complete German dinner at **Wertheim's Gausthaus,** 514 West Sixth Street (859–261–1233).

Suspense and **Suspension**

At first, you think there's a person sitting on the park bench overlooking the river. Gradually, you realize that it's a statue. The seven bronze statues of local historic figures in the riverfront park along Riverside Drive (between Second and Fourth Streets) in Covington will have you doing double takes, particularly the one of abolitionist James Bradley sitting on a bench. Other things to see from this greenspace are the Cincinnati skyline and the blue Roebling Suspension Bridge. Built in 1868, this was the world's first modern suspension bridge, and it was a prototype for the Brooklyn Bridge in New York. (I hope you'll be better prepared than I was to answer questions about what a suspension bridge is!) One of the statues in the park is of the man who engineered this marvel, John Roebling.

Amazing
Kentucky Fact

Daniel Carter Beard, born in Covington, was one of the founders of the Boy Scouts of America.

Devou Park (all ages)

1600 Montague Road, Covington; (859) 292–2151. Open daily. **Free.** To get to the park from I–75/71, take the Twelfth Street Covington exit.

Taking the children to the playground here is especially scenic. Devou (pronounced De-VOO) Park offers one of the best overlooks of the river in the area. At nearly 700 acres, this is also Covington's largest park. In addition to playgrounds there are picnic areas, a small lake for fishing, walking trails, and the Behringer-Crawford Museum. The park's amphitheater hosts **free** plays and concerts in the summer.

Behringer-Crawford Museum (ages 5 and up)

Devou Park, 1600 Montague Road, P.O. Box 67, Covington 41011; (859) 491–4003, www.bcmuseum.org. Open Tuesday to Friday from 10:00 A.M. to 5:00 P.M., Saturday and Sunday from 1:00 to 5:00 P.M.; closed Mondays and holidays. $

From a complete early twentieth-century street car to a two-headed calf, with fossils, art, and model trains in between, this museum in Devou Park has a little something to fascinate everyone in the family. The museum takes its name from William Behringer, an amateur archaeologist who led many of the early excavations at nearby Big Bone Lick and donated many of his collections. Ellis Crawford was the first curator when the museum opened in the 1950s. Housed partly in an 1848 house and partly in a twenty-first-century addition, the museum has lots for kids to see and do. There's an annual holiday show of model trains as well as special activities such as fossil hunts and junior curator programs.

Railway Museum of Greater Cincinnati (ages 4 and up)

315 West Southern Avenue, Covington; (859) 491–RAIL; www.cincirailmuseum.org. Open Wednesday and Saturday from 10:00 A.M. to 4:00 P.M. March through October. There are guided tours on the fourth Sunday of each month at 12:30 and 4:30 P.M. Not wheelchair accessible. $

Train enthusiasts will enjoy strolling through this outdoor museum to see restored cabooses, locomotives, diner cars, and sleepers. You may also see volunteers at work restoring other vintage train cars.

Spiritual Experiences

You can't help but notice the many beautiful churches as you drive through northern Kentucky neighborhoods. There are also some out-of-the-ordinary church-related attractions in the area that may interest your family.

- Did you see the animated film *The Hunchback of Notre Dame?* If so, the **Cathedral Basilica of the Assumption** (Madison Avenue between Eleventh and Twelfth Streets, Covington; 859–431–2060) should look familiar; it's modeled after the Paris cathedral. Though smaller in scale, the gargoyles, sculpture, and flying buttresses look so authentic, you expect to see Quasimodo at any minute. Inside is the world's largest handmade stained-glass window along with eighty-one others, as well as large-scale oil paintings. Open daily from 10:00 A.M. to 4:00 P.M.

- **The Garden of Hope** (699 Edgecliff Drive, Covington; 859–491–1777) is a replica of the tomb of Jesus in Jerusalem, and how it came to be located in Covington is a fascinating story. In 1938, a local minister named Morris Coers visited the Holy Land and was so moved by the experience that he wanted to help others who could not visit there understand what it was like. He spent the next twenty years planning and building this replica tomb, even bringing the caretaker of the Jerusalem garden to Covington to oversee the plans. The garden also includes a chapel patterned after a Spanish mission, a Carpenter Shop, a marble statue of Jesus preaching the Sermon on the Mount, and Holy Land artifacts such as a stone from the Jordan River and ancient tools from Nazareth. The garden is open daily year-round; call to arrange a tour of the buildings (usually not available on Sunday afternoons).

- Northern Kentucky's **Monte Casino House of Worship** made it into *Ripley's Believe It or Not!* as the world's smallest church (just 6 by 9 feet). Only one person at a time can fit inside. It's located across the street from Thomas More College, 2771 Turkeyfoot Road, in Crestview Hills (southwest of Covington and Fort Mitchell). Open from dawn to dusk every day. Take the Turkeyfoot Road exit south off I–275.

Carnegie Visual and Performing Arts Center (all ages)

1028 Scott Boulevard, Covington; (859) 491–2030, www.thecarnegie.com. Open Monday to Friday from 10:00 A.M. to 5:00 P.M., Saturday from noon to 3:00 P.M. Some admissions free, some events $.

This multidisciplinary art center housed in a 1904 Carnegie-built library building includes a theater, galleries, and spaces for educational and hands-on family activities. During the school year, the second Saturday of each month is Carnegie Family Saturday, an afternoon of arts activities, creative play, and fun for parents and children.

Where to Eat

Izzy's, 300 Madison Avenue, Covington; (859) 292–0065. An area institution since 1901, famous for corned beef, Reubens, homemade soups, and potato pancakes. $

LaRosa's Pizzeria, 5880 Merchants Street, Florence; (513) 347–1111 or www.larosas.com. Cincinnati's most famous name in pizza (a local institution since 1954), LaRosa's has numerous locations in the area. The menu features Italian specialties and salads in addition to pizza. This location includes a play area for youngsters. $

Wertheim's Gasthaus, 514 West Sixth Street, Covington; (859) 261–1233. Wiener and other schnitzels, plus other hearty German dishes. Toy box for kids, porch and patio dining. $–$$

Where to Stay

Clarion Hotel Riverview, 668 West Fifth Street, I–75, exit 192, Covington; (859) 491–1200. Indoor pool, revolving restaurant, balconies with great views. $$$$

The Drawbridge Inn, 2477 Royal Drive, Fort Mitchell, off I–75's Buttermilk Pike exit 186; (800) 354–9793 or www.drawbridge inn.com. This castle-themed hotel (complete with moat) is not the newest in the area, but my children enjoyed staying here. The rooms look like normal hotel rooms. Indoor/outdoor pools and several restaurants. $$$

Hampton Inn Riverfront, 200 Crescent Avenue, Covington; (800) HAMPTON. Hot breakfast buffet, indoor pool. $$$

For More Information

Florence Welcome Center, Exit 177 off I–75, Florence; (859) 384–3130. Open daily from 8:00 A.M. to 6:00 P.M. The easiest and most convenient place to get brochures and maps about the northern Kentucky area.

Northern Kentucky Convention and Visitors Bureau, 50 East River Center Boulevard, Suite 100, Covington; (800) STAY–NKY or (859) 261–4677 (hotel reservations and packages); general info (800) 447–8489 or www.staynky.com.

Newport

Newport Aquarium (all ages)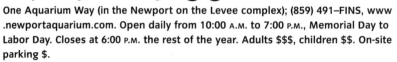

One Aquarium Way (in the Newport on the Levee complex); (859) 491–FINS, www
.newportaquarium.com. Open daily from 10:00 A.M. to 7:00 P.M., Memorial Day to
Labor Day. Closes at 6:00 P.M. the rest of the year. Adults $$$, children $$. On-site
parking $.

"Omigosh, what is that?" "Cool!" "Eeeeyuuuuck!" You'll hear this a lot as you tour the
Newport Aquarium—from fellow adults as much as from children. This small but
nicely laid out aquarium includes a little bit of everything that swims, floats, or soaks.
There are about 11,000 fresh- and saltwater animals, from beautiful tropical fish and
delicate jellyfish to scary-looking eels, several kinds of sharks, and colorful but deadly
dart frogs. You'll see creatures you could hardly imagine, such as the stonefish and
the flashlight fish, along with familiar creatures such as turtles, alligators, penguins,
and an octopus. Seamless acrylic tunnels allow you to view fish swimming above and
below you, creating the illusion that you are surrounded by water. Exhibits include
Shark Alley, with interactive learning stations that allow visitors to get a "shark's-eye
view" of the world and compare their strength to the jaw pressure of a shark; Hidden
Treasures of the Rainforest Islands, featuring Asian otters, Burmese pythons, and lorikeets; and the Shore Gallery, with its Touch Pool, where you can pet a sea star or
horseshoe crab. Older children will enjoy the behind-the-scenes tours (additional
admission), which show how food is prepared for the animals and how they receive
veterinary care. Another extra-admission feature is the Penguin Encounter, a twenty-
minute up-close and personal visit to the penguin house. Call (859) 261–7444 for
reservations for these two tours. An on-site restaurant serves sandwiches and
snacks. NOTE: In summer months, strollers are not allowed before 4:30 P.M. If visiting
earlier in the day, leave the stroller in the car or exchange it in the lobby for a free
loaner backpack that will hold a child weighing up to forty pounds (a good idea, since
you may have to lift younger children to see some exhibits, anyway).

A Day Family Adventure

Viewing animals is always fun, but often the human animals are every bit
as interesting to watch. One time when we visited the Newport Aquarium, we saw a mother and her two daughters closely examining a giant
sea turtle. The younger daughter pressed her face right up against the
glass, eyeball to eyeball with the creature. "He kind of reminds me of
you, Mom," she said in all sincerity. Her older sister glanced mischie-
vously at their mother. "Yeah," she added. "Old and wrinkly."

More to Do at **Newport on the Levee**

- Play more than 200 video, midway, and virtual reality games—plus eat lunch or dinner—at GameWorks (859–581–PLAY). (Children under eighteen must leave at 10:00 P.M.)

- See a movie at the AMC Newport 20—with twenty screens, there's bound to be something you want to see. (859) 261–8100.

- Walk across the Ohio River to Cincinnati on the Purple People Bridge, which is, indeed, purple.

- The complex includes some shops and a variety of eateries, from a pretzel/hot dog stand to full-service seafood, burger, and Italian restaurants.

- Parking is available in an underground garage ($), as well as at nearby pay lots and on the street.

- The complex and surrounding area are the location for concerts and festivals, including the **Newport Italianfest** in mid-June and the **Newport Arts and Music Festival** in late July (859–292–3666).

BB Riverboats (ages 4 and up)

101 Riverboat Row, Newport (behind Newport Aquarium); (859) 261–8500 or (800) 261–8586, www.bbriverboats.com. Cruise year-round; schedule varies. Daily sightseeing cruises in summer. $$$–$$$$

All kinds of excursions are offered aboard this cruise company's three sternwheelers, the *Belle of Cincinnati,* the *River Queen,* and the *Mark Twain.* A one-hour narrated general sightseeing cruise is offered daily; the boats are air-conditioned and have snacks available. Lunch cruises include a buffet meal, entertainment, and games. If you're planning to take a cruise and visit the Newport Aquarium, check into the combination package; it'll save you on the cost of admission. Special holiday and other theme cruises are held throughout the year.

World Peace Bell (all ages)

403 York Street; (859) 581–2971. Always on view. Free.

While you're in the neighborhood, take a few moments to see this large bronze bell; it's a couple of blocks from the levee. Created to honor the new millennium, this 66,000-pound, 12-foot-by-12-foot bronze bell (the world's largest free-swinging bell) was designed by the Verdin Bell Company of Cincinnati, cast in France, shipped to New Orleans, and floated up the Mississippi and Ohio Rivers to Newport. The bell was first rung at the moment 1999 became 2000. Images on the bell include the moon landing; Columbus's ships the *Nina, Pinta,* and *Santa Maria;* and other symbols of human achievement. The bell rings each day at noon, with chimes on the hour.

Other Things to See and Do

Old Courthouse, Fourth and York Streets. Open Monday through Friday from 8:30 A.M. to 4:00 P.M. An 1833 courthouse with skylight depicting the seal of Kentucky.

Stained Glass Theater, Eighth and York Streets; (859) 291–7464. Community theater in a former church building.

Where to Eat

Dewey's Pizza, 1 Aquarium Way; (859) 431–9700. Local favorite; standard toppings plus unusual ones such as goat cheese, capers, and barbecued chicken. Even the crust is good. $

Dixie Chili, 733 Monmouth Avenue; (859) 291–5337. Northern Kentucky tradition since 1929; good chili, plus salads and sandwiches; order at counter. Other locations in northern metro area. Open late. $

Green Derby, 846 York Street; (859) 431–8740. Family owned since 1947; famous for its fried halibut sandwich, "Derby salad" (hot slaw using lettuce), and potato puffs (breaded, fried, mashed potato balls). Good pork chops and fried chicken; cute hand-painted tabletops. $

Pompilio's, 600 Washington Street; (859) 581–3065. Italian favorites. Look for memorabilia from movie *Rain Man.* In summer a bocce ball (lawn croquet) game may be under way out back. $

York St. Cafe, 738 York Street; (859) 261–9675. Eclectic menu, including vegetarian dishes, offered in a converted pharmacy, complete with original floor-to-ceiling wood medicine cases. $$

Where to Stay

Comfort Suites/Riverfront, 420 Riverboat Row, I–471, exit 5; (859) 291–6700. $$$

Travelodge, 222 York Street; (859) 291–4434. $

For More Information

Florence Welcome Center, exit 177 off I–75, Florence; (859) 384–3130. Open daily from 8:00 A.M. to 6:00 P.M. The easiest and most convenient place to get brochures and maps about the northern Kentucky area.

Northern Kentucky Convention and Visitors Bureau, 50 East River Center Boulevard, Suite 100, Covington; (800) STAY–NKY or (859) 261–4677 (hotel reservations and packages); general info (800) 447–8489 or www.staynky.com.

The **Sweet Route**

If you go from Newport to Fort Thomas via Highway 8 (which runs along the river), you'll pass through the community of Bellevue and right by **Schneider's Sweet Shop** (420 Fairfield Avenue, Bellevue; 859–431–3545). Instead of getting ice cream at the Levee Complex in Newport, we waited and bought it at this neighborhood confectionery. Schneider's also sells all kinds of homemade candies, Ice Balls (kind of like snow cones), and Ice Balls with ice cream inside, as well as seasonal treats such as candy apples. Open Monday to Saturday from 10:00 A.M. to 9:00 P.M., Sunday from noon to 9:00 P.M.

Fort Thomas

Blue Marble Books (all ages)
1356 South Fort Thomas Avenue; (859) 781–0602. Open Monday, Friday, and Saturday from 10:00 A.M. to 5:00 P.M., Tuesday to Thursday from 10:00 A.M. to 8:00 P.M. Closed Sunday. Free.

If your children enjoy (or enjoyed) Margaret Wise Brown's *Goodnight Moon,* stop by this independently owned bookstore to see a veritable shrine to this children's classic. Owner Tina Moore has turned an upstairs room into a replica of "The Great Green Room," down to the "bowl full of mush" (which, thankfully, is synthetic). Older readers will also appreciate the "Secret Garden" behind the store. And all young (and would-be) readers and their parents will appreciate the extensive collection of children's books, knowledgeable recommendations, and frequent author signing events.

Tower Park (all ages)
South Fort Thomas Avenue. Open daily. Free.

This eighty-six-acre park is named for the Civil War–era tower designed to provide an overlook of the Ohio River. Today, the tower overlooks a playground and sports fields, but the park's trails take you on a tour around historic buildings that were used as officers' quarters.

Where to Eat

Midway Cafe, 1017 South Fort Thomas Avenue, across from Tower Park; (859) 781–7666. Quesadillas, cheeseburgers, and the house specialty, an Icelandic codfish sandwich, in an 1894 building. $

Wilder

Sunrock Farm (all ages)

103 Gibson Lane; (859) 781–5502, www.sunrockfarm.org. Hours for family tours vary, so call ahead. $$

This rural oasis, only minutes from urban Newport, is the brainchild of "Farmer Frank" Traina. Its mission is to educate children about the importance of conservation by giving them hands-on experiences. Many of its programs are for school and other groups, but families may schedule a one- or two-hour tour, during which parents and children will have the opportunity to milk a goat, bottle-feed kids, gather eggs, and experience the history and natural beauty of this nineteenth-century farm and farmhouse. Maple-syrup tours are offered in February and March.

Butler/Falmouth

Thaxton's Canoe Trails and Paddlers Inn (ages 2 and up)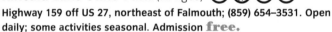

US 27 and Hornbeek Road, Butler; (859) 472–2000. $$$, children under 12 half-price with two paid adult fares.

The Licking River meanders through northern Kentucky from Newport/Covington to Cynthiana. You can follow along by canoe from this outfitter post south of Alexandria. The guides will take you on 6-, 12-, and 18-mile excursions. Children have to weigh at least thirty pounds (so they will fit into a life jacket). Primitive camping and rustic one-room cabins are available for overnight stays.

Kincaid Lake State Park (all ages)

Highway 159 off US 27, northeast of Falmouth; (859) 654–3531. Open daily; some activities seasonal. Admission **free.**

Ever played paddle tennis? (It's kind of a cross between tennis and table tennis.) Give it a try at this recreational park only a half hour south of northern Kentucky's metro area. Equipment is available at the park. You can also rent a boat and go fishing in the 183-acre lake, play miniature golf, walk one of the looped hiking trails, go swimming in the lakeside pool (summer only), enjoy the playgrounds, or have a picnic. There's a nice campground with both tent and RV sites.

Williamstown

Farmer Bill's (all ages)

Windrift Farms, 1790 Baton Rouge Road; (859) 823–1058, www.farmerbill.net. Open June through October; hours vary, so call ahead. Free.

Fall and early December are the best times to visit this farm market. In October there are festival activities on weekends, including a pumpkin patch, corn maze, petting zoo, playground, hayrides, and a haunted barn. In December, you can get your tree and wreaths here while enjoying "Country Christmas" activities such as a live nativity scene and carriage rides. Mam-Maw's Kitchen (see Where to Eat) at the farm serves country cooking for lunch daily and dinner on Saturday nights.

Mullins Log Cabin (all ages)

Scaffold Lick Road, off Highway 36 near Cordova; (859) 322–3082. No regular hours; call ahead. Take exit 154 off I–75, and follow Highway 36 10 miles to Scaffold Lick Road. Overnight stay for a family of up to six people $$.

Want to really get away from it all? Spend the night in this 1800s log cabin—no electricity, no indoor plumbing, and you have to pump your water. This rustic little cabin was saved from destruction by owner Judy Mullins, who with her husband and son dismantled and moved it to its present location. Special events at the cabin include Wild Herb Day, in May, with crafts demonstrations and herb walks.

Where to Eat

The Country Grill, exit 159 off I–75, Dry Ridge; (859) 824–6000. Sandwiches, daily specials, and homemade pie. $

Mam-Maw's Kitchen, 1790 Baton Rouge Road, Williamstown; (859) 391–5301 or www.farmerbill.net. Home cooking for lunch daily, dinner on Friday. $

Where to Stay

Cincinnati South KOA, 331 South Dixie Highway (U.S. Highway 25), Crittenden; (800) 562–9151. Campground with arbore-

tum, stocked lake, paddleboats, game room, and swimming pool. Open March to mid-December. $

Holiday Inn Express, 1050 Fashion Ridge Road, exit 179 off I–75, Dry Ridge; (859) 824–7121. Pets allowed. $$

For More Information

Grant County Tourism and Convention Commission, 1116 Fashion Ridge Road (in the Outlet Center), Dry Ridge; (859) 824–3451.

California

Noah's Ark Farm (all ages)
Koehler Road, off Highway 10; (859) 635–0803. Open April 1 through October 31, Wednesday to Sunday from 10:00 A.M. to 6:00 P.M. $.

Bet you didn't even know Kentucky had a California! I didn't either, until I heard about this fun farm located between Alexandria and Augusta. When you take a tour, you'll see all kinds of animals, from regular farm types, such as sheep and pigs, to peacocks and emus. There are even some Patagonian cavies (giant guinea pigs from South America). You and your kids can bottle-feed lambs and piglets, ask questions of "Dusty the Trick Horse," and watch "Max the Macaw" put on a show. There are also pony rides and picnic areas.

Augusta

Augusta Ferry (all ages)
Ferry Landing; (606) 756–3291. Open daily to vehicle or pedestrian traffic (weather permitting) from 8:00 A.M. to 8:00 P.M. $ per vehicle.

The quaint river town of Augusta was founded in 1795 because it was a location where you could safely cross the river, and a ferry has been carrying folks across since 1798. Today the Augusta Ferry will take you and your car across. A round trip takes only a few minutes (or you can get off and explore Brown County, Ohio), but my children loved this ride and its simple pleasures—seeing the efficient crew at work, peering down into the rushing water, feeling the wind against their faces, and watching the shoreline and its buildings and people recede.

Pace Yourself

From the northern Kentucky metro area, you can get to Augusta and Maysville at a slow and leisurely pace along two-lane Highway 8, which follows the river. A faster route is the very modern AA Highway (Highway 9), which runs from Alexandria at the southern end of Campbell County all the way to the eastern Kentucky city of Ashland.

Amazing Kentucky Fact

Scenes from the movies *Centennial* and *Huckleberry Finn* were filmed in Augusta.

Other Things to See and Do

Dover Covered Bridge, Lee Creek Road off Highway 8 between Augusta and Maysville. Open to traffic.

Historic Walking Tour. Stroll the historic Row House area near Augusta's Riverside Drive. Many of the buildings date to the 1790s. Most of the shops are galleries and antiques stores.

Rosemary Clooney House, 106 East Riverside Drive; (866) 898–8091. Costumes, photos, *White Christmas* memorabilia, and other items relating to the "girl singer" and actress.

Where to Eat

Augusta General Store, 109 Main Street; (606) 756–2525. Sandwiches and hand-dipped ice cream. $

Beehive Tavern, Main Street; (606) 756–2202; reservations recommended. Traditional Kentucky cuisine along with such unusual offerings as Cuban bean soup. With children, lunch is best. $$

For More Information

Augusta Visitor Center, 116 Main Street; (606) 756–2183.

Maysville Area

Kentucky Gateway Museum Center (ages 5 and up)
215 Sutton Street, Maysville; (606) 564–5865. **Open April through December, Monday to Saturday from 10:00 A.M. to 4:00 P.M. Closed Monday from February through March and closed the entire month of January. $**

From life in Limestone to life in miniature—you'll see a variety of history and art exhibits in this new-old building (an 1878 library building with a recent addition). Permanent exhibits here trace Maysville history from settlement days, when it was known as Limestone, to the present and include an eclectic array of dioramas, artifacts, and artworks. Added in 2007 was a collection of miniatures donated by Maysville resident Kaye Browning. Included are thousands of top-quality items crafted to one-twelfth scale—ranging from single pieces of fruit, tiny china, and copies of heirloom chests of drawers to a Kentucky log cabin and a scale model of an eighteenth-century English mansion. "Dollhouse" fans won't want to miss it.

Amazing
Kentucky Fact

Washington, Kentucky, was the first town in America to be named for George Washington. About 500 people lived here in the 1790s; about that same number live here today.

National Underground Railroad Museum (ages 5 and up)
38 West Fourth Street, Maysville; (606) 564–3200 or (606) 564–4413. Open Wednesday, Friday, and Saturday (call first) and other times by appointment. $

Before and during the Civil War, the Ohio River represented a boundary between slavery and freedom, and a lot of Underground Railroad activity occurred in this part of Kentucky. This museum displays a wide range of artifacts, documents, and photographs relating to slavery and the community's role in helping slaves escape. Iron shackles, an original edition of *Uncle Tom's Cabin* by Harriet Beecher Stowe, a rare tobacco press patented by a former slave, and a tin slave plate are a few of the things you'll see. The largest artifact is the house in which the museum is located. The Bierbower House belonged to an abolitionist who came to Maysville with his family specifically to operate a safe house along the Underground Railroad. You can see the original kitchen and slave quarters where fugitive slaves hid under false floors.

Historic Walking Tour
Map of forty-eight sites in Maysville area available from visitor center. Free.

Within walking distance of the Underground Railroad Museum is Phillip's Folly (Third and Sutton Streets), thought to have served as both a holding area for slaves brought to Maysville for sale and later a station on the Underground Railroad. Exterior viewing only. The house is one of forty-eight sites on a city walking tour available at the visitor center. Other sites include a pioneer cemetery and the girlhood home of singer Rosemary Clooney (tell your children that she was George Clooney's aunt). While walking around, you'll also see the Floodwall Murals portraying Ohio River scenes.

Historic Washington (ages 6 and up)

Off U.S. Highway 62/68, south of downtown Maysville; (606) 759–7411, www.washington ky.com. Visitor Center on Main Street open Monday to Friday from 11:00 A.M. to 4:30 P.M., Saturday from 10:30 A.M. to 4:30 P.M., and Sunday from 1:00 to 4:30 P.M., weekends only January through mid-March. Guided tours adults $$, children $.

Although it officially became a part of Maysville in 1990, Historic Washington feels like a separate town. It was, in fact, the first town incorporated west of the Allegheny Mountains (in 1785). Activities are centered on Main Street, where the old buildings house a combination of historic exhibits and modern shops. Start your visit at the Old Washington Visitors Center in the 1790 Cane Brake log cabin, where you can watch a video about the town and sign up for one of the guided history tours (the only way to see the inside of some of the buildings). One-hour tours focus on the Underground Railroad, Washington History, and Log Cabin Learning. If you have the interest and stamina for a longer, more in-depth tour, there's a two-hour Historic District Walking Tour. Highlights include the Simon Kenton Shrine, a re-creation of a 1790 general store; the Harriet Beecher Stowe Slavery to Freedom Museum (while staying here in 1833, the author of *Uncle Tom's Cabin* supposedly witnessed her first slave auction); the Paxton Inn, a former stop on the Underground Railroad (look for the hidden stairwell); and Mefford's Station, one of the few remaining "flatboat houses" built from the timbers of the flatboats that carried the settlers and their possessions down the river to their new home. While in town you may also want to explore the town's shops, which carry everything from candles to looms, and stop by The Carriage Museum on Main Street behind the Carousel Shop. If the kids need to break loose a bit from all this history and shopping, the Maysville Mason County Recreation Park, with an Olympic-size pool, miniature golf course, tennis courts, and twelve-acre fishing lake, is within walking distance.

Festive **Washington**

The little town of Washington is especially fun during these festivals:

- **Chocolate Festival,** weekend before Easter; later if Easter is in March. Chocolate, chocolate contests, and Easter egg hunt. (606) 759–7423

- **Simon Kenton Harvest Festival,** September. Outdoor drama and pioneer-style activities. (606) 564–3559

- **Frontier Christmas,** first weekend in December. Caroling and carriage rides. (606) 759–7411

Other Things to See and Do

Cabin Creek Covered Bridge, off Highway 984, near Tollesboro, east of Maysville. Closed to traffic.

Where to Eat

Caproni's on the River, 320 Rosemary Clooney Street, Maysville; (606) 564–4321. Italian and regional food served in a renovated 1930s landmark. $$

Delites, 222 Market Street, Maysville; (606) 564–7047. Home cooking, burgers, and gyros. $

Hutchison's Grocery, 1201 East Second Street, Maysville; (606) 564–3797. Delicious country ham and other sandwiches to go. $

Magee's Bakery, 8188 Orangeburg Road, Maysville; (606) 759–4882. Pastries and sandwiches on homemade bread to go. $

Where to Stay

Best Western Maysville Inn, US 68 and AA Highway, Maysville; (606) 759–5696. Free breakfast bar; indoor pool. $$–$$$

French Quarter Inn, 25 East McDonald Parkway, Maysville; (606) 564–8000. Outdoor pool, restaurants; some rooms have river view. $$$–$$$$

For More Information

Maysville Tourism Commission, 216 Bridge Street, Maysville; (606) 564–9419, www.cityofmaysville.com. Visitor center is downtown, next to the Simon Kenton Bridge.

Old Washington Visitors Center, P.O. Box 227, Main Street, Washington 41096; (606) 759–7411.

Mount Olivet

Blue Licks Battlefield State Resort Park (all ages)

US 68, P.O. Box 66, Mount Olivet 41064; (859) 289–5507; reservations (800) 443–7008. Open year-round; pool, museum, and minigolf seasonal. Lodge rooms $$–$$$, cabins $$$–$$$$.

This park is kind of a hidden treasure. It has great all-around resort park features—lodge with dining room, cabins, campground, trails, picnic areas, miniature golf, and a pool, plus a **Pioneer Museum**—but is not nearly as crowded or remote as many other resort parks. Between Maysville and Paris off Highway 68 and an easy drive from either direction, it's an easy day trip. The Pioneer Museum includes artifacts relating to prehistoric animals that came here for the salt licks (the mastodon bones are always a big hit) and to Native Americans, pioneers, the Revolutionary War battle fought here in 1782, and the springs that made the area a popular nineteenth-century resort area. Admission charged ($). One of the park's hiking trails takes you past the spot near the Licking River where Daniel Boone was captured by the Shawnee while on a salt-making expedition. In mid-August the park hosts a Battle of Blue Licks Reenactment, with pioneer crafts, music, and animal exhibits.

AnnualEvents in Northern Kentucky

- **Chocolate Festival,** April, Old Washington; (606) 759–7423

- **Kentucky Scottish Weekend,** mid-May, General Butler State Resort Park, Carrollton; (800) 325–4290

- **Maifest,** mid-May, MainStrasse Village, Covington; (859) 491–0458

- **River Days Festival,** early June, Warsaw; (859) 567–5900

- **Italianfest,** early June, Newport; (859) 292–3660

- **Blackberry Festival,** early July, Carlisle; (859) 289–4200

- **Gallatin County Fair and Horse Show,** mid-July, Warsaw; (859) 986–2540

- **Newport Arts and Music Festival,** late July, Newport; (859) 292–3660

- **Grant County Fair,** late July to early August, Crittenden; (859) 824–3451

- **Riverwalk Arts and Crafts Festival,** late August, Maysville; (606) 564–9411

- **Fleming County Covered Bridge Festival,** fourth Saturday in August, Flemingsburg; (606) 845–1223

- **Riverfest,** Labor Day weekend, Newport; (606) 845–1223

- **Oktoberfest,** early September, MainStrasse Village, Covington; (859) 491–0458

- **Trimble County Apple Festival,** early or mid-September, Bedford; (502) 268–3483

- **Dinsmore Homestead Harvest Festival,** late September, Dinsmore Homestead; (859) 586–6117

- **Honey Festival,** October, Maysville; (606) 742–2000

- **Kentucky Wool Fest,** early October, Falmouth; (859) 654–3378

Carlisle

Old Nicholas County Jail and Dungeon (all ages)
121 West Main Street; (859) 289–4200. Open by appointment. Free.

The cell area, or "dungeon," of this early 1800s jail and jailer's house complex is what intrigues most visitors of all ages. (At Halloween, it provides the perfect setting for a fun and scary haunted house. $. Call for dates: 859–289–5174.) You can also step into the restored caboose outside. While you're in town, stroll by the restored 1912 L&N passenger depot at 101 Market Street.

Daniel and Rebecca Boone Home (all ages)
Highway 68 near Carlisle; (859) 289–5174. Open daily; self-guided. Free.

This log cabin was the Boones' last home in Kentucky. If you can find it (in fall and winter you can see it from the road), you're welcome to drive back to it and look around.

A Day **Family Adventure**

I often take day trips with just one child at a time. These are very special and enjoyable opportunities to spend time together, to talk, and to explore each child's interests or those that we share. One of my most enjoyable trips with my daughter was a day visiting covered bridges in northern Kentucky. We set out early one Saturday and took our time, stopping where we pleased. We started at the three bridges in Fleming County, then drove east of Maysville to Tollesboro. We got lost for a while but finally found the 114-foot Cabin Creek Covered Bridge off Highway 984. We stopped in Maysville at the Underground Railroad Museum and visitor center, then drove out to the 63-foot Dover Covered Bridge, just south of Highway 8 on Highway 3113 (Lee Creek Road), between Augusta and Maysville. After a stop in Augusta for a ferry ride (and ice cream), we visited Walcott Covered Bridge, southwest of Augusta off Highway 1159, near the intersection with the AA Highway. On the way home, we went by Johnson Creek Bridge, off Highway 1029 in Robertson County (not far from Blue Licks). Although I was uncertain just how interested a ten-year-old would be, my daughter enjoyed walking through the old bridges and examining the different styles of bracing inside the bridges (and the various states of repair/disrepair and graffiti). I knew the trip had been a success when she asked on the way home, "Can we go back next weekend?"

Amazing
Kentucky Fact

Blue Licks Battlefield State Resort Park was the scene of Kentucky's last battle of the Revolutionary War, in 1782. Among the casualties was one of Daniel Boone's sons.

Flemingsburg

Covered Bridges (all ages)
Highway 32 near Goddard; Highway 158 at Rawlings Road in Ringo's Mill; Highway 111 near Hillsboro; (606) 845–1223. Free.

Three of Kentucky's thirteen remaining covered bridges are in the Flemingsburg area. The prettiest is Goddard White Covered Bridge, off Highway 32. This 60-foot bridge is still open to traffic, and it's a photographers' favorite because it frames a pretty little country church when you look through it from the west side. Grange City Covered Bridge, off Highway 111 near Hillsboro, is an 86-foot bridge that is closed to traffic. Ringo's Mill Bridge, located on Highway 158 at Rawlings Road, is a 90-foot span not open to traffic. Pick up a bridge brochure from Fleming County Tourism (114 West Water Street, Flemingsburg). The drive is pretty, and you'll also pass dairy farms and Amish stores. The fourth Saturday in August, there's a Covered Bridge Festival at Goddard White Covered Bridge.

Lexington

Kentucky is often called "the Bluegrass State," but to Kentuckians "Bluegrass" refers to the city of Lexington and the surrounding counties. Both geographically and symbolically, this lovely region of Kentucky is the heart of the state and a place where your family can experience some of Kentucky's most famous traditions firsthand.

Take horses, for example. Although the Kentucky Derby is run in Louisville, it is at the horse farms in Lexington and the surrounding counties that many Kentucky Derby contenders are bred, born, trained, and, after their racing careers have ended, retired. You can visit some of the farms by appointment, and you'll want to be sure to spend a day at the Kentucky Horse Park, a 1,200-acre farm/educational park.

Teresa's
TopPicks for Lexington

1. Kentucky Horse Park, (800) 678–8813

2. Explorium of Lexington, (859) 258–3253

3. Lexington Children's Theater, (800) 928–4545

4. Lexington Legends, (859) 422–RUNS

5. Lexington History Center, (859) 254–0530

6. McConnell Springs, (859) 225–4073

7. Raven Run Nature Sanctuary, (859) 272–6105

8. Keeneland Race Course, (800) 456–3412

9. Hunt-Morgan House, (859) 233–3290

10. Ashland, (859) 266–8581

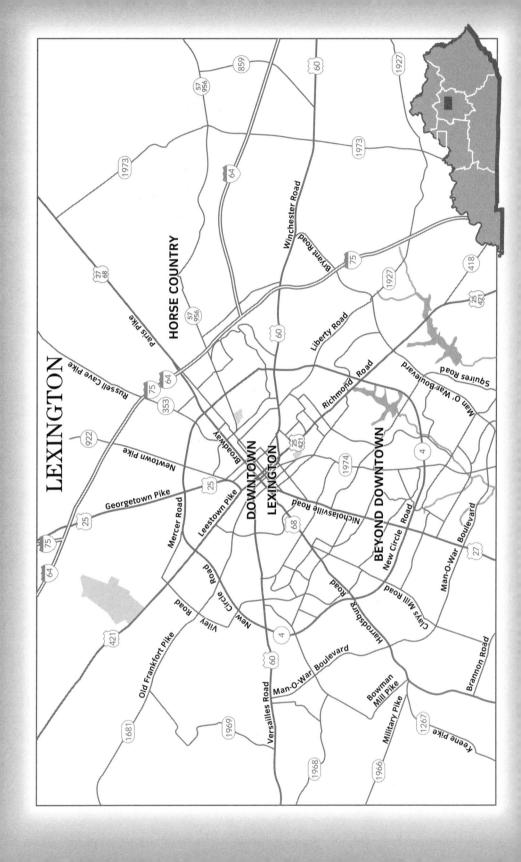

Lexington is also home to an excellent children's museum, children's arts events, and a minor league baseball team, plus a museum celebrating the city's most popular sport—University of Kentucky basketball. Add to this historic and outdoor attractions, and you've got the makings of some great day trips and weekend getaways, almost any time of year.

Lexington is easy to reach: It sits at the crossroads of Interstate 75 north-south and Interstate 64 east-west. Once in town, remember that the city is laid out on a spoke-and-wheel design. Two outer roads—New Circle Road (Highway 4), which encircles the perimeter of the city, and farther out, Man o' War Boulevard—make it almost all the way around. Streets within the city may change names three times as they pass from one end of the city to another. For example, U.S. Highway 27 is Paris Pike north of town, Broadway in town, and Nicholasville Road south of downtown. Go figure! (Get a map.)

Horse Country

Kentucky Horse Park (all ages)
4089 Iron Works Parkway (exit 120 off I–75); (859) 233–4303 or (800) 678–8813, www .kyhorsepark.com. Open year-round; some attractions are seasonal. Open daily March 15 to October 31 from 9:00 A.M. to 5:00 P.M., $$$; closed Monday and Tuesday November 1 to March 14, $$. Children ages 6 and under admitted free year-round. Additional charge for horseback and pony rides. Ticket includes admission to the American Saddlebred Museum.

Horses, horses, everywhere—and you can even take a ride at this 1,200-acre kingdom of the horse. Every family with a horse enthusiast will want to spend a day here, exploring the museum and art gallery, watching a farrier at work, taking a trail ride or horsedrawn carriage ride, and coming face to face with dozens of breeds of horses—racehorses, working horses, riding horses, and even miniature horses. In addition to the permanent exhibits and activities, there's a packed seasonal schedule of horse shows, riding competitions, dog shows, and other events. You can begin your self-guided tour by visiting the grave and bronze statue of Thoroughbred champion Man o' War. Then step into the theater and watch two moving films about horses' roles throughout history. One of our favorite activities is the daily Parade of Breeds (spring through summer), where you get to see familiar and unusual horse breeds strut their stuff; afterward you can walk through the Big Barn for a closer look. The daily Mare and Foal Show (late May through July) is a good opportunity for children and baby horses to come eye to eye. The horse park is also a good place for novice riders to take a trail ride; in fact, it's one of the few places in the region where children under twelve are allowed to ride horses as opposed to guided ponies (mid-March through October for ages seven and up; children must be at least 4 feet tall). There are pony rides, too, for children ages two to twelve. The park includes a restaurant as well as

Horse Basics

Has your young horse lover been bugging you for a horse? The summer Youth Riding Program at the Kentucky Horse Park is a chance for young-sters ages ten to eighteen to learn the basics of horse care, handling, and riding. In these weeklong sessions, each participant is assigned a horse (usually one of the park's mustangs) for the week, and it's his or her responsibility to feed, brush, and care for the horse, including cleaning out the stalls and taking care of the tack. Lodging is not included in the fee, but participants have come from across the United States. Your young rider could go to "summer school" at the Horse Park while the rest of the family goes sightseeing in Lexington and the Bluegrass. Call (859) 259–4206 for session dates and more information.

picnic areas and a campground. Although special events and activities are at their height in spring through fall, the horse park museum can also be a great escape from cabin fever on a winter weekend.

The American Saddlebred Museum (ages 4 and up)

Located next to the Kentucky Horse Park; open same hours. Admission included with Kentucky Horse Park.

This museum traces the history and accomplishments of Kentucky's native breed of horse, the American saddlebred. A film presentation fills you in on the history of the breed—it descended from horses shipped to North America from Britain in the 1600s. In other exhibits you'll see saddlebred champions. Then, in an interactive exhibit, you get to see what you'd look like atop the famous champions Imperator, Sky Watch, and Wing Commander.

Amazing
Kentucky Fact

About 10,000 Thoroughbred horses are born each year in Kentucky, generally from February through July. All of the current year's foals officially become one-year-olds (called yearlings) on January 1 of the following year.

Horsey **Holidays**

The calendar at the Kentucky Horse Park includes some great events for children:

Young riders from across the state compete at the **Kentucky High School Invitational Rodeo,** late May. The "minis" parade, prance, and even dance at the **Miniature Horse Association Julep Cup Show,** mid-July. In late July, collectors of Breyer horse figures gather from around the country for **Breyerfest.** The whole family will enjoy **Southern Lights,** a dazzling drive-through-at-your-own-pace holiday lights show at the Kentucky Horse Park, open nightly mid-November through December 31. The animated displays feature horse themes as well as traditional holiday themes (859–255–5727). Also, watch the calendar for dog agility competitions and other activities. Call the horse park at (800) 678–8813 or visit www.kyhorsepark.com for more information about special events.

Horse Farm Tours (ages 6 and up)

For information about tour companies offering horse farm tours and farms that are currently open, contact the Lexington Convention and Visitors Bureau at (859) 233–7299.

About 150 horse farms are in Fayette County alone (and about 450 if you include the surrounding Bluegrass counties), raising all kinds of horses—from Thoroughbred racehorses to show horses, Morgans, and miniatures. And there are several ways to see horses on these working farms while you're here. Just driving north from Lexington on Paris Pike, Newtown Pike, or Russell Cave roads, you're likely to see beautiful horses, barns, and scenery. Numerous tour companies offer guided tours, some focusing on horse farms, others including horse farms as part of general tours. Tours will range from $$ to $$$$ and usually last from two to three hours. A few farms also allow individual visits by appointment only. Farms offering tours at press time included Three Chimneys Farm and Claiborne Farm (see Versailles and Paris sections of the Bluegrass Region chapter for details).

Keeneland Race Course (ages 6 and up)

4201 Versailles Road; (800) 456–3412 or (859) 254–3412, www.keeneland.com. $ for admission to the races; watching morning workouts or strolling the grounds at other times of the year is free. Take U.S. Highway 60 (Versailles Road) west from downtown Lexington.

Not far past Calumet Farm on Versailles Road is Keeneland, which is not your typical racetrack. With its tall trees, flowering shrubs, and elegant stone buildings and walls, this place looks more like a park. The races run for several weeks in April and October, and at other times of the year the track is a training center. During race meets the track offers Breakfast with the Works, an early morning backside tour that includes special activities for children. Even if your visit to Lexington doesn't coincide with a race meet, your family might enjoy a visit; go out early (6:00 to 10:00 A.M. mid-March through mid-November) to watch the horses working out on the track, then have a hearty breakfast at the track kitchen. The Derby Day celebration at Keeneland (always the first Saturday in May) is much more manageable and family-friendly than Churchill Downs in Louisville, with barbecue, music, and special activities for children.

The Thoroughbred Center (ages 5 and up)

3380 Paris Pike; (859) 293–1853, www.thethoroughbredcenter.com. From April through October, tours are offered Monday to Saturday at 9:00 A.M. No Saturday tours November through March. Adults $$, children $.

Like any athletes, racehorses have to train. They work out, eat right, and have a team of advisers. You can find out how a horse is readied for a race at this private training center on Lexington's Paris Pike (nicknamed "Millionaire's Row" because of the many beautiful farms). The guided training center tour begins with the clocking tour, where you'll have a close view of horses working out on the training track. Then you visit one of the barns and meet an owner/trainer. If you visit April through October, it's a good idea to call ahead for reservations.

Horse Country **Dos and Don'ts**

There are hundreds of horse farms in and around Lexington, and several allow visitors. All things considered, the Kentucky Horse Park is probably the best place for families to see horses in the Lexington area, especially if your children are younger. If you plan to visit a private farm, just keep these points in mind:

- Do call first. Not all farms welcome visitors, and reservations are always required.

- Do keep a close eye on your children for their own safety. Don't let them wander off into stalls, other barns, or fields. Don't let them get close enough to the horses to be bitten or kicked.

- Do be prepared for your kids to learn about the Thoroughbred breeding process. The explanation might be quite detailed.

- Do tip the farm staff member who leads the tour. There's no admission charge for the tours, but a $5 to $10 tip for the guide is customary.

Amazing Kentucky Fact

Keeneland Race Course and other spots in Lexington and the Bluegrass region were shooting locations for the film *Seabiscuit*. Lots of local people served as extras, but the race crowds shown in the movie also included more than 7,000 inflatable dummies specially produced for the film. The dummies had hand-painted individual faces and were topped with period hats.

The Red Mile Harness Track (ages 8 and up) 🐘🍴
1200 Red Mile Road; (859) 255-0752. Racing meets vary. Grounds open year-round from 8:00 A.M. to 5:00 P.M. Free to grounds, races $.

Older children may enjoy seeing harness racing, in which the horses pull riders seated in small carts (the meets run late April through June and a few days in late September). Year-round, you can walk around at this historic track (dates to 1875). Sites to see include the interesting octagonal-shaped Floral Hall building at the entrance, the red soil track from which the name comes, and barn areas. The Red Mile also hosts a variety of other special events, from a chili cook-off on Memorial Day to the Junior League Horse Show, the largest outdoor saddlebred horse show in the nation. Children interested in horses and riding will enjoy seeing the beautiful horses and elegantly dressed riders go through their paces for the judges.

Downtown Lexington

Explorium of Lexington (all ages)
Victorian Square, 440 West Short Street; (859) 258-3253, www.explorium.com. Open Tuesday to Saturday from 10:00 A.M. to 5:00 P.M., and Sunday from 1:00 to 5:00 P.M. $

The interactive exhibits at this bright and lively museum give youngsters a hands-on introduction to science, history, geography, and the arts. Even adults in the group will enjoy the well-designed exhibits. There's also a special area for the youngest visitors: In the Wonder Woods, infants and toddlers can slide down a lightning bug, splash in the water, or curl up in a "nest" while Mom and Dad learn how young brains develop. Older children will enjoy such exhibits as Science Station X (NASA and fighter jet items); Brainzilla, the giant talking brain; and the walk-in anatomy experiences Mighty Mouth and Heartscape. Other favorites include the big bubble fun area and the multicultural Home exhibit, which compares houses around the world. Almost every weekend there are special workshops and activities. Some of the special activities require advance registration, so check to see what's going on while you're in town. In late September, the museum sponsors Museum-Go-Round, an arts festival where youngsters can display their artwork.

University of Kentucky Basketball Museum (ages 5 and up)

Second floor of the Civic Center, Lexington Center, 410 West Vine Street; (800) 269–1953. Open Monday to Saturday from 10:00 A.M. to 5:00 P.M., Sunday from noon to 5:00 P.M. $

If you're into college basketball, you've heard of the UK Wildcats. The Cats have long been a national powerhouse and have captured five NCAA championships. Just a covered pedway walk away from Victorian Square across Main Street, in the Civic Center complex, is an engaging collection of memorabilia relating to the team's history and accomplishments. The hands-on activities are the most fun: You can play trivia at a computer monitor, take your turn at the microphone to call the action of a videotaped play (then listen to yourself), and even shoot some hoops on a small court that includes part of the real floor from the Meadowlands, where UK won one of its championships. Don't miss the Virtual Court, where video cameras and computer technology enable you to go one-on-one against some of Kentucky's top players from the past. For a small additional fee, you can take a guided tour of nearby Rupp Arena, the Wildcats' home court. At the entrance to the museum is a display of some of the art Wildcats created for a citywide exhibit.

Lexington History Center (ages 3 and up)

Old Fayette County Courthouse, 215 West Main Street; (859) 254-0530. Open Friday to Monday from noon to 4:00 P.M. Lexington History Museum opens at 10:00 A.M. on Saturday. Free; donations accepted.

Four local history museums with a wide array of artifacts and curiosities share the big stone building used as Fayette County's courthouse for most of the twentieth century. The **Lexington History Museum** has exhibits on the second and third floors. Among the permanent exhibits is "Athens of the West," which tells the story of the city through photographs, artifacts, and even architectural details from old buildings. ("Athens of the West" was Lexington's nickname in the early 1800s because it was a

Amazing
Kentucky Fact

West to Lexington? Kentucky was the first American frontier, and as its first big city, Lexington was called the "Athens of the West" in the early 1800s.

cultural center on the new western frontier.) Changing exhibits focus on topics relating to local history; past exhibits have included a costume display from the city's Shakespeare festival and exhibits on horse racing. On the first floor, you can visit the **Lexington Public Safety Museum,** with exhibits of badges, equipment, uniforms, photos, and other interesting items relating to the city's law-enforcement and fire agencies; the police and fire dispatch radio is always on. Across the hall is the **Isaac Scott Hathaway Museum,** honoring African-American Kentuckians, including Hathaway, a Lexington-born artist who sculpted busts of famous African-Americans and was the first African-American to design an American coin (a commemorative 50-cent piece honoring George Washington Carver that was issued in 1951). The **Kentucky Renaissance Pharmacy Museum** has displays relating to early Bluegrass drugstores. With all this, there's sure to be something (and probably a number of things) to interest everyone in the family. The Lexington History Center's Web site, www.lexingtonhistorycenter.com, has good activity sheets for youngsters, including a museum scavenger hunt and a family-tree activity.

Lexington Livery Company (all ages)

Make reservations by calling (859) 259–0000, or catch a coach in front of the Radisson Plaza Hotel, Vine Street and Broadway. Evening rides start at 8:00 P.M. daily in summer months, Friday and Saturday in winter months, weather permitting. Cost: $35 for half-hour tour; up to four passengers. www.lexingtonlivery.com.

This horse-drawn carriage tour winds through Lexington's downtown and historic Gratz Park neighborhood, but what youngsters will love most are the giant Percheron draft horses (sweet and pettable) and the thrill of clippity-clopping through the city.

Foucault Pendulum and Horse Clock (all ages)

Lexington Public Library, 140 East Main Street; (859) 231–5500. Library hours are Monday to Thursday from 9:00 A.M. to 9:00 P.M., Friday and Saturday from 9:00 A.M. to 5:00 P.M., and Sunday from 1:00 to 5:00 P.M. The Book Cellar is open Monday to Thursday from 9:00 A.M. to 6:00 P.M., Friday and Saturday from 9:00 A.M. to 4:00 P.M., and the first Sunday of each month from 1:00 to 5:00 P.M. Free.

The atrium of the main branch of Lexington's public library includes a Foucault pendulum suspended 70 feet from the top of the atrium. Also of interest is the handless clock: Sixty horses around the perimeter of the clock face light in sequence to look like a horse racing around the edge. The library also includes a small art gallery off the lobby and a used bookstore, the Book Cellar, on the lower level. The library adjoins Phoenix Park, a good place to rest or have an outdoor lunch in warm weather.

A Fountain **of Fun**

Before or after a visit to the Lexington Children's Museum, UK Basketball Museum, or a Lexington Children's Theater performance, enjoy a soda, malt, milkshake, or sundae at **Hutchinson's Drug Store** (859–252–3554), on the first floor of Victorian Square. This authentic old-time soda fountain is a real treat for modern youngsters. Open Monday to Friday from 9:30 A.M. to 7:00 P.M., Saturday from 12:30 to 4:00 P.M.

Lexington Children's Theater (ages 5 and up)
418 West Short Street; (859) 254–4546 or (800) 928–4545, www.lctonstage.org. $

In a typical season, LCT will bring folk tales, historical characters, and great children's stories to life onstage. Founded in 1938, it's one of the longest operating professional children's theater companies in the United States. The company performs in its own theater just down the street from the Lexington Children's Museum. The performance season runs from October through May. In summer, there are day camps and workshops in which youngsters rehearse and perform plays; if you're planning to be in town for a week or so, this might be a special experience your child would enjoy.

Mary Todd Lincoln House (ages 6 and up)
578 West Main Street; (859) 233–9999, www.mtlhouse.org. Open March 15 through November 30, Monday to Saturday from 10:00 A.M. to 4:00 P.M. Last tour starts at 3:00 P.M. $$, children under 6 free.

At this fourteen-room Georgian-style brick house, you'll learn about the childhood of Mary Todd, who later became First Lady as the wife of Abraham Lincoln. Mary's family lived here, and she and Abe visited after they married. The house features authentic memorabilia of the Todd family, and the tour focuses on Mary's cultured upbringing as a member of a prominent early Lexington family. The house is within easy walking distance of the Lexington Children's Museum and the UK Basketball Museum.

Lexington Cemetery (all ages)
833 West Main Street; (859) 255–5522. Cemetery open daily from 8:00 A.M. to 5:00 P.M. Office open Monday to Friday from 8:00 A.M. to 4:00 P.M. and Saturday from 8:00 A.M. to noon. Free.

With hundreds of varieties of trees and plants, lovely lakes and gardens, and an abundance of birds, this nationally acclaimed arboretum makes an excellent nature walk. There are also many interesting monuments. Stop at the office and pick up the *Children's Tour,* an oversized map with interesting information and a list of things for children to look for as they walk through the arboretum. History and tree guides and a bird list also are available. *NOTE:* Bicycles, picnics, and climbing on monuments are not allowed.

Hunt-Morgan House (ages 8 and up)

201 North Mill Street; (859) 233–3290. Open March 1 through December 22, Wednesday to Friday from 1:00 to 5:00 P.M., Saturday from 10:00 A.M. to 4:00 P.M., and Sunday from 1:00 to 5:00 P.M. Last tours start an hour before closing. $

This elegant Federal-style house just a few blocks north of Main Street has a lot of great history attached to it. It was built by John Wesley Hunt, reputedly Kentucky's first millionaire. Hunt's grandson, who also lived in the house, was a flamboyant figure of the Civil War. Confederate General John Hunt Morgan and his "Raiders" caused trouble all over Kentucky, and his escapades give the house tour guides some great material. Ask about the time Morgan rode his horse into the house—and the ghost with red shoes. A small Civil War museum on the second floor includes uniforms and other artifacts relating to Morgan and his marauders. The surrounding Gratz Park neighborhood was Lexington's poshest suburb in the early 1800s. The small park with its bronze statues and fountain is a pleasant place to rest or romp after a tour.

More Arts for the Kids

Other Lexington arts attractions geared to families include:

- **Lexington Philharmonic.** Three fun one-hour family concerts each season: Halloween, Candy Cane Holiday concert, and spring concert. Performances at Singletary Center, with preconcert Instrument Petting Zoo and games. (859) 233–4226

- **Lexington Ballet** (859–233–3925) and **Kentucky Ballet Theatre** (859–252–5245). The city often has two versions of the popular holiday ballet *The Nutcracker*, as well as other kid-friendly ballet performances.

- **UK Art Museum and Singletary Center for the Arts,** University of Kentucky campus. Variety of works in permanent exhibit; small, easily maneuvered space. Children may also enjoy the contemporary outdoor sculptures on the center grounds. There are many free concerts and recitals at Singletary, as well as paid events by top artists. (859) 257–4929

- **Central Kentucky Youth Orchestras.** Fall, December, and spring concerts by outstanding young musicians. (859) 254–0796

Lexington's **"Transylvania"**

If your family is up for a little more walking, stroll from Gratz Park across Third Street to the campus of **Transylvania University,** the oldest university west of the Alleghenies. Sites to see include a 1783 log cabin and the massive Greek Revival–style administration building, Old Morrison. Despite the name, there are no vampires here, although there is a tomb. Constantine Rafinesque, an eccentric nineteenth-century professor, is buried underneath Old Morrison. Every Halloween students are selected to spend the night in "Rafinesque's tomb."

Lexington Legends (all ages)

Applebee's Park, 1200–1295 North Broadway (next to Northland Shopping Center); (859) 422–RUNS, www.lexingtonlegends.com. Ticket prices from $ to $$$, depending on seat location.

A devoted group of baseball fans worked for years to bring a minor league team to town. The Lexington Legends arrived in 2001 and won the South Atlantic League championship their very first year. Any Legends home game (about seventy per season, April through October) is a winning experience for baseball-loving families. The stadium design puts you very close to the action and includes many family-friendly features, such as picnic areas, family restrooms, and a kids' play area complete with merry-go-round. If you live in the region, you may want to sign up your child for the Kids' Club; for $12, each member gets special perks, including a T-shirt, newsletter, and opportunities to "run the bases" at some games.

More Sports Fun in Lexington

- **University of Kentucky Wildcat football.** Commonwealth Stadium; (859) 257–1818 or (800) 928–2287

- **University of Kentucky Wildcat basketball.** Rupp Arena (tickets can be hard to get); (859) 257–1818 or (800) 928–2287

- **Lexington Horsemen indoor football.** Rupp Arena; (859) 422–PASS

- **Kentucky Boys "Sweet Sixteen" State Basketball Tournament.** Mid-March at Rupp Arena; (859) 299–5472

Haunted Hotel?

Some people have had an absolutely ghostly time at the **Gratz Park Inn,** 120 West Second Street, in downtown Lexington. The ghost of a little girl has been seen playing in the hall. Guests have complained about noise from the rooms on the floor above, only to discover that they are staying on the top floor. And hotel workers have spotted specters in the basement. (Maybe it's not too surprising when you learn that this historic building once housed the city morgue!)

Thoroughbred Park (all ages)
Main and Midland Streets. Open daily year-round, twenty-four hours. Free.

It just isn't a visit to Lexington without snapping a few photos of the family with the life-size, realistic-looking bronze horses that "race" and "graze" in this two-and-a-half-acre park at the east end of downtown.

The Living Arts and Science Center (all ages)
362 North Martin Luther King Boulevard; (859) 252–5222, www.lasclex.org. Open Monday to Friday from 8:30 A.M. to 5:00 P.M.; Saturday from 10:00 A.M. to 2:00 P.M.; closed Saturdays June through August. Free.

Although this center is best known for its workshops and classes, even if you're in town just for a day you may want to stop by to see the changing science and visual arts exhibits.

Beyond Downtown

Ashland, the Henry Clay Estate (ages 8 and up)
120 Sycamore Drive; (859) 266–8581, www.henryclay.org. Tours start on the hour from 10:00 A.M. to 4:00 P.M. Monday through Saturday, 1:00 to 4:00 P.M. Sunday. Closed in January and on Monday from November through March; open in February on weekends and by appointment. Admission for house tour: adults $$, children ages 6 to 18 $, children 5 and under free. Admission to grounds and garden free.

Henry Clay was one of early Kentucky's most prominent citizens, a U.S. senator, secretary of state, and three-time losing presidential candidate. ("I'd rather be right than president," he reportedly said.) Away from Washington, at his 672-acre estate in Lexington, Clay was a gentleman farmer who bred prize livestock and entertained notables such as the Marquis de Lafayette and James Monroe. Twenty acres of Clay's

Lexington estate are preserved as a historic site, including an elegant Italianate house built by his son James. The house includes many family artifacts. Young visitors will enjoy the parklike setting more than the house tour. The formal garden is a fun place to take a walk, and the tombstone of "Gypsy the Ashland Cat" can be seen on the grounds. Pick up a free guide at the visitor center. Check the events calendar during your visit; special children's events range from an Easter egg hunt to Victorian teas. Spring through fall you can have lunch (sandwiches and wonderful desserts) on the grounds at the Gingko Tree cafe.

Lexington Arboretum (all ages)

Alumni Drive, between Nicholasville and Tates Creek Roads; (859) 257–6955, www .ca.uky.edu/arboretum. Open dawn to dusk daily year-round; visitor center open 8:30 A.M. to 4:00 P.M. Free.

Paved pathways and a variety of plant displays make this one-hundred-acre greenspace (Kentucky's Official State Botanical Garden) an enjoyable place for a city hike. The "Walk Across Kentucky" is a 2-mile path encircling the arboretum, with a variety of plants designed to show the geophysical regions of the state. If that's too far for your group, it's just a short stroll from the parking lot to the vegetable, herb, flower, and water-plant display gardens. Stop by the visitor center for maps and information.

Raven Run Nature Sanctuary (all ages)

5888 Jacks Creek Road (from Lexington, take Tates Creek Road to Spears Road to Jacks Creek Pike); (859) 272–6105. Open daily, October through March, from 9:00 A.M. to 5:00 P.M., April through September from 9:00 A.M. to 7:00 P.M. Admission free; **some programs $.**

This 470-acre park includes 8 miles of hiking trails through beautiful meadows and woodlands. Although some of the trails are too rugged for young children, there are some easy options, including a ½-mile Freedom Trail accessible to strollers and wheelchairs. Spring through fall, Raven Run offers terrific evening and weekend programs in which families can explore nature together, including stargazing, "bug walks," nocturnal walks with owl calling and storytelling, and learn-to-camp nights. There are special programs for children under five. The schedule varies and reservations are recommended, so call ahead.

A Day Family Adventure

One spring break, appointments and budget prevented us from taking a trip, so for a few days we checked into a local hotel that had a big swimming pool and game room. We went to free places in the area that we had never visited before and enjoyed the feeling of a getaway without major expense or the long drive.

Play Time

Bring your skateboard when you visit Lexington: The **Skatepark in Woodland Park** (East High Street at Kentucky Avenue; 859–288–2900) offers 12,000 square feet of pipes, platforms, and ramps. **Free.**

Other good spots when it's just time to play include three elaborate wooden **Creative Playgrounds** for climbing, swinging, sliding, and imagining (Jacobson Park, off Richmond Road; Shillito Park, off Reynolds Road; and behind Picadome Elementary School, 1642 Harrodsburg Road). **Free;** (859) 288–2900. If it's raining, take younger kids to **KidsPlace** at the Lexington Athletic Center (3992 West Tiverton Court; 859–272–5433), a two-story indoor playground.

Waveland Historic Home (ages 8 and up)

225 Waveland Museum Lane, 6 miles south of Main Street off Nicholasville Road (US 27 south); (859) 272–3611 or (800) 255–PARK. Open March 1 to mid-December, Monday to Saturday from 9:00 A.M. to 5:00 P.M., Sunday from 1:00 to 5:00 P.M. Adults $$, students $.

Waveland, built by the Bryans, distant relatives of Daniel Boone, offers a glimpse of life on an antebellum Kentucky plantation, from the mansion to the slave quarters. The tour guides tell young visitors about popular children's games of the time, as well as household items that today's children might not be familiar with, such as feather beds. Pack a picnic lunch and let your children play on the playground, or take a family walk on the easy hiking trails near the house. *NOTE:* No wheelchair-accessible restrooms.

McConnell Springs (all ages)

416 Rebmann Lane (from Old Frankfort Pike, turn onto McConnell Springs Drive across from the fire training center and follow signs); (859) 225-4073. Open daily 9:00 A.M. to 5:00 P.M. **Free.**

This twenty-six-acre getaway smack in the middle of an industrial area includes the location of the campsite where early Kentucky settlers heard the big news about the Revolutionary War's Battle of Lexington—and decided to name their settlement in its honor. The city they founded actually grew up a couple miles away, and for years the site seemed lost in time. A citizens' group reclaimed the area, and it's now an interesting natural getaway for bird-watching and hiking. Along the 2 miles of trails you'll see interesting natural features such as sinkholes and bubbling springs as well as the ruins of early nineteenth-century rock fences, barns, and an old mill. The trail includes a ½-mile paved section that is wheelchair and stroller accessible. In the education center, kids can look at books on nature, see a few animals, and use a touch-screen computer program to create "bird raps" and hear other animal sounds. There are lots of special programs throughout the year, from bird counts to geocaching. *NOTE:* Some trails have steep areas, so ask at the education center if you are hiking with younger or less nimble hikers.

Headley-Whitney Museum (ages 8 and up)
4435 Old Frankfort Pike, 6½ miles from downtown Lexington; (859) 255–6653, www.headley-whitney.org. Open Tuesday to Friday from 10:00 A.M. to 5:00 P.M., weekends noon to 5:00 P.M. $, free for children under 5.

Have you ever seen a room in which the walls and doors are covered with thousands of seashells? You'll find one at this eclectic museum, along with a Jewel Room showcasing tiny bibelots encrusted with gems and precious metals. A third building houses a variety of permanent and changing decorative arts exhibits from around the world, from textiles to porcelain. Although there is definitely a "fragile" nature to this museum, older children in particular will enjoy the interesting and odd items on display.

A Day **Family Adventure**

Because I love old houses so much, I've dragged my children through many of them over the years. Even when they were little, I would often give it a try, with varying degrees of success. Here are some "survival" tips for other parents who love historic houses:

- Go through when the house is not crowded (the first or last tour of the day often fits the bill). This gives you and the tour guide more flexibility to shorten the narrative or focus it to children's interests. (A smart tour guide at the Hunt-Morgan House fascinated my children by telling them about the horsehair chair in the parlor.)

- If the tour is self-guided, be prepared to take it all in quickly. Your children won't want to linger, but even a whirlwind walk-through can still be enjoyable.

- Many homes have materials such as scavenger hunts used with school tour groups. Ask for a copy.

- If your child is tired or cranky, come back another time.

- Don't try to cram too many historic houses or passive activities into one day. Balance the historic house tour or educational activity you want your children to see with an activity or attraction they choose. My children quickly discovered that touring an old house made Mom a much more enthusiastic miniature golfer!

The World **Is Coming!**

In 2010, the Kentucky Horse Park in Lexington will host the World Equestrian Games. These are international competitions in dressage, show jumping, driving, vaulting, reining, and other horse-and-rider events. It will be the first time the games have been held in the United States (they're usually held in Europe). More than 800 competitors and 900 horses from around the world are expected to attend. In addition to these exciting competitions, lots of other special activities will be going on. The games will run from September 25 to October 10, 2010. For more information about events and tickets, visit www.feigames2010.org.

Aviation Museum of Kentucky (all ages)

Bluegrass Airport, 4316 Hangar Drive, P.O. Box 4118, Lexington 40544; (859) 231–1219, www.aviationky.org. Open Tuesday to Saturday from 10:00 A.M. to 5:00 P.M., Sunday from 1:00 to 5:00 P.M. $, children under 6 free.

Airplanes big and small are on display in this hangar museum located next to Lexington's Bluegrass Airport (just across Versailles Road from Keeneland). Youngsters can learn about Kentucky aviation pioneers, view an F-4 Phantom jet and other antique and modern airplanes, and try their own hands at flying in a kid-size flight simulator.

Other Things to See and Do

Lexington Farmers' Market, mid-April through early December; Saturdays on Vine Street, Tuesdays and Thursdays at Broadway and Maxwell.

Lexington Walk and Bluegrass Country Driving Tour, pick up at Lexington Convention and Visitors Bureau.

William S. Webb Museum of Anthropology, University of Kentucky campus; (859) 257–8208.

Where to Eat

deSha's, 101 North Broadway in Victorian Square; (859) 259–3771. Varied menu; specialties include meatloaf and honey cornbread. $$–$$$

Gattitown, 2524 Nicholasville Road; (859) 277–2323. Pizza buffet plus bumper cars, cartoons, and video games. $

Jalapeno's, 295 New Circle Road NW; (859) 299–8299; and 1030 South Broadway; (859) 281–5171. Mexican classics in a colorful setting. $$

Joe Bologna's, 120 West Maxwell, near the University of Kentucky campus; (859) 252–4933. Enjoy pizza, huge garlic breadsticks, and other Italian favorites in a former synagogue. $

Magee's Bakery, 726 East Main; (859) 255–9481. Yummy doughnuts, muffins (the pumpkin ones are our favorites), scones, and ham biscuits for breakfast; sandwiches or quiche and cookies for lunch. "Pablo," a painted, almost life-size horse, is on display just inside the front door. This was one of dozens of art horses featured in a citywide exhibit in 2000. $

Mellow Mushroom, 503-507 South Upper Street; (859) 281–6111. Good pizza, salads, and calzones in a casual, fun setting. $–$$

Ramsey's Diner, 496 East High Street; (859) 259–2708. Comfort food such as meatloaf, chicken and dumplings, and locally grown veggies. You can even get a peanut butter sandwich. $$

Where to Stay

Holiday Inn North, 1950 Newtown Pike (exit 11, I–75); (859) 233–0512 or (800) HOLIDAY. Restaurant, indoor pool, huge activity center with video games and table tennis, tennis courts. $$$

Holiday Inn South, 5532 Athens-Boonesboro Road (exit 104, I–75); (859) 263–5241 or (800) HOLIDAY. Indoor and outdoor pools, restaurant, laundry, exercise room, and recreation room. $$$

Kentucky Horse Park Campground, 4089 Iron Works Parkway; (859) 259–4257 or (800) 678–8813, www.kyhorsepark.com. Offers 260 paved campsites with water and electric hookups. Primitive sites also available. Swimming pool, tennis courts, horseshoes, activities pavilion, bathhouse/laundry. $

Marriott's Griffin Gate Resort, 1800 Newtown Pike; (859) 231–5100 or (800) 228–9290. Indoor and outdoor pools, tennis courts, recreation room, restaurant, laundry. $$$$

For More Information

Lexington Convention and Visitors Bureau, 301 East Vine Street; (800) 845–3959 or (859) 233–7299, www.visitlex.com.

Annual Events in Lexington

- **Rolex Three-Day Event,** late April, Kentucky Horse Park; (859) 254–8123

- **Kentucky Derby Day at Keeneland,** first Saturday in May, Keeneland Race Course; (800) 456–3412

- **Kentucky High School Invitational Rodeo,** May, Kentucky Horse Park; (859) 233–4303

- **Founders' Day Celebration,** May, McConnell Springs; (859) 225–4073

- **Annual Egyptian Event,** early June, Kentucky Horse Park; (859) 233–4303

- **Festival of the Bluegrass,** early June, Kentucky Horse Park; (859) 846–4995 or www.festivalofthebluegrass.com

- **Junior League Horse Show,** early July, Red Mile Harness Track; (859) 252–1893

- **Lexington Lions Club Bluegrass Fair,** July, Masterson Station Park; (859) 233–1465

- **Woodland Jubilee,** July, Woodland Park; (859) 288–2925

- **Breyerfest,** late July, Kentucky Horse Park; (973) 633–5090

- **Roots and Heritage Festival,** early September, downtown; (859) 333–8153, www.rootsandheritagefestival.com

- **Museum-Go-Round,** late September, Woodland Park; (859) 258–3256

- **Southern Lights,** mid-November through December 31, Kentucky Horse Park; (859) 255–5727

Bluegrass Region

The Bluegrass region is rich in history. You can tour replicas of pioneer forts in Harrodsburg and near Richmond, the nation's largest restored Shaker community at Shaker Village of Pleasant Hill, and the site of Kentucky's most important Civil War battle at Perryville. You can visit a contemporary landmark—Toyota's state-of-the-art automaking plant in Georgetown—and explore museums featuring everything from a "talking crow" to the inventor of the stop light. This region includes the state capital, Frankfort, with its many museums and public buildings, including the Thomas D. Clark Center for Kentucky History, the state's largest and most comprehensive history museum. Take a riverboat ride, see how dulcimers and quilts are made, watch a pro football team train, and enjoy drama under the stars—so much awaits families in this beautiful and tradition-laden part of the state.

Teresa's TopPicks for the Bluegrass Region

1. Salato Wildlife Education Center and Game Farm, (800) 858–1549

2. Buckley Wildlife Sanctuary, (859) 873–5711

3. Thomas D. Clark Center for Kentucky History, (502) 564–1792

4. Farm fun in Scott County, (502) 863–2547

5. *Dixie Belle* at Shaker Village, (800) 734–5611

6. Hummel Planetarium and Space Theater, (859) 622–1547

7. Old Fort Harrod State Park, (859) 734–3314

8. Fort Boonesborough State Park, (859) 527–3131

9. Toyota Motor Manufacturing Kentucky Inc., (800) TMM–4485

10. Bluegrass Scenic Railroad and Museum, (800) 755–2476

BLUEGRASS REGION

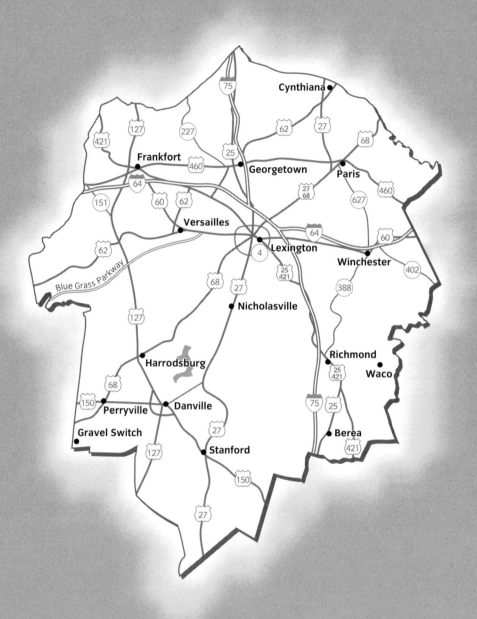

The Bluegrass is a compact region, too. All of the cities mentioned here are an easy day trip from Lexington, northern Kentucky, Louisville, most of north-central and south-central Kentucky, and much of eastern Kentucky. Interstates 75 and 64 can get you to some of the cities, but you're probably going to have to get off the interstates and take the old U.S. highways, such as 68, 62, 27, 127, and 460. In general, these are pretty good roads, though two-lane for the most part. Get a good map, take your time, and enjoy the beautiful view.

Attractions are arranged in a loop around Lexington, starting at the northeast and moving counterclockwise. You'll end up poised to explore eastern Kentucky.

Paris

Claiborne Farm (ages 8 and up)
Highway 627, southeast of Paris; (859) 233–4252. Tours by appointment only. Free (tip for guide is customary).

The Claiborne family has been raising Thoroughbred racehorses for several generations. When you tour this beautiful farm, you'll see the barn areas as well as the grave of great Triple Crown champion Secretariat.

Hopewell Museum (ages 5 and up)
800 Pleasant Street; (859) 987–7274, www.hopewellmuseum.org. Open Wednesday to Saturday from noon to 5:00 P.M., Sunday from 2:00 to 4:00 P.M. Free.

In pioneer times, travelers going from Maysville to Lexington or vice versa hoped they'd make it to this town north of Lexington before dark. But in 1790, the community of Hopewell was renamed Paris to honor America's Revolutionary War allies. In 2000, residents revived the old name for this community museum. Here you can learn about famous Bourbon Countians such as Garrett Morgan, the inventor of the stoplight and the gas mask, and see photographs of local history as well as changing fine arts exhibits. The building itself is a work of art, built in 1909 as the community post office.

Cane Ridge Meeting House and Shrine (ages 5 and up)
Highway 537, off US 460, northeast of Paris; P.O. Box 26, Paris 40362; (859) 987–5350. Open April 1 through October 31, Monday to Saturday from 9:00 A.M. to 5:00 P.M., Sunday 1:00 to 5:00 P.M. Free; donations requested.

If your family is a member of the Christian Church (Disciples of Christ) or Church of Christ denominations, you'll particularly enjoy visiting this shrine and museum. Encased in a golden limestone building is a large log meeting house. Cane Ridge was the site of some of the huge religious revivals of the early 1800s (they attracted 20,000 to 30,000 people), and in 1804 the Reverend Barton Warren Stone and other Presbyterian ministers signed a document here that led to the creation of the new

Christian denominations. The museum includes early church documents, Stone family items, and a collection of nineteenth-century farm and home artifacts. You can picnic on the grounds.

Nannie Clay Wallis Arboretum (all ages)
616 Pleasant Street; (859) 987–6158. Hours vary; call first. Free.

The four-acre backyard of the headquarters of the Garden Club of Kentucky is both scenic and educational. The arboretum features six theme areas: a Walk Garden, Rose Garden, Perennial Garden, Wildflower Garden, Bird Border, and Shade Garden. The trees are marked, and you can borrow a study guide to use as you explore. The fish pond is always a big hit with young visitors. The arboretum is especially pretty in spring, when the dogwoods are in bloom. In early December, there's an open house, with greenery and other natural decorations for sale.

For More Information

Paris/Bourbon County Chamber of Commerce, 525 High Street; (859) 987–3205.

Cynthiana

Cynthiana/Harrison County Museum (ages 5 and up)
112 South Walnut Street; (859) 234–5835. Open Friday and Saturday from 10:00 A.M. to 5:00 P.M. Free.

All kinds of things have been donated by local residents to help this museum tell Cynthiana's story. You'll see old photos, Civil War uniforms, vintage wedding dresses, a model of a long-gone covered bridge, and many other items as you learn about the founding of the town in 1793, Cynthiana's two Civil War battles, and other events large and small in the town's history.

Quiet Trails Nature Preserve (all ages)
Pugh's Ferry Road, off Highway 1284 near Sunrise; (502) 573–2886 or www.nature preserves.ky.gov. Open daily year-round. No restroom facilities. Free.

This lovely preserve offers several easy hiking trails and relatively unspoiled views of the Licking River Valley. There's a box on-site that usually contains trail maps. Pets are not allowed.

Where to Eat

Biancke's Restaurant, 3 Main Street; (859) 234–3443. A local favorite since 1894. Specialties include the Big Joe

Burger, fried green tomatoes, and home-made cream pies. $

Georgetown

Toyota Motor Manufacturing Kentucky Inc. (tour ages 6 and up; visitor center all ages)

2002 Cherry Blossom Way (from I–75, exit 126, head east 2½ miles on Cherry Blossom Way); (800) TMM–4485 or (502) 868–3027, www.toyotageorgetown.com. Visitor center open Monday to Friday from 9:00 A.M. to 4:00 P.M. Tours at 10:00 A.M., noon, and 2:00 P.M. daily, with an additional 6:00 P.M. tour on Thursday. Free.

Learn about the Toyota Production System, *kaizen* (a philosophy of continuous improvement), and Kentucky teamwork at this modern, bright, and noisy automaking facility. About half a million vehicles (Camrys, Camry hybrids, Avalons, and Solaras) and nearly as many engines are made at the Georgetown plant every year. The tour is by tram, and you'll wear headphones to hear the guide over the sound of the factory. The tram visits several areas of the plant: Stamping, where giant presses turn steel into car body parts; Body Weld, where robotic and human welders put the body together; and Assembly, where the engine and other interior components are installed. To go on the plant tours, children must be at least in the first grade and be accompanied by an adult. Reservations are required for the tour. No cameras are allowed on the tour, nor are shorts (for safety reasons). All ages can just stop by to explore the visitor center, which includes interactive exhibits, a video, a music-playing robot, and the first Camry made at the plant in 1986. No purses or bags are allowed inside, and you'll need to show a photo ID.

Cincinnati Bengals Summer Training Camp (ages 5 and up)

Georgetown College Athletic Complex, Lemons Mill Road; (502) 868–6300. Opens mid- to late July and runs a month; days and times vary. Free most days; scrimmage game $, parking $$.

Is there a little (or big) football fan in the house? If so, you may want to brave the sweltering heat to watch Cincinnati Bengals players go through their paces to get ready for the fall season. The daily schedule varies, but the camp includes practice sessions, a scrimmage, and workouts, with some opportunities for autographs and pictures. Warning: It gets very hot sitting in those open-air bleachers—you really gotta love football (or the Bengals).

Up a **Creek**

The Elkhorn Creek is a lovely and historic waterway that flows through six Bluegrass counties. A canoe excursion is a fun way to see the creek and the countryside. You can rent one from **Canoe Kentucky** (7323 Peaks Mill Road, 8 miles north of Frankfort; 502–227–4492, 888–CANOEKY, or 800–K–CANOE; www.canoeky.com. $$$$). Although it's based north of Frankfort, you can make a reservation by phone and meet the guide at a creek entry point. Tell them the ages of the children in your family, your canoeing experience level, and what you're interested in seeing and doing (fishing, history, picnicking, rapids, etc.), and they'll suggest a route. Guided excursions are also available. There are several good entry points to the Elkhorn in and near Georgetown: **Cardome Park** (U.S. Highway 25 North) in Georgetown, **Great Crossings Park** (U.S. Highway 227, off US 460 west of Georgetown), and underneath Switzer Bridge (Highway 1689 off US 460 between Georgetown and Frankfort). At Great Crossings Park, there's a nature trail along the creek, including a short paved section. The trail leads to an elementary school with a playground.

Royal Spring Park (all ages)

South Water and West Main Streets; (502) 863–2547. Log cabin open mid-May through mid-September, Tuesday to Sunday from 10:00 A.M. to 4:00 P.M. View the spring and see the chainsaw sculpture daily year-round. *NOTE:* Cabin not wheelchair-accessible.
Free.

You may see local youngsters fishing near the old stone bridge when you visit this historic site—just as children of Georgetown have done for over 200 years. Royal Spring or Big Spring was discovered by surveyors in 1774, and the town grew up around this amazing water source (which produces some 25 million gallons of water a day). The small park next to the spring includes a viewing area, a Revolutionary War monument (on the bluff above the spring), and two small cabins that were built at other locations. One of the cabins is a museum of pioneer life, with tours and occasional workshops. The sculpture at the park's entrance is of Elijah Craig, a Georgetown founder. Believe it or not, this Baptist minister of the late 1700s is reputed to have made the first batch of bourbon whiskey near the spring. Believe it or not again, the statue was created by local craftsman Sandy Schu using a *chainsaw*.

Farm-Fresh Fun

Fall is an especially fun—and delicious—time to spend a day or weekend in Scott County because the county's numerous farm markets are in full swing. These are great places to pick your Halloween pumpkin, buy farm-grown mums, and take wonderful fall photos of your children.

- **Bi-Water Farm and Greenhouse** (north of Georgetown on US 25; 502–863–3676) holds **AutumnFest** on weekends from mid-September through October. The event features a five-acre corn maze, a Spooky Farmhouse, a petting zoo, and the AutumnFest Express Train. $$

- **Evans Orchard and Cider Mill,** 180 Stone Road (502–863–2255), is the place to get fresh apples, fresh-pressed apple cider, homemade fudge, and homemade apple slushies. There's a petting zoo and other kids' activities, a giant slide down hay bales, and special events include a **Sweet Corn Festival** in July, **Apple Festival** in September, Steps for Pets 5K Race and Fun Walk in October, and **Pumpkin Festival** in October. Some activities $.

- In the midst of all the farm fun comes **Festival of the Horse** (a week-end in late September or early October), with all-horse-drawn parades (including a children's parade on Friday evening), music, and children's activities. Call (502) 863–2547 for more information.

Georgetown/Scott County Museum (ages 5 and up) 🏛️
229 East Main Street; (502) 863–6201. Open Monday to Friday from 9:00 A.M. to 4:00 P.M., Saturday from 10:00 A.M. to 4:00 P.M. Free.

You can learn all about Georgetown history at this interesting museum housed in the town's elegant 1900s post office building. Items on display include paper made by city founder Elijah Craig at his early paper mill, photographs by noted Georgetown landscape and portrait photographer Eugene Bradley, arrowheads, World War II items, pens made in Georgetown, and a changing exhibit about the history of Georgetown College. Some of the exhibits have signage and information in Japanese as well as English, resulting from an exhibit that was on display in Georgetown's sister city of Tahara-cho, Japan. Railroad enthusiasts will want to see the $40,000 model train replica of the 1931 DeWitt Clinton. And be sure to see the animated talking replica of Pete the Crow and get the story on Georgetown's most famous animal resident of the early 1800s.

Cardome Centre/Yuko-En on the Elkhorn (all ages)

800 Cincinnati Pike (US 25) north of downtown Georgetown; (502) 863–1575 (Cardome Centre), (502) 316–4554 (Yuko-En), www.cardomecenter.com, www.yuko-en.com. Open daily dawn to dusk. Free.

Children will love the giant wooden buffalo—more chainsaw art—that "stand watch" in front of this former monastery, just a short drive from Royal Spring Park. Next to Cardome is Yuko-En on the Elkhorn, a five-acre Japanese-style garden and the official "Japanese–Kentucky Friendship Garden." The garden opened in 2002, so exhibits are still growing (literally!), but there are the beginnings of several garden areas, a Zen garden, wooden bridges, statuary, a tiny lake, and huge, interesting wooden doors leading onto it all. At press time, an Environmental Education Pavilion was scheduled to open in late 2007. It's an easy gravel pathway. In late April, Cardome is the site of Georgetown's International Kite Festival (502–863–1575, ext. 44), which features Japanese kite makers and kite flying from Georgetown's sister city, Tahara-cho, Japan—plus hot air balloon rides and a variety of international foods. In early June, Civil War enthusiasts come to Cardome for the reenactment of Morgan's Raid on Georgetown (502–868–0975), with skirmishes, Civil War–era music, costumed historic figures of the time, and "sutlers'" (vendors') tents.

Other Things to See and Do

Elkhorn Creek Nature Trail, off US 227 North at Great Crossing Park; (502) 863-2547. An easy-to-hike 1 ½-mile creekside/countryside trail connecting Great Crossing Park and Western Elementary School (on US 460 West).

Ward Hall, US 460, 1 mile west of downtown Georgetown; (502) 863-2547. Grand antebellum mansion under renovation; open occasional weekends throughout the year.

Where to Eat

Fava's Restaurant, 159 East Main Street; (502) 863–4383. Fava's has been a Georgetown institution since 1910. Join the regular "courthouse crowd" for home cooking, grilled cheese sandwiches and burgers, and homemade pies. There's an all-you-can-eat catfish special on weekends. $

Sam's Truckstop, US 25 South; (502) 863–5872. Before the interstates, US 25 was the main route in and out of Georgetown. These days you'll find more local families than truckers dining at this restaurant south of town. The menu includes everything from steaks to Samburgers. $

Where to Stay

Best Western, 132 Darby Drive; (502) 868–0055 or (877) 868–6555. Breakfast buffet, indoor pool, refrigerators in rooms. $$

Country Inn Suites, 131 Darby Drive; (502) 868–6868 or (800) 456–4000. Complimentary breakfast, indoor pool, laundry. $$

Hampton Inn, 128 Darby Drive; (502) 867–4888 or (800) HAMPTON. Indoor pool, some rooms with kitchenettes. $$$

For More Information

Georgetown/Scott County Tourism,
339 Outlet Center Drive; (502) 863–2547 or
(888) 863–8600, www.georgetownky.com.

Frankfort

Thomas D. Clark Center for Kentucky History (all ages)

100 West Broadway; (502) 564–1792, www.kyhistory.org. Open Tuesday to Saturday
from 10:00 A.M. to 5:00 P.M. and Sunday from 1:00 to 5:00 P.M. $, under 5 free. Price
includes admission to the Old State Capitol and the Kentucky Military History
Museum.

This beautiful, relatively new facility shows off artifacts that the Kentucky Historical
Society has been collecting for decades. The central exhibit is Kentucky Journey, a
chronological look at the state from presettlement to the present day, with numerous
interactive and animated displays. You go through at your own pace, and the open
design is well suited to active children. The history center conducts many special programs for children, including hands-on "Super Saturday" workshops and dramatic
presentations, so check in to the schedule.

State Capitol (ages 5 and up)

Capital Avenue; (502) 564–3449. Guided tours offered Monday to Friday, except holidays, from 8:30 A.M. to 3:30 P.M. Open Saturday 10:00 A.M. to 2:00 P.M. and Sunday from
1:00 to 4:00 P.M. for self-guided tours of main areas. Although all ages can visit, the
tour is for ages 5 and up. Free.

Kentucky's Capitol Building, with its impressive rotunda, was modeled after the federal
Capitol in Washington, D.C. Features include murals of Kentucky history, a collection of
dolls dressed like Kentucky's First Ladies in their inaugural gowns, and the legislative
chambers. Statues of Abraham Lincoln and Jefferson Davis commemorate the fact that
both Union and Confederate presidents during the Civil War were Kentuckians. Behind
the Capitol is the Floral Clock—a 34-foot-diameter clock made of plants and flowers.

Kentucky Governor's Mansion (ages 5 and up)

Adjacent to the Capitol Building; (502) 564–8004. Open Tuesday and Thursday from
9:00 A.M. to 11:00 A.M. Free.

Home to Kentucky's chief executive since 1914, the house was patterned after Marie
Antoinette's summer villa, the Petite Trianon. The tour includes the elegant ballroom,
state dining room, and reception room.

Amazing Kentucky Fact

U.S. Senator George Graham Vest, who coined the famous saying "Dog is man's best friend," grew up in Frankfort. You can tour the house he lived in, the Vest-Lindsey House, at 401 Wapping Street. (502) 564–6980.

Old State Capitol (ages 5 and up)
Broadway and Lewis Streets; (502) 564–1792. Open Tuesday to Saturday from 10:00 A.M. to 5:00 P.M. $ (joint admission with Thomas D. Clark Center for Kentucky History and Kentucky Military History Museum).

The Kentucky legislature met in this building from 1830 to 1910; it's interesting to compare the scale and size of the legislative chambers to the present Capitol. Many early portraits and artifacts are on display, but one of the most interesting features is the unusual self-supporting winding staircase.

Rebecca-Ruth Candy (ages 4 and up)
112 East Second Street; (502) 223–7475 or (800) 444–3766, www.rebeccaruth.com. Tours offered January through October, Monday to Saturday from 9:00 A.M. to noon and 1:00 to 4:30 P.M. Store hours are Monday to Saturday from 8:30 A.M. to 5:30 P.M. Tours $.

Chocoholics the world over know about Frankfort because of Rebecca-Ruth Candy. Take a candy factory tour and find out about the hundreds of confections made here (most famous are its Kentucky Bourbon candies) and about Ruth Hanly and Rebecca Gooch, former schoolteachers who started this candy company in 1919. Best part of the tour: free samples.

Liberty Hall and Orlando Brown House (ages 6 and up)
Liberty Hall: 218 Wilkinson Street; (502) 227–2560 or www.libertyhall.org. Orlando Brown House: 202 Wilkinson Street; (502) 875–4952. Open March through December. Tours at 10:30 A.M., noon, and 1:30 and 3:00 P.M. Tuesday to Saturday; noon, 1:30, and 3:00 P.M. Sunday. $

John Brown, one of Kentucky's first two U.S. senators, built Liberty Hall for his wife, Margaretta, and their family in 1796. The Orlando Brown House next door was built for his son, and lovely lawns and gardens connect the two. The houses remained in the Brown family until they became museums in the 1950s, and many lovely furnishings and family portraits remain. Ghost enthusiasts, take note: Liberty Hall is home to one of Kentucky's most famous ghosts, the "Grey Lady," frequently sighted and thought to be the spirit of an aunt who died while visiting the Browns to help console them over the death of their daughter.

Grave of Daniel and Rebecca Boone (all ages)

Frankfort Cemetery, 215 East Main Street; (502) 227–2403. Open daily from dawn to dusk. Free.

Kentucky's most famous pioneer couple is buried at a lovely site high on a hill overlooking the Kentucky River. This is a large cemetery, with monuments dating to the Revolutionary War period, and some children may like to walk around and look at the interesting Victorian monuments or read the often poetic inscriptions.

Kentucky Military History Museum (ages 7 and up)

East Main Street at Capital Avenue; (502) 564–3265. Open Tuesday to Saturday from 10:00 A.M. to 5:00 P.M. $ (joint admission with Thomas D. Clark Center for Kentucky History and Old State Capitol).

My son's interest in Civil War uniforms led to our first visit here, and sometimes when we're in Frankfort we just stop by. Each time he sees something he never noticed before. It doesn't take long to tour the collection of uniforms, guns, flags, cannons, swords, and other battle memorabilia. The museum covers a time span from before the Revolutionary War to the present day. The building itself is a military artifact: A former Union arsenal building, it looks appropriately fortresslike and sits atop a hill overlooking downtown Frankfort.

Kentucky Vietnam Veterans Memorial (all ages)

Coffee Tree Road. Open daily. Free.

Before visiting, you might explain how a sundial works, so your children can appreciate the unusual design of this monument. The names of Kentuckians who died in the Vietnam War are etched in granite beneath a giant sundial; the gnomon's shadow falls on the veteran's name on the anniversary of his death.

Salato Wildlife Education Center and Game Farm (all ages)

1 Game Farm Road; U.S. Highway 60, west of Frankfort (take exit 53 B off I–64 to US 127 north; travel 1½ miles and turn left on US 60); (800) 858–1549 or (502) 564–7863. Open Tuesday to Saturday from 10:00 A.M. to 5:00 P.M. Free.

Bald eagles, deer, bison, elk, fish, venomous snakes, and wild turkeys live at this state-operated nature complex. There are also two fishing lakes, a songbird area, and picnic grounds. The staff does an excellent job of educating young visitors in an engaging way. One of the fishing lakes is for children ages twelve and under only (and is abundantly stocked to increase the odds of a successful catch). Forgot your pole? No problem—they have some you can use. *NOTE:* Those over sixteen must have a state fishing license, also available at the game farm.

Switzer Bridge (all ages)

Take US 460 east from Frankfort, turn left at Highway 1689.

If you take US 460 from Frankfort to Georgetown, make a side trip to Switzer Bridge. This 120-foot span across Elkhorn Creek was originally built in 1855, when Kentucky had hundreds of "kissing bridges." Today only thirteen are left—but there would be only twelve if not for a bit of luck and a lot of hard work. In 1997, intense spring floods swept the Switzer Bridge off its foundation; luckily, a nearby concrete bridge prevented it from being washed down the creek. An amazing federal/state rebuilding partnership made it nearly good as new. The bridge is closed to traffic, so youngsters can explore it without worry of cars. The small surrounding park is a good place for a summer picnic, splashing in the water, and fishing. It's also a convenient entry point for a Kentucky canoe excursion.

Other Things to See and Do

Capital City Museum, 325 Ann Street; (502) 696–0607. Political memorabilia and other exhibits on local history.

Leslie Morris Park on Fort Hill, enter at Clifton Avenue; (800) 960-7200. Park with panoramic view of city, hiking trail, and remains of Civil War earthen forts.

Where to Eat

Gibby's Deli, 212 West Broadway; (502) 223–4429. Pasta, salads, and sandwiches. $

Jim's Seafood, 950 Wilkinson Boulevard; (502) 223–7448. Fried seafood with kids' menu and scenic view of the Kentucky River. $$

Melanie's on Main, 238 West Main Street; (502) 226–3322. Good lunch place with kids' menu. $

Where to Stay

Bluegrass Inn, 635 Versailles Road, US 60; (502) 695–1800 or (800) 322–1802. Outdoor pool, pets accepted. $

Capitol Plaza Hotel, 405 Wilkinson Boulevard; (502) 227–5100 or (800) HOLI-DAY. Indoor pool, restaurant, exercise room, continental breakfast. $$$

Elkhorn Campground, 165 Scruggs Lane, off US 460; (502) 695–9154. Tent and full hookup sites, pool, showers, playground, laundry. $

Hampton Inn, 1310 US 127 South; (502) 223–7600. Outdoor swimming pool, free breakfast buffet. $$–$$$

For More Information

Frankfort Visitor Center, 100 Capital Avenue; (800) 960–7200 or (502) 875–8687, www.visitfrankfort.com.

Versailles

Three Chimneys Farm (ages 8 and up)
Old Frankfort Pike; (859) 873–7053. Tours Tuesday to Saturday by appointment.
Free.

A classic horse farm with a well-organized tour program, Three Chimneys—home to racing champions Smarty Jones, Silver Charm, and other top stallions—offers tours of the stallion barn, breeding shed, and mare receiving barn. Not advised for younger children or those with short attention spans.

The Castle (all ages)
US 60, west of Bluegrass Airport. Exterior viewing only.

Yes, that really is a stone castle, turrets and all, along US 60 between Lexington and Versailles. What's the story? It was built in 1969 by a businessman who originally intended to live there, but he never finished it. For years it was simply the Bluegrass region's most unusual roadside attraction. In 2004, it was severely damaged by a fire, but another businessman, a Miami lawyer named Tom Post, has been rebuilding it and promises amenities such as a great hall, bowling lanes, shuffleboard, and a whirlpool spa on the roof. He says he plans to rent it out as an event site and overnight accommodation, but at press time, no reservations were yet being taken. You can drive by (pull off US 60 onto Pisgah Pike to snap photos) and see the progress and imagine what you would do with a castle.

Bluegrass Scenic Railroad and Museum (all ages)
Woodford County Park (US 62 at Beasley Road), about 1½ miles west of Versailles, P.O. Box 27, Versailles 40383; (859) 873–2476 or (800) 755–2476. Three excursions on Saturday and two on Sunday, early June through late October. $$

On this railroad the ninety-minute excursion crosses through scenic farmland and stops before returning to allow passengers to walk up to Young's High Bridge, a nineteenth-century railroad trestle over the Kentucky River. In addition to the regular sightseeing excursions, there are numerous themed runs great for families, including

Amazing
Kentucky Fact

Both Versailles, Kentucky, and its French namesake are spelled the same, but they're pronounced differently. In Kentucky, it's not "Ver-SIGH," it's "Ver-SALES."

special Mother's Day and Father's Day excursions, Clown Daze in early October, a Wild West Train Robbery in late June, a Civil War Train Robbery in early September, and Halloween and Santa Claus runs. It's a good idea to get your tickets in advance for these special excursions, since they often sell out. Conclude your day in the museum looking at the 1960s caboose, a restored engine, and other classic rail cars.

Jack Jouett House (ages 5 and up)

Craig's Creek Pike, off McCowan's Ferry Road; (859) 873–7902. Open April through October, Wednesday, Saturday, and Sunday from 1:00 to 5:00 P.M. Free.

Your children may have heard of Paul Revere, but how about Jack Jouett? He has been called the "Paul Revere of the South" for galloping through Virginia countryside to warn of the coming British invasion. His Kentucky house, built around 1797, has just five rooms, a good size for young historians with short attention spans.

Buckley Wildlife Sanctuary (all ages)

1035 Germany Road, between Frankfort and Versailles; (859) 873–5711. Trail and bird blind open Wednesday to Friday from 9:00 A.M. to 5:00 P.M., Saturday and Sunday from 9:00 A.M. to 6:00 P.M. Nature center open Saturday and Sunday from 1:00 to 6:00 P.M. or by appointment. From Versailles, take US 60 west, turn left onto Highway 1681. Take 1681 to Millville, and turn left onto Highway 1659. Go just under 2 miles, and turn right onto Highway 1964. Go 1 mile and turn right onto Germany Road, then keep going straight—do not go left when the road forks—for a little over a mile. $

Though it can be a little tricky to find, this pretty 364-acre sanctuary is worth the effort. There are a variety of hiking trails, educational exhibits, bird blinds, and picnic areas, and you're likely to see all kinds of wildlife, from deer to butterflies. Spring through fall, many weekend events are geared to children. One of the most popular is Fantasy Forest in October, which features hayrides, storytelling, music, and a forest walk in which children encounter animals (costumed volunteers) along the way who tell them about forest life. There's also a Family Fun Day in early August, with animal exhibits and entertainment.

Other Things to See and Do

Boyd Orchards, 1396 Pinckard Pike; (859) 873–3097. Apples and other seasonal goodies; family events; and an onsite cafe.

Where to Eat

McKenzie's Restaurant, 197 South Main Street; (859) 256–0099. Twelve kinds of burgers, barbecue, and even veggie plates. $

Nicholasville

Camp Nelson Heritage Park (ages 6 and up)

Along US 27, about 20 miles south of Lexington and 6 miles south of Nicholasville; (859) 881–5716, www.campnelson.org. White House open Tuesday to Saturday from 10:00 A.M. to 5:00 P.M. Self-guided interpretive trail and restored buggy shed open daily dawn to dusk. **Free.**

After your visit, you can go home and tell your friends you have toured the White House. This White House, however, was the officers' headquarters of a sprawling 4,000-acre Union Army supply depot and enlistment site. After Abraham Lincoln made the Emancipation Proclamation, more than 10,000 African Americans came to Camp Nelson to receive their freedom. Many also came to enlist, followed by their families, who set up camp nearby. The heritage park includes 400 of the original 4,000 acres. In addition to the headquarters' tour, an interpretive trail and a restored buggy shed offer a site overview.

Harry C. Miller Lock Collection (ages 6 and up)

Lockmasters Security Institute, 1014 Main Street; (859) 887–9633. Usually open Monday, Wednesday, and Friday from 1:00 to 4:00 P.M. **Free.**

This is a private company that trains locksmiths, but visitors are welcome to stop by and look at the amazing collection of vintage locks, some dating to the 1300s. The collection was assembled by lock industry legend Harry C. Miller, an inventor of more than forty locks as well as a renowned safecracker. In the 1940s he worked with the federal government to develop locks to protect national security, and later was president of the Sargent & Greenleaf lock company. His descendants own Lockmasters.

For More Information

Nicholasville Tourism Commission,
508 North Main Street; (859) 887–4351.

Amazing Kentucky Fact

Kentucky has its own Brooklyn Bridge, crossing the Kentucky River in the scenic Palisades area. It's on the way from Lexington to Shaker Village/Harrodsburg via US 68.

Harrodsburg

Shaker Village of Pleasant Hill (all ages)

3501 Lexington Road (off US 68); (800) 734–5611 or (859) 734–5411, www.shakervillage ky.org. Open daily except December 24 and 25, April through October from 10:00 A.M. to 5:00 P.M., closes at 4:30 P.M. November through March. Admission: adults $$$, children $$, under 6 free. November through March, some buildings are closed, and admission is reduced.

Children may not want to tour all the buildings that are open, but they'll be interested in the main building, with its kitchen and large cellar, double staircases, and rooms with chairs hung on wooden pegs (an efficient way to keep things neat and clean). They'll also enjoy the animals (the village has an old-breeds preservation program and includes many interesting varieties of farm animals) and wide-open spaces at the nation's largest restored Shaker community. My children were also intrigued by the Shaker premise of separating the men and women, and they enjoyed the singing and dancing presentations. The Shakers lived here from 1805 until 1910. At its height, the community owned 4,000 acres of land and had 500 residents, and was a major producer of tools, animals, and seeds. Many special events throughout the year celebrate Shaker customs and activities as well as the village's role in local history. There are also trails for hiking and, if you bring your own horse, riding. You can walk through the village at your own pace and let the kids run and play for a while if they get restless. Accommodations are spacious rooms in the restored buildings with Shaker-style furniture; the suite holds up to six people. The village inn dining room serves a breakfast buffet, lunch, and dinner daily; children's menu available. The Post Office Snack Shop has sandwiches, soft drinks, homemade potato chips, and Shaker lemon pie.

Dixie Belle (all ages)

Departs several times daily from Shaker Landing May through October; (800) 734–5611. $. If you're going to tour the village and take the boat ride, save money by getting a combo ticket. Buy tickets and get directions to the landing from Shaker Village.

Though their interest in Shaker Village varies from visit to visit, my children always enjoy a boat ride on the *Dixie Belle,* a little sternwheeler that departs from Shaker Landing near the village spring through fall. You may spot people canoeing and turtles sunning themselves on the water, and you're sure to enjoy the beautiful scenery of the Palisades area. This is always a good way to end a day at Shaker Village.

Old Fort Harrod State Park (all ages)

100 South College Street (US 127 and US 68); (859) 734–3314. Open daily 9:00 A.M. to 5:00 P.M. mid-March through October 31, 9:00 A.M. to 4:30 P.M. November through mid-March. Closed Thanksgiving, Christmas week through New Year's Day, and weekends December through February. $

A Day **Family Adventure**

I turned my back for just a second when we were visiting Old Fort Harrod State Park, and when I looked around not a child was in sight. I soon heard a giggle from above. There they were, all three perched on the branches of the giant osage orange tree near the fort's entrance. This immense tree—with some of its huge branches almost parallel to the ground for easy maneuvering—is always a favorite part of our visit to Fort Harrod.

Harrodsburg lays claim to being the first permanent English settlement west of the Allegheny Mountains; it's where James Harrod founded a fort in 1774. The fort here is a full-scale replica of that original fort. The cabins and blockhouses are filled with pioneer artifacts. April through October, costumed craftspeople demonstrate pioneer crafts. We especially enjoyed seeing the blacksmith at work and visiting the schoolhouse. The park's Mansion Museum (open in summer only) includes Native American artifacts, Lincolniana, antique musical instruments, documents relating to George Rogers Clark and Daniel Boone, and many other items relating to Kentucky history. The park also includes the Lincoln Marriage Temple, which houses the cabin where Abraham Lincoln's parents were married (it was moved here from Springfield, Kentucky), and a Pioneer Cemetery.

Olde Town Park (all ages)
Main Street between Poplar and Office Streets; call tourism office at (859) 734–2364 for information. Open daily, twenty-four hours. Free.

If you decide to walk around Harrodsburg and look at the many old buildings (walking-tour guide available from the visitor center), stop and rest at this little park on Main Street. The centerpiece of the park is an interesting cascading fountain by Harrodsburg artist Zoe Strecker. The fountain was inspired by the rock and cliff formations in the nearby Palisades area of the Kentucky River.

Where to Eat

Beaumont Inn, US 127 south, 638 Beaumont Inn Drive; (859) 734–3381 or (800) 352–3992. Open for lunch daily, for dinner Wednesday to Sunday. Homey atmosphere and Kentucky specialties, plus an excellent Sunday brunch. $$–$$$

Kentucky Fudge Company, 225 South Main Street; (859) 733–0088. Sandwiches, ice cream, and twenty kinds of fudge served in an 1860 drugstore building. $

Where to Stay

Beaumont Inn, US 127 south, 638 Beaumont Inn Drive; (859) 734–3381 or (800) 352–3992, www.beaumontinn.com. Though historic (a former girls' school), this hotel is very family friendly. Rooms are housed in several buildings in the neighborhood and decorated with period antiques. Outdoor pool. $$–$$$$

Bright Leaf Golf Resort, 1742 Danville Road; (859) 734–5481 or (800) 469–6038. Rooms and villas, restaurant, outdoor pool, thirty-six-hole golf course. $$–$$$$

Chimney Rock Campground, 160 Chimney Rock Road; (859) 748–5252. Open April through October. Tent camping and hookups, laundry, showers, and pool. $

Days Inn, 1680 Danville Road; (859) 734–9431 or (800) 329–7466. Outdoor pool, large rooms, continental breakfast. $$–$$$

For More Information

Harrodsburg/Mercer County Tourism Commission, 103 South Main Street, P.O. Box 283, DEPT KTG01, Harrodsburg 40330; (859) 734–2364 or (800) 355–9192, www .harrodsburgky.com.

Herrington **Lake**

A 3,600-acre manmade lake, Herrington Lake is accessible from Highway 33 or Highway 152. The lake is pretty but gets very crowded, especially on weekends. You can rent a fishing boat or pontoon at

- **Cane Run Fishing Marina,** 360 Cane Run Camp Road; (859) 748–5487

- **Chimney Rock Marina,** 250 Chimney Rock Road; (859) 748–9065

- **Pandora Marina,** #1 Pandora Cove; (859) 748–9121

- **Royalty's Fishing Camp,** 940 Norman's Camp Road; (859) 748–5459

- **Cummins Falls Marina,** 2558 Cummins Ferry Road (Highway 1988); (859) 865–2003; also rents canoes and paddleboats

Danville

Constitution Square State Historic Site (all ages)

134 South Second Street; (859) 239–7089. Buildings open daily 9:00 A.M. to 5:00 P.M.; grounds open until dusk. **Free.**

Younger children won't necessarily take in all the history, but they'll enjoy exploring the mix of original and replica pioneer buildings in this small park in Danville. The collection commemorates Danville's role as the center for political activity that led to Kentucky statehood in 1792. The self-guided tour includes a replica of the courthouse where early political leaders held ten constitutional conventions to prepare for statehood, a replica of an early jail made of 9-inch-thick logs, an original pre-1792 post office, and a replica of an early meetinghouse. At the center of the park is a bronze statue of Kentucky's state seal surrounded by plaques denoting Kentucky governors. The old brick buildings adjacent to the park date to the early 1800s and house art galleries and a local museum operated by the Danville/Boyle County Historical Society. There's a small charge to tour the museum, which includes an eclectic collection of items relating to Danville history.

McDowell House, Apothecary, and Gardens (ages 6 and up)

125 South Second Street; (859) 236–2804, www.mcdowellhouse.com. Open Monday to Saturday, 10:00 A.M. to noon and 1:00 to 4:00 P.M., Sunday 2:00 to 3:30 P.M. Closed Monday November through February. $

On Christmas Day 1809, in a back bedroom of this house, Dr. McDowell removed a twenty-pound ovarian tumor from Jane Todd Crawford without benefit of anesthesia. (Mrs. Crawford, who rode more than 60 miles on horseback to get to Danville, recited psalms during the operation.) Five days after surgery, she was making her own bed, and twenty-five days later, she returned home. The operation became a milestone in modern medicine. Adults, more than children, are fascinated by this harrowing tale of America's first abdominal surgery, but all ages will enjoy touring the house and attached apothecary shop to see interesting items such as a comb-back rocker and early dental tools.

Lunch on the Square

Get a sandwich from Burke's Bakery, 121 West Main Street (859–236–5661), across the street from Constitution Square, and have lunch at the picnic tables in the park.

Top **Brass**

Danville has one of the best musical events in the state—the annual **Great American Brass Band Festival** in mid-June. Dozens of bands and some 40,000 people from around the world converge on Danville for a weekend of Dixieland, march tunes, even Civil War music using authentic period instruments. Concerts are free at various locations on the Centre College campus and around town. Other events include a hot air balloon race.

J. F. C. Museum (ages 4 and up)
1389 Stanford Road; (859) 236–7057 or (858) 236–3442. Open Saturday and Sunday from 10 A.M. to 6 P.M. or by appointment during the week.

Youthful collectors can see lots of cool stuff and meet a kindred spirit at this eclectic museum. The rocks, artifacts, Civil War memorabilia, stamps, and local history items on display are the personal collections of Danny Curtsinger. He started collecting rocks at the age of four and continues, four decades later, to expand his interests. He named his museum after his father, Joe Francis Curtsinger.

Pioneer Playhouse of Danville (ages 6 and up)
840 Stanford Road; (859) 236–2747 or (866) 597–5294, www.pioneerplayhouse.com. Performances Tuesday to Saturday. Tickets can be purchased for dinner and the play ($$$$) or just the play ($$). Children under 12 $.

Not all the plays at the open-air Pioneer Playhouse will be of interest to young children, but usually at least a couple of shows each season are appropriate. Come just for the show, or come early to look at the pioneer-style shops and to have dinner in the on-site restaurant.

Old Crow Inn and Elements Pottery (ages 5 and up)
471 Stanford Road; (859) 236–1808.

All kinds of interesting stuff is going on here—a pottery studio and shop, hiking trails, the beginnings of a winery. There's also overnight lodging.

Kentucky School for the Deaf (ages 6 and up)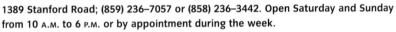
South Second Street; (859) 239–7017. Open Monday to Friday from 8:30 A.M. to noon and 1:00 to 4:00 P.M. Free.

This school, founded in 1829, was the first state-supported institution created to educate deaf children. The small museum located in Jacobs Hall includes a re-creation of an 1850s classroom and student dorm. A video and exhibits of photographs, letters, historical records, and auditory aid equipment also are on display.

Amazing
Kentucky Fact

John Travolta is among the famous actors who have performed at Pioneer Playhouse.

Where to Eat

Bluegrass Beach House, 127 North Fourth Street; (759) 236–6642. Sandwiches, salads, smoothies, and shakes.

Freddie's, 126 South Fourth Street; (859) 236–9884. Terrific Italian favorites plus daily specials. $

Where to Stay

Comfort Suites, 864 Ben Ali Drive; (859) 936–9300. Continental breakfast, indoor pool. $$

Country Hearth Inn, U.S. Highway 150 Bypass; (859) 236–8601. Outdoor pool, restaurant; pets allowed. $$

Gwinn Island Fishing Resort and Marina, off Highway 33 north; (859) 236–4286. Rustic cabins on Lake Herrington. Marina, boat rental, swimming pool. $$

Holiday Inn Express, US 150 Bypass; (859) 236–8600. Outdoor pool, continental breakfast. $$

Pioneer Campground, Pioneer Playhouse; (859) 236–2747. Hookups and tent sites; showers. $

For More Information

Danville/Boyle County Convention and Visitors Bureau, 304 South Fourth Street; (800) 755–0076 or (859) 236–7794, www.danville-ky.com.

Perryville

Perryville Battlefield State Historic Site (all ages)

1825 Battlefield Road, on Highway 1920, just north of the junction of US 68 and US 150; (859) 332–8631. Grounds and trails open daily year-round, from 9:00 A.M. to 9:00 P.M. Museum open daily April through October from 9:00 A.M. to 5:00 P.M., November through March from 10:00 A.M. to 3:00 P.M., weather permitting. Admission to museum $; admission to grounds free.

On October 8, 1862, Kentucky's deadliest and most important Civil War battle was fought here. More than 6,000 soldiers were casualties in this last serious effort of the Confederacy to claim Kentucky. Today the battle is commemorated with monuments to the soldiers of both sides and a museum detailing the history of the battle. There are also trails that allow families to take a self-guided walking tour over these historic grounds. The gift shop has a large selection of books about the Civil War. The first weekend in October, reenactors and spectators gather for a battle reenactment complete with "sutlers'" (merchants') camps, a ghost trek, and a living history tour.

Gravel Switch

Penn's Store (all ages)

257 Penn Store Road, off Highway 243; (859) 332–7715 or (606) 332–7706; call for hours of operation.

This is a real old-timey country store, right down to the cigar-box cash register. In fact, it's the oldest continuously operating family store in the United States, in business since 1850. Your children will enjoy the old-fashioned candies, homemade dolls, potbellied stove, and general tumbledown appearance.

Stanford

William Whitley House State Historic Site (ages 4 and up)

625 William Whitley Road, off US 150, east of Stanford; (606) 355–2881. **Tours offered April through November, Monday through Saturday from 9:00 A.M. to 4:30 P.M., November through March, Tuesday through Friday from 10:00 A.M. to 3:00 P.M. $**

This beautiful estate, built in 1788, was one of the first brick houses in Kentucky. It was the home of William Whitley, a Revolutionary War veteran and Indian fighter. One of its most fascinating features for children is the hidden staircase, so the family could hide in case of Indian attacks, a real possibility in pioneer Kentucky. Whitley's long rifle and engraved powderhorn hang over one of the fireplaces. The lovely grounds make a nice place for a picnic (tables available), and there's playground equipment for the children.

Historic Stanford L&N Depot (all ages)

1866 North Depot Street; (606) 365–4518. **Free.**

You're welcome to stop by the restored 1860s depot and see such items as a velocipede (a machine used to do small errands on the railroad tracks) and large brass bell. A restored caboose is set up to show a cabooseman's home away from home.

Where to Eat

Cree-Mee Drive-in, 816 East Main Street; (606) 365–9100. Burgers in a '50s atmosphere. $

Kentucky Depot Restaurant, 119 Metker Trace; (606) 365–8040. Home cooking and daily specials. $

Berea

Berea College Tours (ages 6 and up)

Register for tours at Boone Tavern Hotel, College Square; (859) 985–3000, www.berea .edu. Historical tours offered Monday, Wednesday, and Friday at 9:00 A.M. and 1:00 and 3:00 P.M.; Tuesday at 9:00 and 10:00 A.M. and 1:00 and 3:00 P.M.; and Saturday at 9:00 A.M. and 2:00 P.M. College Craft tours Monday to Friday at 10:00 A.M. and 2:00 P.M. Free.

Berea College's past and present are equally interesting. The school was founded in 1859 with the goal of dividing its student population evenly between blacks and whites—an interracial college in the South, and this was before the Civil War. Today Berea is known for its student industries, which enable low-income students from Kentucky's mountains to obtain a quality college education. All students must work, but they pay no tuition. The historical tour focuses on the college's story and historical buildings. Most children will find the crafts tour, with its demonstrations of blacksmithing, weaving, and woodworking, more enjoyable.

Berea Artisan Shops (ages 6 and up)

Shops are concentrated in the College Square area and Old Town (North Broadway area, near visitor center). Hours vary.

Berea is internationally renowned for its craftspeople and artisans who work and display here, making everything from pottery to jewelry in both traditional and contemporary styles. Some shops are working studios; others are display galleries. If your children enjoy shopping and/or crafts, they might like to explore some of the stores; mine have become impatient after a few stops.

If your time (or your children's patience for shopping) is limited, you can get a one-stop look at a wide range of artisans' works at the **Berea Artisan Center,** located right off I–75 at exit 77 (975 Walnut Meadow Road; 859–985–5448). From fun to fine, jewelry to furniture, you'll find it here. There might even be an artisan at work when you visit. The center also includes a casual restaurant with reasonably priced food and snacks.

If you drive into town, one of our favorite places to stop is **Warren A. May Woodworker,** 110 Center Street (859–986–9293). Young musicians in particular will enjoy seeing Mr. May's beautiful handmade mountain dulcimers. The **Log House Craft Gallery** in College Square (800–347–3892) showcases student-made pottery, weaving, woodworking, candles, jewelry, and other items. There are numerous small shops with everything from handblown glass to cornhusk dolls in the **Old Town** area near the Berea Welcome Center, 201 North Broadway.

Valley View **Ferry**

If you're heading to Richmond or Berea from Lexington, make a free ride on the Valley View Ferry a part of your route. This ferry has been in operation since 1785, making daily crossings over the Kentucky River between Jessamine and Madison counties. Many people who work in the Lexington/Bluegrass area use it to help them get to work and back each day. To get to the ferry from Lexington, take Tates Creek Road (Highway 169) all the way south to the Kentucky River. Once you get across you can take Highway 169 into Richmond, and from there get on I–75 or US 25 if you're continuing to Berea. The ferry runs year-round, river conditions permitting, Monday to Friday from 6:00 A.M. to 8:00 P.M., Saturday from 8:00 A.M. to 6:00 P.M., and Sunday from 9:00 A.M. to 6:00 P.M. Call (859) 885–4500 or (859) 258–3611 for more information.

Kentucky Guild of Artists and Craftsmen Spring and Fall Fairs/ Berea Craft Festival (all ages) 🔒

Indian Fort Theater, Highway 21 east, 3 miles east of Berea; depending upon weather conditions, the fair may also be held in Memorial Park in Old Town Berea; (800) 598–5263. Guild fairs weekends in mid-May and mid-October; craft festival in mid-July. $

Berea's open-air fairs are an enjoyable way for families to see a wide variety of crafts and craft demonstrations. You'll see everything from garden art and painted gourds to textiles and fine jewelry. There's also entertainment, as well as traditional foods. Artisans must have their work juried to join the guild, and only members display at these two fairs. The Berea Craft Festival brings in top-quality craftspeople from across the United States.

Where to Eat

Main Street Cafe, College Square; (859) 986–0703. Salads, quiches, sandwiches; some vegetarian entrees. $

Papaleno's, College Square; (859) 986–4497. Pizza and pasta. $

Where to Stay

Boone Tavern Hotel, 100 Main Street; (859) 986–9358 or (800) 366–9358. Historic hotel decorated with handmade crafts and staffed by Berea College students. $$$

Holiday Inn Express, at I–75, exit 77; (859) 985–1901 or (800) HOLIDAY. Continental breakfast, indoor pool. $$

For More Information

Berea Welcome Center, 201 North Broadway (in restored L&N Railroad Depot); (859) 986–2540 or (800) 598–5263, www.berea.com.

Waco

Bybee Pottery (ages 6 and up)

610 Waco Loop (Highway 52), 9 miles east of Richmond; (859) 369–5350. Self-guided tours Monday to Thursday from 8:00 A.M. to noon and 12:30 to 3:00 P.M. and Friday from 8:00 A.M. to 3:00 P.M. Free.

The log Bybee Pottery building looks ancient—this family-owned company has been making pottery here since 1845, maybe since 1809, if local legend is correct. The simple-lined, solid-colored and speckled pieces are made from local clay that is ground and stored in a vault before it is hand-thrown, glazed, and fired. Visitors are welcome to walk through the production area and see the process firsthand. Bybee makes some cute piggy banks and other items children will like. If it's shopping you're most interested in, call ahead to see which days the kiln will be emptied, selection is best on those days, usually two a week.

Richmond

Hummel Planetarium and Space Theater (all ages)

Kit Carson Drive, Eastern Kentucky University campus; (859) 622–1547, www .planetarium.eku.edu. Children's shows at 6:00 P.M. Thursday and Friday and 2:00 and 6:00 P.M. Saturday; main features at 7:30 P.M. Thursday and Friday and 3:30 and 7:30 P.M. Saturday. $

"Explore" Mars, get an astronomical glimpse of the future or distant past, see how the sky would look from the space shuttle—visions like these are available on Earth through the equipment of the Hummel Planetarium. With a starball capable of pro-jecting up to 10,164 stars, a multimedia system capable of creating special effects, and Dolby sound, this is one of the largest and most sophisticated planetariums in the world. Programs for younger children incorporate characters, stories, and games. Both the children's and the main program topics change several times a year. Each program includes a "Star Talk" about that night's sky.

Irvinton House Museum (all ages)

345 Lancaster Avenue; (859) 626–1422 or (800) 866–3705. Open Monday to Friday from 8:00 A.M. to 4:00 P.M. Free.

This beautiful early 1800s house is located in Irvine McDowell Park, and the Richmond Visitor Center is at the back of the house. So touring is very convenient; when you stop to pick up a map or brochures, see if the curator is around to take you through. (And if you have restless little ones, let them play in the park before or after.) The tour is highly personalized and friendly, and the elegant house includes an eclectic collection of items relating to local history. The vintage clothes are great, and children will enjoy seeing the Revolutionary War uniform and artifacts from Boonesborough.

Lake Reba Recreational Complex (all ages)

876 Eastern Bypass; (859) 623–8753. Open daily. Free.

This 450-acre park features a variety of recreational facilities, including nature and walking trails, picnic areas, and volleyball courts. The seventy-five-acre fishing lake is stocked with largemouth bass, bluegill, and catfish.

White Hall State Historic House (ages 6 and up) 🏛

500 White Hall Shrine Road; follow the signs from the I–75 Winchester–Boonesboro exit; (859) 623–9178. Open daily April 1 through Labor Day from 9:00 A.M. to 4:30 P.M. (last tour starts at 4:30 P.M.); Labor Day through October 31, open Wednesday to Sunday, 9:00 A.M. to 4:30 P.M.; November 1 through March 31, tours are Wednesday to Friday at 10:00 A.M., noon, and 2:00 P.M. $

Cassius Clay, this house's most famous resident, was quite a character. At various points in his life he was an emancipationist, newspaper publisher, flamboyant U.S. ambassador to Russia under Abraham Lincoln, and local eccentric (there's a hole in one of the walls where he shot at an unwanted visitor). The house itself is a bit eccentric. It's actually a house within a house, an older Federal-style building over which an elegant Italianate structure was built. A costumed guide fills you in on the details as you tour the house; the forty-four rooms include many family items and interesting early bathroom facilities. Picnic facilities are available on the grounds.

Amazing
Kentucky Fact

The famous scout and pioneer "Kit" Carson was born on Christmas Eve 1809, in a log cabin near Richmond, Kentucky.

A Boone for You?

According to local tradition, it's good luck to rub the foot of the Daniel Boone statue on Eastern Kentucky University's campus. The Daniel Boone Monument is located on University Drive. (859) 628–8474.

Deer Run Stables (all ages)

2001 River Circle Drive, off Highway 627 between White Hall and Fort Boonesborough (take exit 97 from I–75); (859) 527–6339. Open year-round Tuesday to Friday (call ahead for weekday visits), Saturday and Sunday from 12:30 to 3:30 P.M. Closed some Mondays. Trail rides $$$$, pony rides $$.

Deer Run offers one-hour trail rides for ages eight and up. The guided ride at a walk pace takes you up and down hills, along a creek, and past an old cabin or cemetery. Younger children can take a thirty-minute pony ride around the grounds. Only groups of six or more need reservations. If you're driving along Highway 627 heading from Fort Boonesborough to White Hall, look for the sign.

Fort Boonesborough State Park (all ages)

4375 Boonesboro Road (between Richmond and Winchester); follow the signs from I–75, exit 99; (859) 527–3131. Most attractions open daily, April through October. There are separate entrances for the park and for the fort. Fort admission $.

Start your visit to this pioneer fort, a re-creation of the settlement founded in this area by Daniel Boone in the 1770s, with a short video presentation. Then walk around the village to see how pioneers in the eighteenth century lived and to watch artisans demonstrate weaving, rifle making, baking, pottery, soap making, and wool carding. There's also a small general store with maple candy and other treats and souvenirs. In the center of the fort is a blacksmith shop with a giant bellows that is certain to fascinate young ones. Once you have finished touring the old fort, you can enjoy more modern fun in this state park, including a junior Olympic-size pool with a waterslide, fountain, special children's area, and a rain tree. There are also picnic shelters, a fishing area, and nature trails. From the park, you can see the locks on the Kentucky River, where you can watch the interesting process of boats "locking through." To find out more about the river, visit the park's Kentucky River Museum, located in a restored lock house, with exhibits relating to commerce on the river.

AnnualEvents in the Bluegrass Region

- **Raggedy Ann Festival,** April, Cynthiana; www.cynthianaky.com

- **International Kite Festival,** late April, Georgetown; (502) 863–1575

- **Kentucky Guild of Artists and Craftsmen Spring Fair,** late May, Berea; (800) 598–5263

- **Horsey Hundred Bicycling Weekend,** Memorial Day weekend, based in Georgetown; (859) 271–6001

- **Kids' Fishing Day,** early June, Shaker Village of Pleasant Hill; (800) 734–5611

- **Fort Harrod Beef Festival,** early June, Old Fort Harrod State Park, Harrodsburg; (859) 734–3314

- **Hero on Horseback: Jack Jouett Patriot Day,** early June, Versailles; (859) 873–7902

- **Kentucky River Heritage Weekend,** mid-June, Fort Boonesborough State Park; (859) 527–3131

- **Great American Brass Band Festival,** mid-June, Danville; (859) 236–7794

- **Woodford County Fair and Rodeo,** mid-June, Versailles; (859) 879–0670

- **Morgan's Raid on Georgetown Civil War Reenactment,** mid-June, Georgetown; (502) 863–1575

- **Scott County Fair,** late June, Georgetown; (502) 863–2547

- **Sweet Corn Festival at Evans Orchard,** July, Georgetown; (502) 863–2255

- **Berea Crafts Festival,** mid-July, Berea; (800) 598–5263

- **Kentucky Shaker Music Weekend,** late July, Shaker Village of Pleasant Hill; (800) 734–5611

- **Annual Pleasant Hill Craft Fair,** early August, Shaker Village of Pleasant Hill; (800) 734–5611

- **Family Fun Day,** early August, Buckley Wildlife Sanctuary, Versailles; (859) 873–5711

- **Daniel Boone Pioneer Festival,** Labor Day weekend, Winchester; (800) 298–9105

- **Apple Festival at Evans Orchard,** September, Georgetown; (502) 863–2255

- **Kentucky Folklife Festival,** September, downtown Frankfort; (502) 564–1792

- **Spoonbread Festival,** mid-September, Berea; (800) 598–5263

- **Constitution Square Festival,** late September, Danville; (859) 239–7089

- **AutumnFest at Bi-Water Farm,** weekends mid-September through October, Georgetown; (502) 863–3676

- **Festival of the Horse,** late September, Georgetown; (502) 863–2547

- **Pumpkin Festival at Evans Orchard,** October, Georgetown; (502) 863–2255

- **Perryville Battle Reenactment,** early October, Perryville; (859) 332–8631

- **Bluegrass Festival and Burgoo Festival,** early October, Winchester; (800) 298–9105

- **Kentucky Guild of Artists and Craftsmen Fall Fair,** mid-October, Berea; (800) 598–5263

- **Storytelling at the River,** late October, Shaker Village of Pleasant Hill; (800) 734–5611

Other Things to See and Do

Camp Catalpa Bird Sanctuary, US 25 east off Eastern Bypass; (859) 623–8753. One-mile scenic walking trail through shaded forest. Shelters, playgrounds, and picnic tables.

Driving Tour of Battle of Richmond, guide to 1862 Civil War battle sites; available at visitor center; (859) 626–8474.

Where to Eat

Burns Family Restaurant, 107 Big Hill Avenue; (859) 623–8265. Home cooking, varied menu. $

Casa Cafe, 709 Big Hill Avenue; (859) 623–8582. Traditional Mexican food made from scratch each day. $

Woody's Restaurant and Bar, 246 West Main Street; (859) 623–5130. Eclectic menu with interesting lunch and dinner specials. $$

Where to Stay

Days Inn, I–75, exit 90; (800) 325–2525. Continental breakfast, outdoor pool, pets allowed. $$

Econolodge, I–75, exit 87; (800) 424–4777. Continental breakfast, outdoor pool; pets allowed. $$

Fort Boonesborough State Park Campground, 4375 Boonesboro Road; (859) 527–3131. April through October. Primitive and full hookup camping. Showers, laundry, access to park pool, grocery. $

For More Information

Richmond Visitor Center, 345 Lancaster Avenue; (800) 866–3705 or (859) 626–8474.

Winchester

Downtown Area (all ages)

Main Street and surrounding streets; (859) 744–0556. Free.

Winchester has a cute, old-fashioned downtown area, and you can pick up a guide for a short walking tour at the Tourist Information Center, 2 South Maple Street. Sites include the county courthouse, where a portrait of Daniel Boone hangs; the *Spirit of the American Doughboy* statue by E. M. Visquesney on the courthouse lawn; and the restored Leeds Theatre, a performing arts center that features some drama and music performances appropriate for children.

Ale-8-One Bottling Plant and Company Store

25 Carol Road; (859) 744–3484, www.ale-8-one.com. Plant tours Friday at 10:50 A.M. Store open Monday to Friday from 8:30 A.M. to 4:30 P.M. Reservations required. Free.

Ale-8-One is a sweet, gingery soft drink made only in Winchester, with many devoted fans in the region. If you've never heard of it, be sure to try one while you're in the area. (It's sold in vending machines as well as at some restaurants in Lexington and the Bluegrass region.) Ale-8-One has been made since the 1920s using a secret formula developed by a Winchester entrepreneur named G. L. Wainscott. He held a contest to name his new soft drink, and since other soft drinks were already on the market, a little girl suggested "A Late One." Wainscott changed her suggestion a little to become Ale-8-One, or so the story goes. Take a company tour and see how it's made and bottled. The company store carries clothing and souvenirs with the Ale-8-One logo, as well as memorabilia and, of course, Ale-8-One.

Bluegrass Heritage Museum (ages 5 and up)
217 South Main Street; (859) 745–1358. Open Tuesday, Wednesday, and Friday from noon to 5:00 P.M., Thursday and Saturday from noon to 4:00 P.M. $

This large house with a rounded three-story tower was Winchester's hospital from the 1920s to the early 1970s. Today it houses an array of artifacts and photographs relating to various aspects of local history. There are exhibits on agriculture, the Civil War, and the old hospital, as well as a large collection of telephones.

Where to Eat

Hall's on the River, 1225 Athens-Boonesboro Road, near Boonesborough, between Winchester and Richmond; (859) 255–8105. Popular family restaurant overlooking the Kentucky River. Famous for its fish, fried battered banana peppers, and beer cheese. Children's menu available. $$

Where to Stay

Days Inn, I–64, exit 96; (859) 744–9111. Outdoor pool, free continental breakfast. $$

Holiday Inn Express, 5250 Revilo Road (I–64, exit 94); (859) 745–3009. Indoor pool, free continental breakfast. $$

Eastern
Kentucky

astern Kentucky is a region of incredible natural beauty, abundant recreational opportunities (especially if you like to hike, camp, or fish), and constant surprises. You never know what you might find around the next bend—a classy performing arts center, a coal-mining museum (or a coal mine), a craft shop, or a snake venom research collection center. Rolling in the north, mountainous in the south, this area contains some of Kentucky's most rugged and interesting geography. There are lush forests, massive stone arches, and rushing waterfalls. State parks are the prime ways to take advantage of the outdoor opportunities.

Interstate 64 runs through the northern part of eastern Kentucky to the largest city in this region, Ashland, and Mountain Parkway and Hal Rogers Parkway are four

Teresa's
TopPicks for Eastern Kentucky

1. Natural Bridge State Resort Park, (606) 663–2214

2. Highlands Museum and Discovery Center, (606) 329–8888

3. East Kentucky Science Center, (606) 889–0303

4. Kentucky Reptile Zoo, (606) 663–9160

5. Carter Caves State Resort Park, (606) 286–4411

6. Jenny Wiley State Resort Park, (606) 886–2711

7. Kentucky Opry/Mountain Arts Center, (888) 622–2787

8. Kentucky Folk Art Center, (606) 783–2204

9. Appalshop, (606) 633–0108

10. Hindman Settlement School, (606) 785–5475

EASTERN KENTUCKY

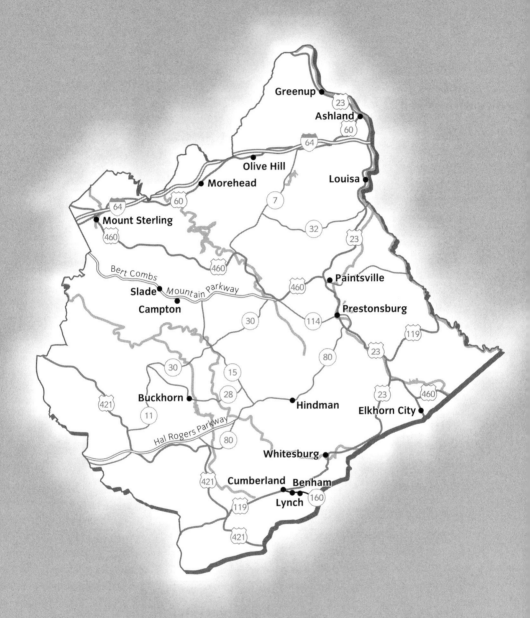

Greenup
Ashland
23
60
64
Olive Hill
Morehead
Louisa
60
7
Mount Sterling
64
32
460
23
460
Bert Combs
460
Paintsville
Slade
Mountain Parkway
460
Campton
Prestonsburg
30
119
114
30
80
23
15
23
460
28
Buckhorn
Hindman
Elkhorn City
421
11
Hal Rogers Parkway
80
Whitesburg
421
Cumberland
Benham
119
Lynch
160
421

lanes for at least part of the way. But in many places you will be on winding two-lane highways. As a result, travel time is longer, so bring along plenty of books, CDs, tapes, and games for your passengers. Some areas have little development, so don't defer necessity stops assuming there will be another place just up the road.

Attractions are listed in a circuitous route that begins east of Winchester, heads northeast to Ashland, then south along Kentucky's eastern border and west to the Cumberland Gap area. This will position you to explore south-central Kentucky.

Slade

Natural Bridge State Resort Park (all ages)

2135 Natural Bridge Road (off Highway 11); (606) 663–2214; reservations: (800) 325–1710. Admission and many activities **free;** sky lift ride $. Lodging $$–$$$$; dining $.

Because it's so close to Lexington (just about an hour and a half via I–64 and Mountain Parkway), this getaway spot is very popular and often crowded. Nonetheless, we've always had a good time. The park takes its name from its huge natural stone arch, one of many in the area. The main trail up to the arch is scenic and fairly easy— I've done it with a four-year-old walking and an infant in a front pack. The worst part is seeing your little one go scampering across the top of the arch: There are no side rails. (The arch is fairly wide, but for your own peace of mind, be ready to hold a younger child's hand.) You can also take a sky lift to a level walking trail at the top (April through October). Other features include pedal boat rental, a small nature center, miniature golf, picnic areas, playgrounds, and weekly square dances and music on Hoedown Island. Some activities are seasonal. There are nine hiking trails, ranging from ½ mile to 8½ miles in length, with interesting views year-round (in winter you can see the rock formations more clearly, since there's less vegetation). The park includes a small lodge, cottages, and two seasonal campgrounds. The lodge dining room offers a buffet and regional specialties.

A Day **Family Adventure**

With its beautiful scenery, eastern Kentucky is a great place for photography. On one of our day trips to Natural Bridge we took along several cameras so everyone would be able to take photos of the rock formations, trees, wildlife, and, of course, each other. We had a great time sharing and comparing our shots and perspectives.

Red River **Gorge**

Natural Bridge State Resort Park is a good place to begin exploring the Red River Gorge Geological Area. This federally designated 26,000-acre geological area is located within Daniel Boone National Forest and is the state's most visited hiking area. The more than eighty natural stone arches add a special beauty to the landscape, and the area is abundant in wildflowers and wildlife. Red River Gorge is popular with rock climbers as well as hikers, and there are so many trails that entire books have been written about this area alone.

Take the 30-mile driving loop, beginning at Highway 15, west of the Slade exit off Mountain Parkway. Along the way are scenic overlooks and other points of interest:

- **Nada Tunnel,** on Highway 77, is an 800-foot-long tunnel cut in the early 1900s to give trains access to timber in the area.

- **Gladie Creek Cabin,** a restored 1884 cabin, also has a blacksmith shop, a buffalo herd, and logging exhibits.

- At the **Gladie Creek Forest Service station,** you can pick up maps and information, essential for safe hiking. It's open daily in summer; hours vary other times of the year. (606) 663–2852.

The gorge is beautiful, but it's a place where you should know what you're getting into if you plan to hike or camp (backcountry camping allowed with permit and small fee). The steepness and the remoteness of the area make many trails inappropriate for novice hikers and younger children, and every year even experienced back-packers are injured here. Keep in mind that the area is also open to hunting.

Another way to see the gorge is a canoe excursion on the Red River. Canoe Kentucky offers both guided and unguided trips (800–522–6631).

Fall **Color**

Eastern Kentucky is a great place to catch color, and the state tracks the turning of the leaves to help visitors time their travels. ColorFall Kentucky reports are posted weekly at www.kentuckytourism.com from late September through the end of October.

Kentucky Reptile Zoo (ages 4 and up)
1275 Natural Bridge Road; (606) 663–9160. Open daily Memorial Day through Labor Day from 11:00 A.M. to 6:00 P.M., weekends only at other times of the year. $

The big painting in front of this place of a man riding an alligator should get your children's attention. Don't worry: This isn't a tacky tourist trap but an educational center run with a good sense of humor. Reptile and amphibian fans in the family will want to see the turtles, alligators, lizards, and hundreds of varieties of snakes from around the world and learn how poisonous snakes are "milked" to obtain venom used for medical research.

Where to Eat

Miguel's Pizza, 1890 Natural Bridge Road; (606) 663–1975. Open March through Thanksgiving. A favorite hangout for serious rock climbers in the area, this small spot serves delicious pizza made with homegrown veggies. $

Rose's Restaurant, 1289 Natural Bridge Road; (606) 663–0588. Beans and cornbread, sandwiches, and daily specials. $

Where to Stay

Bee Rocks Village, 184 L&E Railroad Place; (606) 663–9199. Cottages and seasonal camping. $$

Hemlock Trail Cabins, 415 Natural Bridge Road; (859) 230–3567. A-frame cabins with fully equipped kitchens and picnic tables. $$–$$$

For More Information

Gladie Creek Information Center, Stanton Ranger District, 705 West College Avenue, Stanton; (606) 663–2852.

Powell County Tourism, 478 Washington Street, Stanton; (606) 663–1161, www.powellcountytourism.com.

Campton

Torrent Falls Family Climbing Adventures (ages 10 and up)

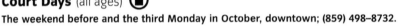

1435 Highway 11; (606) 668–6613. Open daily in summer from 9:00 A.M. to about 8:30 P.M.; last climbers admitted around 6:30 P.M. Over 17 $$$$, children 10–17 $$. From exit 33 off Mountain Parkway, go right.

If you and your older children enjoy those rock-climbing walls, here's a chance to go big time. This is an outdoor activity based on a European sport called *via ferrata*. The idea is to climb and maneuver around a vertical hiking/climbing path. You use a harness and steel cables to climb up and around iron rungs that have been drilled into the rock around a U-shaped canyon. (This isn't for those with a fear of heights—it goes about 100 feet up!) Admission is for an all-day pass, so you climb at your own pace and where you want to. The course includes a suspension bridge and ledges to rest along the way. You'll get a short training session; also, guides are available for an additional hourly fee and are required for minors not climbing with a parent. Sturdy shoes are a must, and gloves are also a good idea since your hands will get sore. Climbers must be at least ten years old, and you're required to sign a liability waiver. Food is available on-site.

Mount Sterling

Court Days (all ages) 🔒

The weekend before and the third Monday in October, downtown; (859) 498–8732. Free.

The main event in the pretty little town of Mount Sterling is this wild swapfest. Court Days has been going on here for some 200 years: Back in the early 1800s, each county court met once a month, and the days became occasions for celebration and trading. This event gets incredibly crowded; some 100,000 people converge upon this town of 5,400 over the three days (go on Monday if you can, when it's less

Good Old **Days**

Have a chili hot dog and shake for dinner at **Berryman's Tasty Treat,** 639 East Main Street in Mount Sterling (859–498–6830), then catch the show at the **Judy Drive-in,** 4078 Maysville Road, Mount Sterling (859–498–1960). (Both are closed in winter.)

crowded). But it's fun, even for youngsters. Just make sure you bring a stroller or pack carrier for little ones. Vendors offer just about everything—old stuff, new stuff, strange stuff—plus barbecue, funnel cakes, and other delicious festival fare.

Ruth Hunt Candies (all ages)

550 North Maysville Street; (859) 498–0676. Open Monday to Saturday from 9:00 A.M. to 5:30 P.M., Sunday from 1:00 to 5:30 P.M.

Ever hear of a Blue Monday? It's a dark chocolate candy bar with pulled cream in the center, the creation of Ruth Tharpe Hunt, who started this candy business in 1921. Other homemade goodies include caramel, sweet chocolate balls, and hot cinnamon suckers. Take a peek in the kitchen, where they make the candy in huge copper kettles.

For More Information

Mount Sterling/Montgomery County Tourism Commission, 51 North Maysville Street; (859) 498–8732, www.mountsterling-ky.com.

Morehead

Kentucky Folk Art Center (ages 5 and up)

102 West First Street; (606) 783–2204, www.kyfolkart.org. Open Monday to Saturday from 9:00 A.M. to 5:00 P.M., Sunday from 1:00 to 5:00 P.M. $, 12 and under free.

This museum features fascinating walking sticks, carved animals and figures, paintings, assemblages, painted furniture, and other folk art created by Kentuckians. You may see anything from figures of Elvis and Abe Lincoln to clothing woven from strips of plastic bags. Like Minnie Adkins, who makes the wonderful carved foxes and chickens, some of the artists live nearby in eastern Kentucky, but urban Kentuckians create folk art, too. Your family will get a broadened perspective of what art is, and you're bound to see something that will make you smile.

Cave Run Lake (all ages)

Off Highway 801 (take I–64, exit 133). Forest Service visitor center on Highway 801: (606) 784–5624. Open year-round. Day-use fees in recreational areas for noncampers. $

On a summer weekend at this lovely 8,270-acre lake at the northern end of Daniel Boone National Forest, you'll see fishing boats and maybe even a sailing regatta. It's a big muskie fishing area. Both the U.S. Army Corps of Engineers, which built the dam, and the U.S. Forest Service manage recreational areas here for camping and day use. Two major areas are Zilpo, a 355-acre wooded peninsula (606–768–2722), and Twin Knobs (606–784–8498). Both have campgrounds, picnic areas, hiking, and boat ramps. Stop at the Cave Run Lake Morehead Ranger Station on Highway 801, 2 miles off U.S. Highway 60 for lake information and to see exhibits about the area.

For a scenic overview, drive the Zilpo National Scenic Byway, an 11-mile route from US 60 in Salt Lick to Highway 211 south to Forest Service Road 129; you'll end at Tater Knob Fire Tower, where there's an interpretive trail.

Minor Clark State Fish Hatchery (all ages)

120 Fish Hatchery Road (Highway 801; take I–64, exit 133); (606) 784–6872. Open Monday to Friday from 7:00 A.M. to 3:00 P.M. Free.

Where do fish come from? The fish in Cave Run and many other Kentucky lakes come from this 300-acre hatchery, one of the largest warm-water hatcheries in the nation. You can view breeding ponds of muskie and bass and learn about the hatching process.

Where to Stay

Twin Knobs Recreation Area, Highway 801, 7 miles from I–64, exit 133; (606) 784–8816. U.S. Forest Service campsites on Cave Run Lake. $

For More Information

Morehead Tourism Commission, 150 East First Street; (606) 780–4342 or (800) 654–1944, www.moreheadtourism.com.

Forest Info

Daniel Boone National Forest covers 672,000 acres in eastern and south-central Kentucky, offering all kinds of spectacular sites and recreational opportunities, from camping and picnicking to whitewater rafting and rock climbing. The Sheltowee Trace National Recreation Trail runs 257 miles from one end to the other (now there's an ambitious family project!). There are six ranger stations throughout the forest, which are great sources of information and maps. The stations in eastern Kentucky are

- **Morehead** (Cave Run Lake), (606) 784–6428

- **Stanton** (Red River Gorge), (606) 663–2852

Or visit www.fs.fed.us/r8/boone.

Olive Hill

Grayson Lake State Park (all ages)

314 Grayson Lake Park Road (Highway 7, south of Grayson); (606) 474–9727. Open daily year-round. Admission and many activities **free;** outdoor drama $$.

The main attractions here are the fishing in the 1,500-acre lake and the serene atmosphere. Mid-June through mid-July a historical drama about the Civil War, *Someday*, may be performed in the outdoor amphitheater Friday and Saturday nights. Call (606) 286–4522 to see if it's being offered.

Carter Caves State Resort Park (all ages)

344 Caveland Drive (Highway 182 off US 60 and I–64); (606) 286–4411 information, (800) 325–0059 (reservations). Open year-round. Last cave tour leaves between 4:00 and 6:00 P.M., depending upon cave. Admission and many activities **free;** tours $ each cave. Lodge rooms $$–$$$, cottages $$$$, campground $. Dining $.

Three of the twenty caves located in this scenic state resort park are open for guided tours. These are good cave tours for children: The tours are generally easy walking, and they don't last too long (a half hour to ninety minutes). Families with older children may be able to tour all three in a day. The biggest and prettiest tour is of Cascade Cave, which includes a small waterfall. The Saltpetre Cave tour is more historically oriented, and there are fewer formations in the cave, but you'll learn how saltpeter was mined to make gunpowder. X Cave has the coolest name and the shortest tour (about a half hour); it's just two tunnels that make an X. If you're really into spelunking, plan to come for the park's Crawlathon Weekend in late January. There are also Ghosts in the Cave tours at Halloween. Aboveground activities abound as well: You can canoe, swim, play miniature golf, picnic, or take a hike. The park offers a lodge with a restaurant, cottages, and a campground.

Greenup

Greenbo Lake State Resort Park (all ages)

Highway 1, 18 miles from I–64, Grayson exit; information: (606) 473–7324, reservations: (800) 325–0083. Admission and some activities **free.** Lodge rooms $$, campground $. Dining $.

Not all of eastern Kentucky is mountainous, as a visit to this 3,008-acre park demonstrates. There are easy hiking trails along even to gently sloping terrain. Good as a day destination as well as for longer stays, Greenbo has a public swimming pool with wading pools and a waterslide, a lake for fishing and pontoon sightseeing (boat rentals available), miniature golf, bicycle rentals, and tennis courts. The lodge is named for Jesse Stuart, the famous Kentucky author and poet who lived nearby, and

Covered **Bridges**

Two of Kentucky's thirteen remaining covered bridges are located near Greenbo Lake State Resort Park. On your way to or from the park, stop to see 192-foot-long **Oldtown Bridge,** off Highway 1, 9 miles south of Greenbo Lake State Resort Park. This bridge is closed to traffic. You can drive through the 155-foot-long **Bennett's Mill Bridge,** north of the park, on Highway 3112, off Highway 7.

in the reading room at the lodge you can sample his works and learn about his life. The fieldstone lodge overlooks the lake and is open year-round; the campground is open seasonally. The dining room features a buffet and regional specialties.

Ashland

Highlands Museum and Discovery Center (all ages)

1620 Winchester Avenue; (606) 329–8888, www.highlandsmuseum.com. Open Tuesday to Saturday from 10:00 A.M. to 4:00 P.M. $

Hands-on fun for preschoolers on up is the order of the day here. Permanent exhibits range from an area set up like a nineteenth-century one-room schoolhouse to a science exploration area based on the PBS children's show *FETCH!* Children can pilot "Little Joe," a small tugboat at the "Poage's Landing: Life on the River" exhibit and enter a treehouse and explore the world of bugs, birds, and flowers. Another area celebrates Ashland's country music heritage, with exhibits on the Judds, Billy Ray Cyrus (and his daughter, Hannah Montana). There are special activities and areas for those under five.

Jesse's **Stories**

Jesse Stuart (1906–1984) wrote short stories, novels, and beautiful poems about his native eastern Kentucky. His books for elementary-school-age children include *The Beatinest Boy, A Penny's Worth of Character,* and *Andy Finds a Way.* You'll find them at Greenbo Lake State Resort Park and other resort park gift shops, as well as at the Jesse Stuart Foundation, 1645 Winchester Avenue; (606) 326–1667 or www.jsfbooks.com.

Road **Music**

US 23, the main highway running from Ashland in northeastern Kentucky to the Virginia border in southeastern Kentucky—passing through Paintsville, Prestonsburg, and Pikeville along the way—has been named the "Country Music Highway." Signs along the route note the many country stars who are from this area of the state, including Loretta Lynn and Dwight Yoakam.

Paramount Arts Center (ages 6 and up)
1300 Winchester Avenue; (606) 324–3175, www.paramountartscenter.com.

This lavish art deco–style 1931 movie house has been beautifully restored and now hosts music and theatrical presentations, some of which are appropriate for older children. If you're there when nothing is scheduled, ask to peek inside.

Where to Eat

Gattiland, Midtown Shopping Center; (606) 329–8381. Game room and Italian buffet. $

JJ Restaurant, 5260 Thirteenth Street; (606) 325–3816. Home-style cooking. $

Rajah's, US 60 west, Meads; (606) 928–3382. Despite the name, it's not an Indian restaurant; good home cooking. $

Where to Stay

Ashland Plaza Hotel, Fifteenth Street and Winchester Avenue; (606) 329–0055. High-rise with river or skyline view. No pool. $$$

Hampton Inn, 1321 Cannonsburg Road; (606) 928–2888. Indoor pool, continental breakfast. $$$

Holiday Inn Express, 4708 Winchester Avenue; (606) 325–8989. Indoor pool, continental breakfast. $$$

For More Information

Ashland Area Convention and Visitors Bureau, 1509 Winchester Avenue; (606) 329–1007 or (800) 377–6249, www.visitashlandky.com.

Louisa

Yatesville Lake State Park (all ages)

Highway 3 off U.S. Highway 23, near Louisa; (606) 673–1492; campground: (606) 673–1490. Open daily year-round. Admission **free;** camping $.

Fishing for bluegill, bass, and crappie is the main activity at this 808-acre park. There are picnic areas, three hiking trails with lake views, and boat rentals. The campground is open April through October only.

Paintsville Area

Mountain Homeplace (all ages)

Located in Paintsville Lake State Park, off Highway 40, west of Paintsville; (606) 297–1850. Open Tuesday to Saturday from 8:30 A.M. to 5:00 P.M. (last tour at 3:15 P.M.). Adults $$, children $.

Visiting this attraction is a little like dropping in on a nineteenth-century family. Costumed interpreters go about their lives and work as they might have done in the mid-1800s at a self-sufficient homestead, so what you'll see depends on the time of the year, from spinning to taking care of animals to making sorghum. The complex includes a blacksmith shop, grist mill, and schoolhouse in addition to the main house—it's enlightening to see how much hard work it took just to get through the day.

US 23 Country Music Highway Museum (all ages)

Highway 40, just off US 23, adjacent to the Paintsville Information Center; (606) 297–1469. Open Monday to Friday from 10:00 A.M. to 5:30 P.M., Saturday from 10:00 A.M. to 5:30 P.M., and Sunday from noon to 5:00 P.M. $

Guitars, costumes, and other memorabilia relating to country music stars from this area of Kentucky are on display here. You can sing karaoke to songs they made famous. One of the most interesting exhibits is the nickelodeon, a full-band player piano.

Loretta Lynn Birthplace (all ages)

Butcher Hollow, Highway 302 southeast of Van Lear; (606) 297–1469. No set hours; tours generally available most days year-round. $

Country music fans will enjoy seeing the birthplace of singer Loretta Lynn, of *Coal Miner's Daughter* fame. This board-and-batten cabin at her birthplace was rebuilt for the 1980 movie about Lynn's life. To take a tour, stop by Webb's Grocery nearby, owned by Lynn's brother Herman Webb.

Van Lear Historical Society Coal Miner's Museum (all ages)

Highway 302, near Van Lear; (606) 789–8540. Open by appointment. $, 10 and under **free.**

One of several attractions in eastern and southeastern Kentucky that cover the area's coal-mining industry and its history, this small museum includes a model of a typical early-twentieth-century company town. The museum is located in the former offices of Consolidated Coal Company.

Where to Stay

Paintsville Lake State Park Campground, Highway 40, off U.S. Highway 460, 4 miles west of Paintsville; (606) 297–8486. Primitive and hookup camping, plus showers, laundry, and full-service marina. $

Ramada Inn, 624 James Trimble Boulevard; (606) 789–4242 or (800) 951–4242. Indoor-outdoor pool, restaurant, game room. $$

For More Information

Paintsville Tourism Commission, 304 Main Street; (800) 542–5790.

Prestonsburg

East Kentucky Science Center (ages 4 and up)

207 West Court Street; (606) 889–0303. Open Tuesday through Saturday 11:00 A.M. to 4:30 P.M. Laser shows Friday and Saturday at 7:00 P.M. $

Located on the campus of Prestonsburg Community College, this center includes a planetarium and science exhibit hall. The planetarium offers three general astronomy show times in the afternoon and three laser show times on Saturday evenings; both shows feature an excellent sound system and more than 8,000 stars projected by a high-tech GOTO Chronos Star Projector. In the exhibit hall, youngsters can explore hands-on traveling exhibits. The center also hosts special events such as live music and theater exhibits.

The Real McCoys **(and Hatfields)**

Pikeville, Kentucky, about 35 miles southeast of Jenny Wiley State Resort Park, was the site of the famous Hatfield–McCoy feud. Some of the McCoy family are buried in the city's Dils Cemetery. The families' modern-day members have made peace and gather each June in Pikeville for the Hatfield–McCoy Reunion Festival. (606) 432–5063.

Jenny Wiley State Resort Park (all ages)
75 Theatre Court, off US 23/460; information: (606) 886–2711, reservations: (800) 325–0142. Open daily year-round. Many activities free.

This very popular and scenic mountain resort park takes its name from a pioneer woman who was captured by Indians in 1789 and escaped eleven months later. (The summer theater at this park includes a production that tells her story.) Present-day Kentuckians escape to the park for outdoor fun—there are swimming, boating, and fishing in the 1,100-acre Dewey Lake, as well as hiking, miniature golf, a nine-hole regulation golf course, and a 3-mile mountain-bike trail. Picnic areas and boat rentals are available. Daily mid-May through Labor Day and weekends through October, weather permitting, the Mountain Parkway Chair Lift will take you up 4,700 feet for hiking and scenic views atop Sugar Camp Mountain. Recent additions to the park include an eighteen-hole disc golf course (this is like golf, played with a Frisbee) and Elk Viewing Tours ($$$$), van excursions onto reclaimed surface mine areas where herds of elk are being re-established. The park dining room has a glorious view of the lake, and lodging includes rooms, cottages, and camping.

Jenny Wiley Theatre (ages 6 and up)
Jenny Wiley State Resort Park Amphitheatre; (606) 886–9274 or (877) CALL–JWT. Evening and some matinee performances mid-June through mid-August; call for specific schedule. Adults $$$, under 21 $$.

Children old enough to sit still for a couple of hours will enjoy the music, bright costumes, and lively onstage action at the amphitheater at Jenny Wiley State Resort Park. The theater presents classic Broadway musicals and comedies, along with a historical drama about pioneer Jenny Wiley. The show goes on rain or shine—in bad weather, the performance moves indoors to the Wilkinson-Stumbo Convention Center next to the amphitheater. Ask about family night specials: On these occasional dates, two children are admitted free with the purchase of two adult tickets. Also, some hotels in the Prestonsburg and Paintsville area offer packages including accommodations and theater tickets.

Kentucky Opry/Mountain Arts Center (ages 5 and up)

Mountain Arts Center, 50 Hal Rogers Road; (606) 886–2623 or (888) 622–2787. Performance dates vary; most Kentucky Opry performances are June through August and late November through mid-December. You can order advance tickets by phone. Ticket office open Monday to Friday from 10:00 A.M. to 6:00 P.M., Saturday from 10:00 A.M. to 4:00 P.M. Ask about one-price family admission. Tickets $$$. Self-guided tour **free.**

The Kentucky Opry, a lively family showcase of country, bluegrass, gospel, oldies, and Top 40, is the house attraction in the modern, 1,050-seat performance hall locals refer to as "MAC." The show frequently features young performers. Other concerts with regional and national performers are scheduled from time to time. You can stop by during the day and walk through this 47,000-square-foot entertainment complex, which often has art exhibits.

Where to Eat

Billy Ray's Restaurant, 101 North Front Street; (606) 886–0001. Home cooking. $

Where to Stay

Comfort Suites, 51 Hal Rogers Drive; (606) 886–2555. Indoor pool, free continental breakfast. $$–$$$

Holiday Inn, 1887 North US 23; (606) 886–0001 or (800) 466–5220. $$$

Microtel Inn, 85 Hal Rogers Drive, next to Mountain Arts Center; (606) 889–0331. Exercise room, free continental breakfast. $$

For More Information

Prestonsburg Tourism Commission, 113 South Central Avenue; (606) 886–1341 or (800) 844–4704, www.prestonsburg ky.org.

Elkhorn City

Breaks Interstate Park (all ages)

Highway 80 at the Kentucky–Virginia border; mailing address: P.O. Box 100, Breaks, VA 24607; (540) 865–4413 or (800) 982–5122. Open daily year-round. Park admission $. Lodge rooms $$; cottages $$$; camping $; dining $.

The huge 5-mile canyon within this park is sometimes called the "Grand Canyon of the South" for its 1,000-foot cliffs and breathtaking views. It's the largest canyon east of the Mississippi River. The park, jointly operated by Kentucky and Virginia, is popular with sightseers as well as hikers and experienced white-water rafters. Stop at the visitor center to view exhibits about the area's formation some 250 million years ago before heading to the four terrific scenic overlooks, or explore the area via hiking trails and trail rides on horseback. Pony rides offered for younger children. The lodge hugs the rim of the canyon, offering breathtaking views from the balconies of the rooms and from the dining room. Two-bedroom cottages also are available.

Nature Preserves

In addition to the excellent state parks, nature lovers can explore Kentucky's preserves. Of the forty-one legally designated and protected areas in the state, twenty-one are open to the public from dawn to dusk daily.

Unlike the state parks, however, nature preserves are not operated mainly with visitation in mind. Just the opposite: The idea is to preserve these beautiful and important natural areas. Except for preserves located within state parks, there are no restroom facilities, and there may not be maps and guide information on-site. They are for foot traffic only—no bikes or horses—and picnicking, camping, pets, and radio/tape decks are not allowed. Nature preserves open to the public in the area covered by this chapter are

- **Bat Cave/Cascade Cavern**—ask at Carter Caves Park for information and cave tours

- **Jesse Stuart**—W-Hollow Road off Highway 1; includes land once owned by the famous author

- **Natural Bridge**—located in the park

- **Pilot Knob**—Brush Creek Road, off Highway 15 in Powell County

- **Bad Branch**—off Highway 932 near Whitesburg

- **Blanton Forest**—off Highway 840 in Harlan County

- **Kingdom Come**—in state park

For more information on Kentucky's nature preserves, call (502) 573–2886, or visit www.naturepreserves.ky.gov.

Whitesburg

Appalshop (ages 5 and up)
91 Madison Avenue; (606) 633–0108, www.appalshop.org. Open Monday to Friday from 9:00 A.M. to 5:00 P.M. Reservations needed for guided tour. Free.

Appalshop is a not-for-profit community and media organization that produces documentary films about Appalachian culture, sponsors community events, concerts, and theater performances, and even has its own recording label and radio station. If you just stop by, you may be able to watch a video and see the art gallery and some activities, but if you want to be assured of a tour, make reservations. While you're there, ask about the nearby J. B. Caudill Store and History Center, which includes all kinds of artifacts. In June, Appalshop sponsors Seedtime on the Cumberland, with crafts, music, and food.

Where to Eat

Courthouse Cafe, 127B Main Street; (606) 633–5859. Sandwiches, salads, and daily specials; local crafts on display. $

Some Things I've Learned (the Hard Way) **about Family Hiking**

Eastern Kentucky has hundreds and hundreds of miles of hiking trails, from very easy and accessible paths to extremely rugged and remote areas. The temptation is to get out there and explore. But first:

- Be sure all family members (including toddlers) are wearing athletic shoes or hiking boots with good traction—not sandals!

- Take along (filled) water bottles, preferably one per person.

- Know how long and how difficult the trail is before you go; you should have a map. (What we assumed, mistakenly, was a short, easy walk along an unmarked trail turned out to be a tough 7-mile trek—and it was ninety degrees outside. Some of us thought we were going to die!)

- Don't be hard-headed—turn back if the trail is getting too long or difficult.

- If you have a toddler, strongly consider bringing a back or front carrier—you'll get awfully tired carrying him or her in your arms.

- With younger children, stick to the short and easy trails near facilities. There's no reason to push little ones. (Remember, their legs are shorter than yours.) You can always come back and hike the longer trails when they're older. (Believe me, before you know it, you'll be the one lagging behind!)

If you are serious hikers, get a hiking guide to the region, such as Globe Pequot Press's *Hiking Kentucky*.

Amazing
Kentucky Fact

About 96 percent of Kentucky's electricity is generated by coal, a non-renewable fossil fuel. It takes about a pound of coal to power a 100-watt lightbulb for ten hours—so turn off those lights when you're not using them!

Hindman

Hindman Settlement School (all ages)
Highway 160, off Highway 80, northeast of Hazard; (606) 785–5475. Open Monday to Friday from 8:00 A.M. to 5:00 P.M.; large groups should call first. Craft shop open Monday to Friday from 10:00 A.M. to 4:00 P.M., Saturday 10:00 A.M. to noon. Free.

The Hindman Settlement School was founded in 1902 and was the first rural social settlement school in the United States. The goal now, as it was then, is to provide educational opportunities and services with respect to the local heritage. Today this is a wonderful place to learn about Appalachian culture and folkways. If you stop by, you can watch a video about the school's history and get to see some of the buildings with their lovely handmade furniture and crafts. You'll also visit the Marie Stewart Craft Shop, which sells quilts, pottery, baskets, and other items made by local craftspeople; children will love the wooden trucks and animals.

Kentucky Appalachian Artisan Center (all ages)
16 West Main Street; (606) 785–9855. Open Monday to Friday from 10:00 A.M. to 6:00 P.M., Saturday from 10:00 A.M. to 4:00 P.M. Free.

Stop by this center in downtown Hindman to view changing arts and crafts exhibits. There's also a small sales shop.

Oh, **Man!**

Bet you've never seen a 10-foot-plus gingerbread man! The world's largest gingerbread man is the star attraction of the annual **Gingerbread Festival** in Hindman. Why gingerbread? It's part of the area's political history; politicians used to give out gingerbread to woo voters. The festival starts the Thursday after Labor Day and continues through Sunday. For a taste of the gingerbread man, come on Saturday. (606) 785–5329.

Cumberland/Benham/Lynch

Kingdom Come State Park (all ages)

502 Park Road, off U.S. Highway 119, Cumberland; (606) 589–2479. Open daily year-round. Many activities **free.**

DO NOT FEED THE BEARS. You expect to see this warning posted in Yellowstone National Park in Wyoming, but in Kentucky? There were a lot of bears in eastern Kentucky a century ago, but they virtually disappeared because of logging and hunting. They're venturing back from Virginia and West Virginia. There's no guarantee that you'll see one, but they've become prevalent enough in Kingdom Come State Park that the park is calling itself the "Black Bear Capital of Kentucky," bear-proofing its trash cans, and warning campers not to leave any food in their tents. In case you don't see a bear, other things to do here include fishing, pedal boating, miniature golf, and hiking to Log Rock, a sandstone arch, and Raven Rock, a huge rock that reaches 250 feet in the air. The fourteen trails range in length from ⅛ to ⅞ mile. The park offers primitive camping only.

Lilly Cornett Woods (ages 6 and up)

Highway 1103, off Highway 7, north of Kingdom Come State Park, Allie; (606) 633–5828. To tour, call for an appointment. **Free.**

Your children need to be able to walk about 2 miles/two hours to take this guided hike through one of Kentucky's rare remaining areas of old-growth forest. Many of the trees are more than 200 years old.

Godbey Appalachian Center (ages 6 and up)

700 College Road, Cumberland; (606) 589–2145, ext. 2047.

Stop by this cultural center on the campus of Southeast Community College to view a collection of Appalachian photographs, crafts, and art.

Kentucky Coal Mining Museum (ages 4 and up)

Main Street (Highway 160), Benham; (606) 848–1530. Open Monday to Saturday from 10:00 A.M. to 5:00 P.M., Sunday from 1:00 to 4:00 P.M. $

When Benham was an International Harvester company town, this building was the commissary. Now it houses a variety of exhibits about mining and life in a mining camp. Children can climb onto a 1940s electric locomotive on the grounds, don hard hats, and wiggle through a mock coal mine in the basement. Other exhibits include tools, mining equipment, and artifacts from the hospital and school. A collection of items relating to country singer Loretta Lynn is on the third floor.

AnnualEvents in Eastern Kentucky

- **Carter Caves Crawlathon,** late January, Carter Caves State Resort Park; (606) 286–4411, www.cartercaves.com

- **Hillbilly Days,** mid-April, Pikeville; (800) 844–7453

- **Mountain Mushroom Festival,** late April, Irvine; (606) 723–2450

- **Herpetology Weekend,** late April or early May, Natural Bridge State Resort Park; (800) 325–1710

- **Wildflower Weekend,** early May, Natural Bridge State Resort Park; (800) 325–1710

- **Poke Sallet Festival,** early June, Harlan; (606) 573–2600

- **Seedtime on the Cumberland Festival of Mountain Arts,** early June, Appalshop, Whitesburg; (606) 633–0108

- **Breathitt County Honey Festival,** Labor Day weekend, Jackson; (606) 666–3800

- **Gingerbread Festival,** September, Hindman; (606) 785–5329

- **Poppy Mountain Bluegrass Festival,** late September, Morehead; (606) 784–2277

- **Black Gold Festival,** late September, Hazard; (606) 436–0161

- **Kentucky Highland Folk Festival,** late September, Prestonsburg; (800) 844–4704

- **Morgan County Sorghum Festival,** late September, West Liberty; (606) 743–3330

- **Letcher County Mountain Heritage Festival,** late September, Whitesburg; (606) 632–1200

- **Cave Run Storytelling Festival,** late September, Morehead; (800) 988–1075

- **Kentucky Apple Festival,** early October, Paintsville; (800) 542–5790

- **Cumberland Mountain Fall Festival,** early October, Middlesboro; (800) 988–1075

- **Court Days,** weekend before and third Monday of October, Mount Sterling; (850) 498–8732

- **Jenny Wiley Pioneer Festival,** mid-October, Prestonsburg; (606) 886–2335

- **Lee County Woolly Worm Festival,** late October, Beattyville; (606) 464–2888

Portal 31 Mine Tour and Lamphouse Museum (ages 4 and up)

Highway 160, Lynch, southeast of Benham; (606) 848–1530, www.portal31.org. Museum open Monday to Friday from 9:00 A.M. to 5:00 P.M. $

Just a couple of miles from the Coal Mining Museum is the entrance to the old mine. Kentucky's first underground coal mine tours are in development. Plans are that you'll don safety gear and ride a transport into the mine, where projected images will give the impression of miners at work. In the meantime, you can see mining equipment and miners' hats on display at the 1920s lamphouse.

Where to Eat

Benham School House Inn, 100 Central Avenue, Benham; (606) 848–3000. Lunch and dinner. Fried chicken, catfish, sandwiches, daily special. $

Where to Stay

Benham School House Inn, 100 Central Avenue, Benham; (606) 848–3000.

Rooms and suites in a school building built in 1926 for children of the coal-mining camp. $$$

Portal 31 RV Park, Main Street, Lynch, right across from Portal 31; (606) 848–1530. Open year-round. Primitive and hookup sites. $

Family **Folk Week**

During the second week of June, the Hindman Settlement School offers a wonderful family vacation. Parents and children stay in the school dorms and attend all kinds of workshops on crafts, storytelling, music, and folk dancing. There are sessions for children ages four to twelve as well as for teens and adults, and all ages come together for some events. Each evening there are performances by the teachers (these are open to the public if you happen to be in the area). Many families return year after year for Family Folk Week, so make your reservations early. For information about tuition, call the school at (606) 785–5475.

Log **Cathedral**

While in the Buckhorn area, take a short drive on Highway 28 to Buckhorn, about 16 miles southeast of the state park, to see the Log Cathedral (606–398–7382; **free**), a beautiful log church with amber stained-glass windows, a large bell tower, and a huge pipe organ inside. It was built in 1907 as part of a Christian school founded by New Yorker Harvey S. Murdoch.

Buckhorn

Buckhorn Lake State Resort Park (all ages)

4441 Highway 1833; information: (606) 398–7510, reservations: (800) 325–0058. Many activities **free.** Lodge rooms $$–$$$, cottages $$$$. Dining $.

The 1,200-acre lake is the centerpiece of this mountain resort park. You can bring your own boat or rent one; pontoon sightseeing boats also available (rentals April through October only). The lodge dining room overlooks the lake. Work up your appetite with the 1½-mile easy walking trail or a round of miniature golf. There's a public beach, but the swimming pool is for lodge and cottage guests only. No campground.

South-Central Kentucky

I n this region you can explore Kentucky from just about every angle—the top of a mountain, on water, even deep beneath the surface of the earth. South-central Kentucky is really three vacation zones in one. The easternmost section features mountain scenery and traditional cultural attractions. Then you get to water world— fishing and boating enthusiasts flock to Laurel Lake, Cumberland Lake, Dale Hollow Lake, and Green River Lake. Heading west, the lakes give way to cave country. Mammoth Cave, the nation's longest cave system, and a bevy of other underground caverns offer natural air-conditioning and cool formations. At the western edge of the region is Bowling Green, Kentucky's fourth largest city. Throughout are an array of

Teresa's
TopPicks for South-Central Kentucky

1. Kentucky Down Under, (800) 762–2869

2. Mammoth Cave National Park, (270) 758–2180

3. Cumberland Gap National Historical Park, (606) 248–2817

4. Barren River Imaginative Museum of Science, (270) 843–9779

5. Dinosaur World, (270) 773–4345

6. Big South Fork Scenic Railway, (800) GO–ALONG

7. Kentucky Museum, (270) 745–2592

8. Kentucky Music Hall of Fame Museum, (606) 256–1000

9. Wolf Creek National Fish Hatchery, (270) 343–3797

10. Cumberland Falls State Resort Park, (606) 528–4121

SOUTH-CENTRAL KENTUCKY

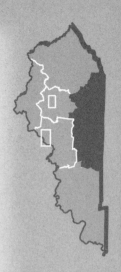

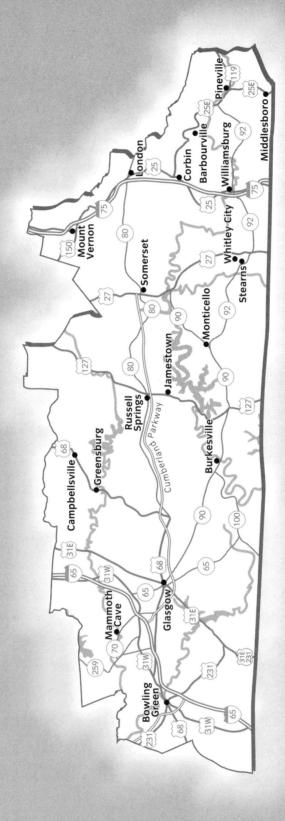

interesting and fun museums and attractions, relating to everything from coal to chicken to kangaroos.

Interstate access is good through much of this region: Interstate 75 runs south from the Bluegrass; from there you can go west to Somerset and pick up the Louie B. Nunn Parkway (a toll road), which hooks into Interstate 65 at Bowling Green. I–65 connects the cave area and Bowling Green with the Louisville area. Many chain hotels and restaurants are located along the interstate corridors.

Middlesboro

Cumberland Gap National Historical Park (all ages)

U.S. Highway 25E south, P.O. Box 1848, Middlesboro 40965; (606) 248–2817. Open daily except Christmas 8:00 A.M. to 5:00 P.M. Admission and many activities free. Cave and Hensley Settlement Tours $.

If you were doing a tour of Kentucky in chronological order, you'd start here, for this is where Daniel Boone and other early explorers and settlers first entered the state through a natural break in the Cumberland Mountains. Native tribes had used the gap, but their "Warriors' Path" to Kentucky became known as the Wilderness Road as European settlers poured through in the late 1700s. The road was later paved, but after the modern tunnel through the adjacent mountain opened (see next entry), the old US 25 highway was removed, and the Wilderness Road path was restored in recent years. It's about ⅞ mile long, a fairly easy hike from the parking lot off Pinnacle Road to the gap. You'll also want to drive up to Pinnacle Overlook to see three states (Kentucky, Tennessee, and Virginia). There are many ranger-guided activities in this 50,000-acre park, including two- to four-hour tours of Hensley Settlement and Cudjo's Cave (for a fee), as well as kids' hiking and history activities. (Did you know that Daniel Boone *didn't* wear a coonskin cap?)

Cumberland Gap Tunnel (all ages)

US 25E, Kentucky to Tennessee; (606) 248–2482. Free.

Leave and reenter Kentucky like a modern pioneer: Drive through the mountain via these ultramodern 4,600-foot twin portals under Cumberland Mountain. The project was completed in 1996 to make passage safer.

Coal House and Museum (all ages)

106 North Twentieth Street; (606) 248–1075. Open Monday to Friday from 8:00 A.M. to 4:00 P.M. Free.

An entire house made of coal? Actually, this building housing the Bell County Chamber of Commerce is just faced with bituminous coal, but it's still a lot of coal—about 40 tons. The house was built in 1926. Next door is the Coal House Museum, which features various mining artifacts.

Amazing
Kentucky Fact

Middlesboro, Kentucky, is the only U.S. city known to be located within a meteor crater.

Where to Eat

J. Milton's Steak and Buffet, US 25E; (606) 248–0458. Steaks, chicken, and seafood. $

Webb's Country Kitchen, 602 Colwyn Avenue, Cumberland Gap (just over the state line in Tennessee); (423) 869–5877. Country cooking with live music on Friday nights. $

Where to Stay

Best Western Inn, 1623 Cumberland Avenue; (606) 248–5630, www.bestwestern kentucky.com. Complimentary breakfast, outdoor pool. $$$

Boone Trail Hotel, 1252 North Twelfth Street; (606) 248–1340. Complimentary breakfast, outdoor pool. $$

Pineville

Pine Mountain State Resort Park (all ages)

1050 State Park Road (off US 25E, 1 mile south of Pineville); information: (606) 337–3066, reservations: (800) 325–1712. Open daily year-round. Many activities free. Lodge rooms $$-$$$$, cottages $$$$. Dining $.

The beautiful tall trees and enchanted feel of this park attract bird-watchers and nature lovers along with golfers and would-be beauty queens (the park's main event is the crowning of the Mountain Laurel Queen each April at the natural amphitheater). The 8½ miles of hiking trails include a trek to Chained Rock (about ½ mile if you drive to the Chained Rock parking lot first; about 3 miles if you're hiking from the lodge). This giant rock is chained to the mountaintop to supposedly keep it from falling on the city of Pineville below (a 1920s publicity stunt). The park's challenging eighteen-hole championship course, Wasioto Winds, was designed by renowned golf course architect Michael Hurdzan. If you have a youngster who is interested in golf, check out the separate four-hole course; Pine Mountain is part of the World Golf Foundation's "First Tee" program for children ages seven to seventeen. NOTE: The park swimming pool is for lodge and cottage guests only.

Henderson Settlement School and Log House Craft Shop

(all ages)

Highway 190, 18 miles southwest of Pineville; Settlement School: (606) 337–3613, Log House Craft Shop: (606) 337–5823. Open Monday to Friday from 8:00 A.M. to 4:30 P.M. **Free.**

You're welcome to walk around this 1,300-acre United Methodist Church mission complex that includes orchards, gardens, and a community greenhouse. Handwoven items and other locally made crafts are sold at the crafts shop.

For More Information

Bell County Tourism Commission, 2215 Cumberland Avenue, Middlesboro; (606) 248–2482 or (800) 988–1075, www.mountaingateway.com.

Barbourville

Dr. Thomas Walker State Historic Site

Highway 459, off US 25E; (606) 546–4400. Grounds open daily year-round; facilities seasonal. **Free.**

Though not as famous as Daniel Boone, Dr. Thomas Walker, a physician and surveyor, played an important role in opening Kentucky for settlement. He led the first expedition through the Cumberland Gap in 1750 and was the first settler from the east to build a log cabin in Kentucky. This was the place; the cabin is a replica. (Of course, there weren't picnic tables, miniature golf, a basketball court, playgrounds, and concession stands back then.)

Barbourville Recreational Park/Brickyard Waves Water Park

(all ages)

Allison Avenue; (606) 546–6197. Open daily; water park seasonal. Many activities **free;** water park $.

Cool off in this activities-packed city park. Brickyard Waves Water Park has a wave pool, giant slide, lazy river, and kiddie pool. (Smile as you hit the water— sometimes the slide action is broadcast on the local access cable channel!) Other features include batting cages, pedal-boat rentals, miniature golf, and free fishing, picnic areas, and playgrounds.

Where to Eat

Vintage House Restaurant, 101 North Main Street; (606) 546–5414. Across from the courthouse. Lunch Wednesday through Friday (quiche and sandwiches $); dinner Thursday through Saturday (prime rib, fresh fish $$).

Where to Stay

Best Western Wilderness Trail, 1476 South US 25E; (606) 546–8500. Pool, restaurant, free continental breakfast. $$

For More Information

Barbourville Tourism and Recreation Commission, P.O. Box 1300, Barbourville 40906; (606) 546–6197, www.barbour ville.com.

Williamsburg

Cumberland Museum (all ages)

649 South Tenth Street; (606) 539–4050. Open Monday to Saturday from 8:30 A.M. to 6:00 P.M. $

You don't expect to find a polar bear in Kentucky, but this eclectic museum operated by Cumberland College has not one but two, along with hundreds of other preserved animals displayed in natural settings. And that's just the beginning. There's also a collection of 6,000 crosses, animated Christmas figures (Santa himself is around in December), and mountain crafts and artifacts.

Hal Rogers Family Entertainment Center and Kentucky Splash Water Park (all ages) 🏊 ⚾ 🎠 🎡

1050 Highway 92 west; (606) 549–6065, www.kentuckysplash.com. Water park seasonal; other attractions open year-round. Open Monday to Thursday from 11:00 A.M. to 9:00 P.M., Friday and Saturday from 11:00 A.M. to 11:00 P.M., and Sunday from 12:30 to 6:30 P.M. Hours may vary seasonally. Water park $$$; other activities individual fees. All-day activity pass $$$$.

This large family amusement center features an array of family activities. The water park includes an 18,000-square-foot wave pool, triple twisting slides, a drift pool, and Tad Pole Island for younger children. There's a go-kart track for older children, as well as a kiddie track, batting cages, and a big arcade. Snacks, burgers, and sandwiches are available.

Where to Eat

Athenaeum Restaurant, Cumberland Inn, 649 South Tenth Street; (606) 539–4100. Operated by Cumberland College. Breakfast, lunch, and dinner. Order from the menu, or try the extensive buffets. $

Where to Stay

Cumberland Inn, 649 South Tenth Street; (606) 539–4100. Rooms and suites, plus sixty-bedroom log house. Indoor pool. Operated by Cumberland College as part of student work/study program. $$$–$$$$

Days Inn, U.S. Highway 25W and Highway 91; (606) 549–1500. Free continental breakfast, outdoor pool. $$

For More Information

Williamsburg Information Center, exit 11 off I–75; (606) 549–0530 or (800) 552–0530, www.williamsburgky.com.

Corbin

Cumberland Falls State Resort Park (all ages)

7351 Highway 90, near Corbin; information: (606) 528–4121, reservations: (800) 325–0063. Open year-round. Many activities **free.** Lodge rooms $$–$$$$, cottages $$$–$$$$, camping $. Dining $.

After you snap some family photos in front of the scenic falls (67 feet tall and 150 feet wide, the "Niagara of the South"), enjoy the swimming, hiking, miniature golf, tennis, and horseback riding. Within the park itself is 44-foot-high Eagle Falls, about a 1-mile hike from Cumberland Falls. The stone lodge built in the 1930s includes a pleasant sitting room, game room, and exhibits relating to the local area. Pick up the visitor guide at the lodge for directions to other waterfalls and a scenic arch. In the summer, there are weekly square dances at the park pavilion.

Sheltowee Trace Outfitters (ages 7 and up)

Entry points vary depending on type of excursion; based in Whitley City; (800) 541–RAFT. Mid-May through October; schedule and rates vary depending on activity.

This company offers water outings in the Cumberland Falls/Big South Fork area that range from mild to wild. At Cumberland Falls State Resort Park on weekends Memorial Day through Labor Day, you can take a Rainbow Mist Tour Ride to the bottom of the falls (children must weigh at least twenty-five pounds; trip dependent on water levels and weather; call the day before your planned visit). Lunch cruises are offered on Lake Cumberland aboard a 65-foot double-decker riverboat. Some of the more adventurous rafting, canoeing, and duckie boat outings are for ages thirteen and up only, but a few are available for participants as young as seven.

Name **Game**

Can you guess why Corbin calls its annual community event the **NIBROC Festival?** Study the name for a while, and it might come to you. Or just show up mid-August and ask while you enjoy street dances, a dog show, a parade, children's activities, and other events. (800) 528-7123.

Falls Mountain Craft Center (all ages)

Highway 90 west of Cumberland Falls State Resort Park; (606) 376-3463. Open daily except Wednesday from 10:00 A.M. to 6:00 P.M.

This shop, located in 1840s log buildings, carries a variety of arts and crafts produced locally—everything from painted gourds, ornaments, and candles to large cedar chests. It's operated by a nonprofit organization, and the selection changes often—whatever local craftspeople decide to make. The manager lives next door, so even if you come on a Wednesday, you may be able to visit the shop.

Harland Sanders Cafe and Museum (all ages)

US 25E; (606) 528-2163. Open daily from 10:00 A.M. to 10:00 P.M. Admission free; charge for food.

The world's most famous chicken—and the "Colonel" who invented it—got its start here. Visit this restaurant/museum where, in 1940, Harland Sanders perfected his recipe of "secret herbs and spices" and began serving chicken so good that he decided to try to franchise it. The rest is finger lickin' history. There's memorabilia on display, and the place still serves KFC.

Where to Stay

Comfort Suites, I-75, exit 29, 47 Adams Road; (606) 526-6646. Indoor pool. Rooms and suites, free continental breakfast. $$

Holiday Inn Express, I-75, exit 25, 1973 Cumberland Falls Parkway; (606) 523-4000. $

For More Information

Corbin Tourist and Convention Commission, 101 North Depot Street; (606) 528-6390 or (800) 528-7123, www.corbin ky.com.

More **Egg-citement!**

Corbin has the Colonel Sanders Cafe, but nearby London has the **World Chicken Festival** each year in late September. See the world's largest stainless steel skillet!

Amazing
Kentucky Fact

If you visit Cumberland Falls State Resort Park during a full moon when there's a clear sky, go to the falls area after dark—you might see a nighttime rainbow. There are only two places in the world where "moonbows" occur: Cumberland Falls, Kentucky, and over Victoria Falls on the Zambezi River in Africa.

London

Levi Jackson Wilderness Road State Park (all ages) 🌊 🏛 👫 ⛺
998 Levi Jackson Mill Road; (606) 878–8000. Park open year-round; museum open April through October. Many activities **free**; museum admission $.

Pioneer artifacts are an added attraction at this 800-acre park. Two historic hiking trails, Wilderness Road and Boone's Trace, come through this park. At the Mountain Life Museum, a reproduction of a pioneer settlement, costumed guides tell about pioneer life, and you can see tools, household items, and other relics. One of the seven buildings is a reproduction of McHargue's Mill, with authentic interior works. The mill building is surrounded by a large collection of millstones. After all that history, you can have some modern fun at the park's miniature golf course, swimming pool, playgrounds, and picnic areas.

London/Corbin Area **Lakes**

- **Laurel River Lake,** This 6,000-acre lake is located within Daniel Boone National Forest. There are two marinas and several Forest Service recreation areas. Stop at the ranger station on US 25 (606–864–4163) for maps and information. A state record smallmouth bass (eight pounds, seven ounces) was caught here in 1998.

- **Wood Creek Lake,** Highway 80 off I–75, exit 41, at the edge of Daniel Boone Forest, may be small—672 acres—but it has a big claim to fame. The state record largemouth bass—thirteen pounds, ten ounces—was caught here on April 14, 1984.

Mount Vernon

Kentucky Music Hall of Fame Museum (ages 6 and up)

US 25 off I-75, exit 62, 2590 Richmond Road; (606) 256-1000 or (877) 356-3263, www .kymusichalloffame.com. Open Monday to Saturday 10:00 A.M. to 6:00 P.M., Sunday 9:00 A.M. to 3:00 P.M. Admission $, recording studio $$.

"What's that song?" my daughter asked. "Bye, Bye Love," an old tune by the Everly Brothers, was being piped through the speakers as we toured this museum (opened in 2002). Although your children may not recognize all the stars whose music is played and costumes and artifacts displayed, young musicians will enjoy seeing the antique instruments and exploring pitch, rhythm, and timbre in the interactive area. You can go into the museum's recording studio and make a CD of a favorite song from the studio's array of music.

Renfro Valley (all ages)

US 25 off I-75, exit 62, Renfro Valley; (800) 765-7464, www.renfrovalley.com. Shows March through December; schedule and ticket prices vary. Shop hours also vary; most open Wednesday to Saturday from 10:00 A.M. to 9:00 P.M. spring through fall and during Christmas season. Motel $-$$, cabins $-$$, RV campground $.

Renfro Valley has been holding jamborees and barn dances since 1939. The schedule includes headliner concerts featuring well-known artists as well as a full array of performances featuring local and regional performers—up to a dozen shows a week in the summer. Regular features are the Saturday Barn Dance at 7:00 P.M., the Saturday Jamboree at 9:00 P.M., and the Sunday Gatherin' (gospel music) at 8:30 A.M. There's also a "village" of shops, including a cute gristmill general store, plus two restaurants, a motel, cabins, and an RV campground.

How 'Bout These Apples

Follow your appetite to Liberty for the annual **Casey County Apple Festival.** Held the last week in September, this festival features a giant chocolate chip cookie on Wednesday, a giant pizza on Thursday, and the world's largest apple pie on Saturday (it takes a forklift to get it into the oven). If you happen to still be hungry, stop by Bread of Life Cafe, 5369 South U.S. Highway 127, for good home cooking.

For More Information

Renfro Valley Visitors Center, I–75, exit 62, Renfro Valley; (606) 256–2638 or (800) 765–7464.

Mount Vernon/Rockcastle County Tourist Commission, P.O. Box 1261, Mount Vernon 40456; (606) 256–9814 or (800) 252–6685.

Somerset/Monticello Area

1840s Mill Springs Mill (all ages)

Highway 1275 off Highway 90, near Monticello; (606) 348–8189. Open daily May through the end of October from 9:00 A.M. to 5:00 P.M. **Free.**

Stop by to see this antique waterwheel—one of the largest overshot waterwheels in the world, at 40 feet, 10 inches in diameter. You can buy cornmeal ground at the mill in the gift shop; to see the grinding in action, come by Saturday or Sunday at 2:00 P.M. Picnic areas available.

SomerSplash Water Park (all ages)

1700 North US Highway 27, Somerset; (606) 679–7946. Open June through September, Monday to Friday from 10:00 A.M. to 8:00 P.M., Saturday from 10:00 A.M. to 9:00 P.M., and Sunday from 11:00 A.M. to 9:00 P.M. May stay open later in July. $$$

The biggest attraction at this twenty-acre water park is the 30-foot tower with three slides. There's also a huge wave pool, a lazy river, a kiddie area for younger swimmers, arcade, and concession stand. Children must be at least 48 inches tall to go on the slides.

General Burnside Island State Park (all ages)

8801 South US 27, Burnside (about 9 miles south of Somerset); (606) 561–4104 or (606) 561–4192. Some activities **free.**

We got a kick out of just driving over to this park since it's on an island. The golf course is a big attraction, but there are also picnic areas and fishing.

Civil War History

Mill Springs Mill is one of the sites relating to the Civil War Battle of Mill Springs. Other sites include Union and Confederate cemeteries and the site of the fighting at Zollicoffer Park near the town of Nancy. (606) 679–1859.

Whitley City/Stearns

Big South Fork Scenic Railway (all ages)

Board at 21 Henderson Street, Stearns; (800) 462–5664 or (606) 376–5330, www.bsf sry.com. Excursions offered Tuesday to Saturday in April; Wednesday to Sunday May through September; Tuesday to Sunday in October; and Thursday to Saturday in early November. Weekday departures are at 11:00 A.M., Saturday departures are at 11:00 A.M. and 2:30 P.M., and Sunday departures are at 2:30 P.M. Also open on Memorial Day and Labor Day. Halloween, Santa, and other special excursions have different departure times; call for info. Ticket office opens ninety minutes before departure. For regular excursions, tickets are on a first-come, first-served basis; reservations taken only for groups of 10 or more. Reservations required for Halloween and other special excursions. Adults $$$, children ages 3–12 $$.

This is really four attractions in one. The ticket price includes admission to the Stearns Museum, with its exhibits about the town and the coal-mining heritage of the area. The train ride itself is a spectacularly scenic (especially in fall) 16-mile, 600-foot descent into the gorge of the Big South Fork National River. The route includes a section that goes through what was once Worley, a large mining community; interpretive panels about the community are viewed from the train. Passengers depart to tour Blue Heron Coal Mining Camp and its "ghost structures." Life-size photos, push-button oral histories, and artifacts tell the story of life in this camp, which operated from 1937 to 1962. You can walk across the river on the tipple bridge. After about forty-five minutes at Blue Heron, you reboard and return to the Stearns station. This is a fun and interesting experience, but keep in mind, particularly with younger children, that total excursion time is two and a half to three hours and that there are no restrooms on the train. (There are facilities, as well as a concession stand, at Blue Heron.) Younger children would especially enjoy the Trick or Treat Train for Tots the last Friday and Saturday nights in October and the Santa Express the first three Saturdays in December. There's a scarier Haunted Hollow Express for older children and adults. Older children (and adult train enthusiasts) may also want to make reservations to ride in the locomotive ($$$$). If you're also a canoe enthusiast, ask about the combination packages with Sheltowee Trace Outfitters.

Amazing
Kentucky Fact

The term *sideburns* came from the hair and beard style of Union Civil War general A. E. Burnside, who had headquarters in this area.

Big **South Fork**

The Barthell and Blue Heron Mining Camps are part of a 125,000-acre national recreational area that stretches into Tennessee, offering abundant hiking, sightseeing, and canoeing/rafting opportunities. The area has beautiful gorges, rock ledges, and waterfalls. The **National Park Service Visitor Center** in Stearns (Highway 92) is a good place to get a map, advice, and answers to any questions (606–376–5073). It's open April through October from 9:30 A.M. to 4:30 P.M. Monday through Saturday and noon to 4:30 P.M. Sunday; hours vary from November through March.

Barthell Mining Camp (all ages)

Off Highway 742, 7 miles west of Stearns; (888) 550–5748. Tuesday to Saturday 9:00 A.M. to 5:00 P.M. Closed January through March. $$

The Koger family spent five years rebuilding this mining camp and now offers guided tours as well as overnight lodging. The tour includes the Old Doctor's Office, a 1920s barber shop, bath house, one-room school, church, and mine openings. The Motor House includes a collection of 1909–1934 cars and trucks as well as mining equipment. The gift shops have some cute and inexpensive souvenirs for children, including handmade wooden train whistles and toys and corn husk flowers. You can get a sandwich or snack at the Coal Miner's Daughter restaurant.

Blue Heron Mining Camp (all ages)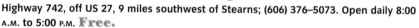

Highway 742, off US 27, 9 miles southwest of Stearns; (606) 376–5073. Open daily 8:00 A.M. to 5:00 P.M. Free.

This is one of the stops on the Big South Fork Scenic Railway, or you can drive to it. A thriving mining camp from the late 1930s through the early 1960s, this camp now lives on as one of Kentucky's most intriguingly designed historic attractions. Unusual open-air "ghost structures" and life-size photographic figures suggest the buildings important in camp life—church, school, store, and homes—and, at the push of a button, you can hear the real voices of people who lived at Blue Heron tell their stories. Children may not have the patience to listen to all the recordings, but they will find the atmosphere interesting and enjoyable. The coal tipple and mine openings are part of the tour. A hiking trail leads to a scenic overlook. In summer months, there's a concession stand.

A Day **Family Adventure**

When we got down to Yahoo Falls, my daughter and I had a good laugh, wondering how many other people get here and say, "That's *it?*" Here's the story: Yahoo Falls is promoted as the state's tallest waterfall (about 130 feet), but it's a very thin stream of water. In summer (the time of our visit), it may even dry up completely. The good thing about Yahoo Falls is that it's very accessible—you can drive to the head of a roughly ½-mile trail, and there are even restrooms in the parking area. (For easier hiking, take the left part of the loop down—there are metal steps—and you'll hike up the easier, more gradual part of the loop.) Even though the falls was less than overwhelming—especially after seeing Cumberland Falls—we enjoyed the rock formations, the forest, and the toads we saw along the way.

McCreary County Museum at Stearns (all ages)
1 Henderson Street, Stearns; (606) 376–5730. Open mid-April through October, Tuesday to Sunday 9:00 A.M. to 5:00 P.M. $; admission included in scenic railway ticket.

Learn about the area's coal-mining and other history in this museum located in the former Stearns Coal and Lumber office building near the train depot.

Where to Eat

Stearns Restaurant, Highway 1651, 14 Henderson Street, Stearns, next to the depot; (606) 376–5354. Good daily specials with vegetables, great cornbread, sandwiches, and homemade pies. Friendly service. Try a Coal Miner's Special (beans and cornbread). $

Where to Stay

Barthell Mining Camp, off Highway 742, 7 miles west of Stearns; (888) 550–5748. Secluded one- and two-bedroom cabins with full baths and kitchens, porch swings; linens supplied. Restaurant at the camp. $$$–$$$$

Holiday Inn Express, 1116 US 27, Whitley City; (606) 376–3780. Outdoor pool, continental breakfast, laundry. $

Licensed to Catch

Remember: Anglers over age sixteen need a state fishing license ($$$), available at most lakes and bait shops. The one exception is the first weekend in June, Free Fishing Days in Kentucky.

Jamestown/Russell Springs

Lake Cumberland State Resort Park (all ages)

5465 State Park Road, off US 27, Jamestown; information: (270) 343–3111, reservations: (800) 325–1709. Open year-round. Many activities **free.** Lodge rooms $$$$.

Both water lovers and landlubbers will find plenty to do at this 3,117-acre park. Rent a fishing boat and go after bass and crappie in one of the state's largest lakes, or rent a pontoon boat and spend the day just tooling around on the water. Ages six and up can take a trail ride from the park's horse stables. And then there's swimming (an outdoor pool open to day visitors as well as an indoor pool for lodge guests), miniature golf, a nine-hole regulation course, tennis, picnicking, and playgrounds. Lure Lodge offers panoramic views of the lake and has a good restaurant and an indoor swimming pool. Lodging is also available in the more secluded ten-room Pumpkin Creek Lodge. The park also has cottages and a campground.

Wolf Creek National Fish Hatchery (all ages)

50 Kendall Road, off US 127, 13 miles south of Wolf Creek Dam, Jamestown; (270) 343–3797. Open daily from 8:00 A.M. to 7:00 P.M. **Free.**

This nursery for rainbow and brown trout definitely has kid appeal. For starters, there are seemingly millions of fish—from tiny, speck-sized ones inside to the growing youngsters getting exercise in the "raceways" outside. For a nickel you can buy fish food (bring a cup since it's more than you can hold in your hand) and feed the outdoor babies. The tanks are low enough that kids can get a good view. There's fishing for all ages in the nearby fishing stream (over sixteen must have a fishing license and trout stamp), and in early June there's a special fishing derby for youngsters with prizes in various age categories and a special kiddie fishing pool for ages one to four.

Lake **Cumberland**

No wonder this is one of Kentucky's most popular fishing and boating spots. This lake is huge—more than 50,000 acres with 1,200 miles of shoreline extending into seven counties. The lake was created by the construction of a dam across the Cumberland River in 1950. Be sure to stop at the Wolf Creek Dam Powerhouse and Overlook off US 127 south.

Home **Afloat**

You can rent just about any kind of boat, from pontoon to a luxurious floating home-away-from-home, on Lake Cumberland. The lake's eleven marinas are the place to rent boats; some also feature restaurants, camping areas, and cabins for rent. Eight of the eleven marinas rent houseboats for floating vacations, including the state dock at Lake Cumberland State Resort Park (888–782–8336). Houseboat rental isn't cheap—you can pay up to $5,200 a week or so for the biggest, fanciest ones (and you still have to bring your own towels). For a "standard luxury" houseboat, expect to pay a couple thousand dollars a week in summer, less in spring and fall. Weekend rentals are also available. Pontoon and fishing boats can be rented by the hour or by the day. For a listing of places that rent houseboats on Lake Cumberland and other Kentucky lakes, visit www.statedock.com.

Where to Eat

Jamestown Cafe, 105 Jefferson Street, Jamestown; (270) 343–5550. Varied menu, music on weekend evenings. $

Little Chop Shop, US 127 and Lakeway Drive, Russell Springs; (270) 866–7711. All kinds of smoked food, pork chops, steaks, hot dogs, and chicken. Homemade fudge. Carryout and picnic tables only. $

The Porch, US 127 south of Highway 80, Russell Springs; (270) 866–8988. Home cooking, fresh salads, homemade pies (even the crust). $

Where to Stay

KOA Campground, 1440 Highway 1383, Russell Springs; (270) 866–5616. Open April through October. Primitive and full hookup sites. Snack bar, restaurant, tennis court, game room, miniature golf, bait store, and grocery. $

Pinehurst Lodge, 1115 West Cumberland Avenue, Jamestown; (877) 855–4143 or (270) 343–4143. Z-shaped pool, family units with multiple beds as well as units with kitchens. Game room, basketball court. May require two-night minimum during summer weekends. $–$$

Amazing
Kentucky Fact

The first oil well in America was located near Burkesville (off Highway 61 on Renox Creek).

Scuba in Kentucky

The 27,700-acre Dale Hollow Lake has a reputation for being one of the clearest in the state. In fact, it's where scuba divers from all over Kentucky go to earn their certification and to dive. The closest dive shop is at Willow Grove Marina across the lake (or about two hours by car) near Allons, Tennessee (931–823–4794; ages ten and up only).

Burkesville

Dale Hollow Lake State Resort Park (all ages)

6371 State Park Road (Highway 1206 off Highway 449 off Highway 90); information: (270) 433–7431, reservations: (800) 325–2282. Open year-round. Many activities **free.**

Another popular spot for fishing (the lake is famous for smallmouth bass), this state park features full-service amenities for day or longer visitors. Along with hiking trails, there are bike and horse trails (but no stables or bike rentals). Boat rentals are available. The lodge is perched high above the lake, and you can eat in the dining room or outside on a patio. The park also has a campground.

Campbellsville

Green River Lake State Park (all ages)

179 Park Office Road, Highway 1061, off Highway 55; (270) 465–8255. Open year-round. Many activities **free.**

A little bit more laid back than Lake Cumberland (but still crowded on a summer weekend), this 8,200-acre lake is a popular day and camping destination. The park includes a sandy beach on the lake, picnic and playground areas, miniature golf, and a year-round campground with marina, laundry, and boat ramp. Trails for horseback riding and biking (no rentals), as well as hiking, are available.

U.S. Army Corps of Engineers Visitor Center/Atkinson-Griffin House Museum (all ages) 🏛 🚻 🥤 🚗

Off Highway 55; (270) 465–4463. **Free.**

This is a good place to stop for information about the lake, as well as trail brochures and a Battle of Tebbs Bend Civil War driving tour. The visitor center also has exhibits, and you can pick up the keys to see the Atkinson-Griffin House Museum a short walk away. This 1840 log cabin served as a hospital and displays Civil War artifacts.

Fancy **Footwork**

If you go to Greensburg (southwest of Campbellsville), try taking the 445-foot bridge that leads from Courthouse Square to surrounding neighborhoods. Pop into the courthouse too—it's the oldest west of the Alleghenies.

Where to Stay

Best Western Campbellsville Lodge, 1400 East Broadway; (270) 465–7001 or (800) 770–0430. Outdoor pool. $$

Emerald Isle Marina and Resort, Highway 372; (888) 815–2000 or (270) 465–3412. Three-bedroom condominiums, restaurant, boat rentals. $$$$

For More Information

Taylor County Tourist Commission, 107 West Broadway; (270) 465–3786 or (800) 738–4719.

Glasgow Area

Barren River State Resort Park (all ages)

1149 State Park Road, Lucas (off US Highway 31E, 12 miles southwest of Glasgow); information: (270) 646–2151, reservations: (800) 325–0057. Open year-round. Many activities free.

Another popular lake with Kentucky anglers, Barren River is known for its bass, bluegill, channel cats, and crappie. You can rent fishing boats, pontoon sightseeing boats, and houseboats for use on the 10,000 acres of water. On-land activities include trail rides (ages six and up), a beach for swimming (the pool is for lodge and cottage guests only), basketball and tennis courts, an eighteen-hole golf course, picnic areas, and playgrounds. There also are 4 miles of nature trails. The lodge and dining room overlook the lake. Two-bedroom cottages, both lakeside and tucked away in the woods, are available, along with a seasonal campground.

Scotland in Kentucky

Glasgow, Kentucky, was named after the city in Scotland, and every year it celebrates Scottish heritage with a huge gathering of clans. The **Glasgow Highland Games,** held the weekend after Memorial Day, features bagpipe and harp competitions, concerts, and highland dancing, plus all kinds of athletic competitions (caber throwing, anyone?). The numerous activities for children include athletic competitions scaled to ages four to sixteen. Many events take place in Barren River State Resort Park; call (270) 651–3141, or visit www.glasgowhighlandgames.com for more information.

Mammoth Cave Area (Cave City/ Horse Cave/Brownsville)

Mammoth Cave National Park (all ages)

Highway 70 from I–65, exit 48, or South Entrance Road from I–65, exit 53; follow signs. P.O. Box 7, Mammoth Cave 42250; information: (270) 758–2180, tour reservations (recommended): (877) 444–6777, www.recreation.gov. Open daily except Christmas. Many activities free; cave tour admission varies $–$$$.

Mammoth Cave is the kind of place you're likely to visit time and again, yet do something new and different each time. The cave—the longest known system in the world, with 350 miles of charted tunnels—is the star attraction, but don't forget the aboveground area, too—some 52,830 acres. On some visits, we've enjoyed the hiking and the boat ride as much as the underground tours.

Cave Tours. Tours ranging from seventy-five minutes to six-and-a-half hours are offered, with up to forty cave tours per day in the busiest summer months. The Travertine is recommended for preschoolers (also a good option if the family group includes older folks who can't walk long distances). Part of the time is spent on a bus going over to the entrance. This tour has the fewest steps of any of the tours, but you can still see some interesting cave features. With older children who aren't afraid of heights (and can walk for two hours), you can take the Historic Tour, which includes areas used by Native Americans thousands of years ago, as well as saltpeter-mining areas; and the Frozen Niagara, an expanded Travertine Tour route, on which you see huge domes and many formations. The Trog Tour is a special tour for children eight to twelve (proof of age required) in which youngsters get to don helmets and lights and do some crawling as well as walking (parents go along for the first fifteen minutes of the two-and-a-half-hour adventure). Families with children ten to fifteen might

A Day **Family Adventure**

Being the kind of traveler who likes to jump in the car on the spur of the moment and decide routes and lodging along the way, I've had to make some adjustments as a traveling parent. (It's no fun trying to find a hotel room with a screaming toddler—or cranky older child—in the car.) But old habits are hard to break. Pooh-poohing all the advice about advance reservations for Mammoth Cave tours in busy summer months, we headed out and arrived at the park mid-morning. I began to sweat as I saw all the SOLD OUT signs. I think we got the last four tickets for the last tour of the day. Next time I'll make reservations and avoid "Mammoth" anxiety!

also enjoy the Introduction to Caving, a more adventurous three-and-a-half-hour excursion that includes crawling, climbing, and visits to passages not on the regular tour routes. Whatever tour you take, be sure children (and you) are wearing sturdy shoes, and take sweaters or jackets along; the temperature is in the 50s and 60s. Strollers are not allowed, and you're urged to use caution if you carry your child, since some ceiling areas of the cave are very low. In the summer season, tours sell out, so get advance tickets to be sure of getting the tour of your choice.

Trails. There are numerous hiking trails, including short and easy woodland trails that families can walk at a leisurely pace. The Heritage Trail is the easiest; it's paved, and you can take a stroller. More challenging trails are available for older hikers.

Miss Green River II. We like to end the day with this leisurely and scenic boat ride; various departures daily April through October (adults $$, children $). You'll see deer and other animals and hear enjoyable stories about the area. This mellows everyone out for the long drive home. (270) 758–2243.

Kentucky Down Under (all ages)

At I–65, exit 58, Horse Cave; (800) 762–2869, www.kdu.com. Open daily April through October from 8:00 A.M. to 8:00 P.M., November through March from 9:00 A.M. to 4:00 P.M. Closed Thanksgiving Day, Christmas Day, and New Year's Day. Adults and children 5–14 $$$, children under 5 **free.**

If you have time to visit only a few places in south-central Kentucky, make this Australian-themed animal attraction a priority. It's very well done and mixes education with fun. The park encompasses a variety of areas that you can visit at your own pace, in the order you prefer, along with a forty-five-minute guided cave tour. There are plenty of hands-on encounters and memorable photo opportunities, from the kangaroo "walkabout" to the walk-in bird cage where colorful lorikeets perch on your head and shoulders, looking for a treat. At the sheep station, children get to catch and bottle-feed lambs, and the whole family can take a crack at milking a cow. Scheduled activities focus on Australian culture, and the park personnel not only are knowledgeable but also seem genuinely enthusiastic about what they do. There's also an Outback Cafe, open in summer, and a gift shop with a good selection of books for children about caving, Australia, and animals.

American Cave Museum/Hidden River Cave (ages 4 and up)
119 East Main Street, Horse Cave; (270) 786–1466, www.cavern.org. Open daily year-round from 9:00 A.M. to 5:00 P.M. Monday through Friday; may stay open until 7:00 P.M. in summer and on weekends. $$

Another attraction that effectively mixes education and fun, the museum combines exhibits about caves, karst, and groundwater with tours of Hidden River Cave. The tours emphasize the cave's remarkable story: Not too long ago, Hidden Cave was anything but hidden. All you had to do was follow your nose! Pollution made the cave smell so bad that it affected the entire downtown area. A dedicated group of citizens worked to reclaim the cave, and now it's a model of cave recovery and management.

Caves and **More Caves**

Mammoth and Lost River aren't the only caves in the area. Here are some others open for touring:

- **Crystal Onyx Cave,** I–65, exit 53, at Cave City; (270) 773–2359. One-hour tours year-round. Includes many crystalline draperies and formations and working archaeological site. $$

- **Onyx Cave,** I–65, exit 53, at Cave City; (270) 773–3530. Onyx waterfall and other formations. $$

- **Diamond Caverns,** Mammoth Cave Parkway, I–65, exit 48; (270) 749–2233 or www.diamondcaverns.com. Numerous formations and drapery deposits. $$

Dinosaur World (all ages)

711 Mammoth Cave Road, Cave City (exit 53 from I–65); (270) 773–4345, www.dino world.net. Open daily except Christmas Day, 8:30 A.M. to sunset. $$

You can't miss the giant dinosaur that stands by the side of I–65, just a sample of what you'll see when you visit. Over one hundred immense and brightly painted Plexiglas dinos—your children will probably know their names even if you don't—are displayed in family and herd groupings along a shaded walkway. An indoor museum with fossils and other informative displays opened in 2004. A favorite part of a visit is the Fossil Dig. Each child gets to take home three finds, which include shark's teeth, sponges and shells, and bits of amber. One of my son's favorite souvenirs—a wonderful example of a plastic inflatasaurus—came from the extensive gift store here.

Mammoth **Amusements**

Driving to Mammoth Cave from the interstates is a little like running a gauntlet: If you stopped at every place that tempted your children, you'd never get there. Suffice to say that before or after your cave tour you'll find something to amuse the whole family. Some of the options:

- **Guntown Mountain,** Highway 70 at I–65, Cave City; (270) 773–3530, GuntownMountain.com. Take the skylift or shuttle bus up to Wild West town with rides, games, shows, haunted house, and petting zoo. All-day pass available.

- **Kentucky Action Park/Jesse James Riding Stables,** 3057 Mammoth Cave Road, Cave City; (800) 798–0560 or (270) 773–2560, www .kentuckyactionpark.com. The action here includes alpine slide, go-karts, bumper cars, minigolf, old-time photos, and trail rides.

- **Hillbilly Hound Fun Park,** I–65, exit 53, Cave City; (270) 773–4644. Go-karts, minigolf, game room, with a cartoon theme.

- **Mammoth Cave Wax Museum,** I–65, exit 53, Cave City; (270) 773–3010. From Abe Lincoln to Marilyn Monroe, wax figures.

- **Mammoth Cave Wildlife Museum,** I–65, exit 53, Cave City; (270) 773–2255. Preserved animals from around the world.

- **Big Mike's Mystery House,** 566 Old Mammoth Cave Road, Cave City; (270) 773–5144. Mirror and gravity illusions; gift shop includes many rocks and minerals.

Wigwam Village 2 (all ages)

601 North Dixie Highway (US 31W), Cave City; (270) 773–3381. Open daily March through November. $–$$

Here you can "sleep in a wigwam," but even if you don't plan to stay here, drive by to see this wonderful world-famous motel. This complex of concrete tepees was built in the 1930s, before interstates with chain lodgings and restaurants homogenized American travel. At one time there were seven Wigwam Villages in the South and West; this is one of only two remaining. It's listed on the National Register of Historic Places. There's a huge gift shop.

Where to Eat

Mammoth Cave Hotel, located in the national park; (270) 758–2225. Restaurant and coffee shop serving breakfast, lunch, and dinner. Varied menu. $

Mammoth Cave National Park Campground, four locations in park; make reservations through www.recreation.gov or call (800) 365–CAMP. No hookups. $

Where to Stay

Mammoth Cave Hotel, located in the national park; (270) 758–2225. Motel rooms and cottages, tennis courts, laundry. $$–$$$

For More Information

Edmonson County Tourism Commission, P.O. Box 628, Brownsville 42210; (800) 624–8687, www.cavesandlakes.com.

National Park Service, www.nps.gov.

Bowling Green

The National Corvette Museum (all ages)

350 Corvette Drive (at I-65, exit 28); (270) 781–7973 or (800) 53–VETTE, www.corvette museum.com. Open daily from 8:00 A.M. to 5:00 P.M. except Thanksgiving Day, December 24, and December 25. Adults $$, children 6–16 $, children 5 and under free. Family rate available.

If you're driving on I-65, somebody in the car is likely to spot this museum and ask "What's that?" The building design is really unusual—a bright yellow cone-shaped structure with a red spire. Inside you'll find classic Corvettes going back to '53—the first year they were made—plus exhibits about how they're designed and experimental models—68,000 square feet in all. Keep in mind that there are no interactive exhibits (and this is definitely NOT a "hands-on" kind of museum). Serious Corvette enthusiasts or not, most kids will enjoy the animal-cracker-style boxes of Corvette-shaped cookies sold in the gift shop.

Amazing Kentucky Fact

South-central Kentucky gave America cake and coffee: Duncan Hines was from Bowling Green (in June, at the Duncan Hines Festival, the town bakes a 950-pound brownie in his honor), and Joel Owsley Creek of Burkesville developed Maxwell House coffee.

Corvette Assembly Plant Tour (ages 7 and up)

I–65, exit 28, adjacent to The National Corvette Museum; (270) 745–8419, www.bowling greenassemblyplant.com. Tours twice daily Monday to Friday except during plant shutdown periods. Reservations required. $

Corvettes have been assembled in Bowling Green since 1981, and every Corvette made comes from this modern plant. The one-mile walking tour lasts about an hour and includes body weld and assembly areas as well as the "First Start" and line drive-off. If you've never been inside a modern automaking plant, it's quite an experience, from the robotic welders to the speed and efficiency with which vehicles come together. Children must be at least seven to take the tour. You must wear closed-toe shoes, and no cameras, purses, or backpacks are allowed. Plant shutdown times (no tours) vary but usually include the last week in December, the Friday and Monday of Labor Day weekend, and other holidays. Check the phone number for tour status, since business factors can also affect tours.

Barren River Imaginative Museum of Science (all ages)

1229 Center Street; (270) 843–9779. Open Thursday to Saturday from 10:00 A.M. to 3:00 P.M., Sunday from 1:00 to 4:00 P.M. $

Participation is the rule, not the exception, at this museum, where children can try all kinds of activities that illustrate principles of science—from mirror fun to generating electricity by pedaling a bicycle. The information arranged into What to Do and What's Going On makes getting the point easy.

Kentucky Museum (ages 5 and up)

Kentucky Building, Western Kentucky University; (270) 745–2592. Open Monday to Saturday from 9:00 A.M. to 4:00 P.M., Sunday from 1:00 to 4:00 P.M. $

What was it like to be a child in the mid-1800s? What toys would you have played with? What kinds of clothes would you have worn? What would have been expected of you? Your children can learn the answers at this museum's Growing Up Victorian display, just one of the fascinating exhibits at this gem of a museum tucked away on the Western Kentucky University campus. Budding archaeologists can see arrowheads and other early artifacts at Taking the Mystery Out of Prehistory. Other exhibits relate to early downtown Bowling Green (fun to compare with a modern-day walk), Kentucky guitar maker Hascal Haile, and Bowling Green native Duncan Hines. Next to the main museum building is the Felts House, an authentic 1815 cabin that was moved to the campus and contains reproduction early-nineteenth-century tools and household items. Ask about the family activities guide for the Victorian exhibit, and check out the teachers' guides and other books in the gift store.

Lost River Cave and Valley (all ages)

2818 Nashville Road; (866) 274–CAVE or (270) 393–0077, www.lostrivercave.com. Tour offered daily year-round; schedule varies, so call for times. Adults $$, children $.

Now, here's something different and fun: a boat cave tour. Some time ago, Mammoth Cave offered them, but it hasn't for years (in fact, the boats used at Mammoth are now here at Lost River). A forty-five-minute tour begins with a twenty-minute guided walk along the river and the twenty-five-minute boat tour inside this cave. The cave has a huge opening and short but deep river. It was used by Native Americans 11,000 years ago and may have been a hiding place for the Jesse James gang; it even has a night-club that was popular from the 1930s through the 1960s (it's been renovated). You're also welcome to walk the easy trails near the cave opening, which includes "Blue Holes," where the river rises to the surface before becoming "lost" again under the city of Bowling Green.

More **Unusual Buildings**

The National Corvette Museum isn't the only unusual-looking building in south-central Kentucky. Check out the following:

- **John B. Begley Chapel,** on the Lindsey Wilson College campus in Columbia. (270) 384–8400. This interesting double-domed chapel was designed by one of the world's foremost chapel architects, E. Fay Jones. Other attractions in Columbia include the restored log home of Kentucky author Janice Holt Giles and a local historical museum in the 1820s Trabue-Russell House. Columbia is between Lake Cumberland and Green River Lake via the Louie B. Nunn Parkway or Highway 55. (270) 384–6020.

- **Octagonal Hall,** 6040 Bowling Green Road, Franklin. This is an eight-sided brick building. While in Franklin, also learn about local African-American history at the African-American Heritage Center, 501 Jefferson Street, and see life-size drawings made on the walls of the Old Jail by Civil War soldiers. (270) 586–3040.

Beech Bend Raceway Park (all ages)

798 Beech Bend Road; (270) 781–7634, www.beechbend.com. Drag races March through October, Tuesday and Saturday nights. Adults $$, children under 12 free with adult. Amusement park and water park open weekends May and September, daily Memorial Day through Labor Day, from 10:00 A.M. to 6:00 P.M. Admission ($) includes water park; all-day unlimited rides $$$$.

Older children may enjoy the drag races, but the main attraction for families here is the amusement park. Its big new attraction is the Kentucky Rumbler, a very twisted wooden coaster with thirty crossovers. It joins the Wild Mouse Spinning Coaster, the Looping Star, and Dragon Coaster for four coasters in all. There's a wide variety of other thrill rides for all ages (some rides require minimum height of 54 inches), and the park's Splash Lagoon has large tube slides, a four-level interactive splash/play area, and a large swimming pool.

Race World (ages 6 and up)

255 Cumberland Trace (I–65, exit 22); (270) 781–RACE. Open March through October, Tuesday to Thursday from 5:00 to 10:00 P.M. Closed when it rains. Pay by attraction.

Older children and adults can get into racing action themselves at this park, which has two tracks, racing displays, and an arcade. One track is for ages sixteen and over only. A smaller "Naskart" track is for younger children; they must be 53 inches tall to compete in the nightly races. Displays include a car that belonged to NASCAR great Dale Earnhardt. There's food on-site and a seasonal Halloween House geared toward older children, teens, and adults.

Riverview at Hobson's Bend (ages 6 and up)

End of Main Street at Hobson Grove Park; (270) 843–5565. Open Tuesday to Saturday from 10:00 A.M. to 4:00 P.M., Sunday from 1:00 to 4:00 P.M. $, children under 6 free.

Historic house fans will enjoy seeing this elegant Italianate building and learning about the Hobson family, who owned it from 1857 to 1952. Particularly interesting are the interpretive tours given the third Saturday of each month at 10:00 A.M. on various topics ranging from holiday celebrations to servant life. The house is located in a park, so if everybody isn't into old houses, one parent can entertain kids outside while the other parent tours.

Race Days

Bowling Green is race car crazy year-round but especially so in April, when the **Junior Achievement Mini Corvette Challenge** is held. Mini-Corvettes race Grand Prix–style on the streets of downtown. (270) 782–0280.

Bookworms Take Note!

At the annual **Southern Kentucky Festival of Books** in Bowling Green, children (and adults) can meet authors and celebrate the fun of reading. Children's authors who have attended in the past include R. L. Stine, who writes the popular *Goosebumps* horror series. Many children's activities take place during the two-day event, including music, drama, and hands-on creative fun, along with author signings. It's held in mid-April at the Sloan Convention Center, and admission is free. Call (270) 745–5016, or visit www.sokybookfest.com for the latest news about which authors are coming.

Other Things to See and Do

Capitol Arts Center, (877) 694–ARTS.

Civil War Driving Tour, (800) 326–7465.

Flea Land of Bowling Green, weekends indoor/outdoor; (270) 843–1978.

Fountain Square Park, downtown; (800) 326–7465.

Hardin Planetarium, Western Kentucky University; (270) 745–4044.

Phoenix Theatre, (270) 781–6233.

Russell Sims Aquatic Center, pool, slides and play areas; (270) 393–3271.

Where to Eat

Brickyard Cafe, 1026 Chestnut Street; (270) 843–6431. Brick-oven pizza and pastas, homemade breads, and desserts. Located in historic house, but casual. Kids will love the Bambino Pizza for lunch. Lunch and dinner. $

Chaney's Dairy Barn, 9191 Nashville Road; (270) 843–5567. Sandwiches and homemade soups, ice cream, cakes, and pie. $

Mariah's, 801 State Street; (270) 842–6878. Casual atmosphere in a restored historic house. Steaks, sandwiches, seafood. $$

Teresa's Restaurant, 509 Gordon Avenue; (270) 782–6540. Home cooking in a friendly atmosphere. Breakfast and lunch only. $

Where to Stay

Beech Bend Campground, 798 Beech Bend Road; (270) 781–7634. Open year-round. Full hookups (including some sites with modem hookups), bathhouses. $

Bowling Green KOA, 1960 Three Springs Road; (270) 843–1919. Pool, game room, playground. $

Courtyard by Marriott, 1010 Wilkinson Trace; (270) 783–8569. Indoor pool. $$$

Hampton Inn, 233 Three Springs Road; (800) HAMPTON. Outdoor pool, continental breakfast. $$$

University Plaza Hotel, 1021 Wilkinson Trace; (800) 801–1777. High-rise hotel, indoor pool, restaurant. $$$–$$$$

AnnualEvents in South-Central Kentucky

- **Eagle Watch,** late January, Dale Hollow State Resort Park; (800) 255–PARK

- **Family Fishing Fun Weekend,** late March, Dale Hollow State Resort Park; (800) 255–PARK

- **Southern Kentucky Festival of Books,** mid-April (during National Library Week), Bowling Green; (270) 745–5016 or www.sokybook fest.org

- **Junior Achievement Mini Corvette Challenge,** late April, Bowling Green; (270) 782–0280

- **Mountain Laurel Festival,** late May, Pine Mountain State Resort Park; (606) 337–3066

- **Glasgow Highland Games,** late May to early June, Glasgow; (270) 651–3141

- **Catch a Rainbow Kids Fishing Derby,** early June, Wolf Creek National Fish Hatchery, Jamestown; (270) 866–4333

- **Wayne County Fair,** early July, Monticello; (606) 348–3064

- **Laurel County Fair,** mid-July, London; (800) 348–0095

- **Master Musicians Festival,** mid-July, Somerset; (888) FUN–JULY

- **Russell County Fair,** late July, Russell Springs (near Jamestown); (270) 343–3191

- **NIBROC Festival,** mid-August, Corbin; (606) 528–2163

- **Monroe County Watermelon Festival,** early September, Tompkinsville; (270) 487–5504

- **Cow Days,** late September, Greensburg; (270) 932–4298

- **Casey County Apple Festival,** late September, Liberty; (606) 787–6747

- **World Chicken Festival,** late September, London; (606) 878–6900

- **Colonial Trade Fair,** early October, Cumberland Gap National Historic Park; (606) 248–2817

- **Aussie Fest,** early October, Kentucky Down Under; (800) 762–2869

- **Cumberland Mountain Fall Festival,** early October, Middlesboro; (800) 988–1075

- **Winter Lights,** late November through December, Bowling Green; (270) 782–3660

For More Information

Bowling Green Area Convention and Visitors Bureau, 352 Three Springs Road; (800) 326–7465 or (270) 782–0800.

Western Kentucky

Most people think of water when they think of western Kentucky. The state's largest lakes, Lake Barkley and Kentucky Lake, and the wild area they border, known as the "Land Between the Lakes," are great places to enjoy the great outdoors, from fishing to seeing elk and American bald eagles. There are four state resort parks in the region, three of them along the lakes, as well as dozens of privately operated marinas and resorts. But as vast as the lake region is, it's just the beginning. At area museums, attractions, and events, tap your foot to the sound of bluegrass and blues, learn about Native American heritage, view fine art, and discover the unexpected. This region gets my vote for the most unusual attractions—and in Kentucky, that's an accomplishment! Paintings by a World War II prisoner of

Teresa's
TopPicks for Western Kentucky

1. Land Between the Lakes National Recreation Area, (800) LBL–7077

2. John James Audubon State Park, (270) 826–2247

3. Owensboro Museum of Science and History, (270) 687–2732

4. Wickliffe Mounds, (270) 335–3681

5. Ben E. Clement Mineral Museum, (270) 965–4263

6. Columbus Belmont State Park, (270) 677–2327

7. Trail of Tears Commemorative Park, (270) 886–8033

8. Adsmore, (270) 365–3114

9. International Bluegrass Music Museum, (270) 926–7891

10. River Heritage Museum, (270) 442–8856

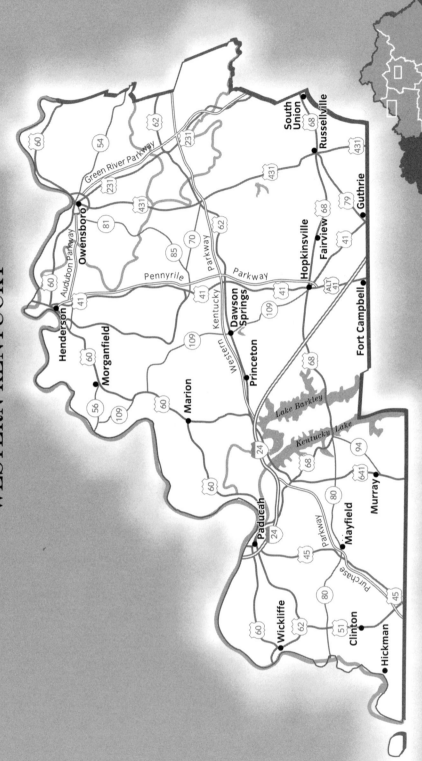

WESTERN KENTUCKY

Area Code Alert!

Most cities listed in this section will get a new area code—364—in mid-2008. Owensboro, South Union and Russellville are among cities keeping the 270 area code. Henderson, Hopkinsville, Princeton, Marion, Murray, Mayfield, and Paducah (and all areas in the westernmost part of the state) will use the new area code. For a short time after the change, the 270 area code will continue to work in areas changing to 364.

war, a giant chain and anchor once stretched across the Mississippi River, an eighteen-statue memorial, a replica of King Arthur's Round Table—you'll find all this and more in western Kentucky. And don't forget to try the region's food specialty: barbecue. One thing is certain: Once you experience western Kentucky, you'll want to come back for more.

Attractions are listed beginning with the southern part of the region, moving west from Bowling Green, then circling northeast to end in Kentucky's third largest city, Owensboro. Travel is a combination of interstates, limited-access parkways, and generally good two- to four-lane U.S. highways. *FYI:* This part of the state is in the central time zone. Times listed are local times.

South Union

South Union Shaker Village (ages 6 and up)

Off US Highway 68, 10 miles west of Bowling Green; (800) 811-8379. Open March through November, Monday to Saturday from 9:00 A.M. to 4:00 P.M.; open until 5:00 P.M. May through October. Open Sunday from 1:00 to 5:00 P.M. $$, ages 6–12 $, children under 6 free.

The Shakers, a religious community, lived here from 1807 to 1922. As you tour the forty-four-room main building and outbuildings, including the smokehouse and milk house, you'll learn about the community's many industries—it sold products ranging from seeds to silk handkerchiefs—as well as Shaker religious beliefs. The numerous artifacts and large collection of furniture are all authentic. An especially enjoyable time for families to visit is during special events such as the Shaker Summer Nights music entertainment in mid-July, the Civil War encampment in August, Shaker Farm Day in early October, and Christmas at Shakertown, late November through December.

Outlaws

While in Russellville, drive by the old Southern Deposit Bank building at the corner of Main and Sixth. This was the scene of the city's most famous crime: On May 20, 1868, Jesse James and his gang dropped by and made an unauthorized withdrawal, getting away with $9,000.

Russellville Area

Lake Malone State Park (all ages)

Highway 973 off US Highway 431, Dunsmore; (270) 657–2111. Free.

Centered around a 788-acre lake whose shorelines range from sandy beach to 200-foot rock cliffs, Lake Malone State Park is a lovely spot for a day of picnicking and fishing. Boats are available in summer, and you can swim at the beach. Hike along 1½-mile Laurel Trail.

Dogwood Lake Fun Park (all ages)

7777 Highway 973, Russellville; (270) 657–8380. Open Memorial Day through Labor Day, Monday to Friday from 10:00 A.M. to 5:00 P.M., Saturday and Sunday from 9:00 A.M. to 6:00 P.M. $

The swimming pool at this family amusement center near Lake Malone State Park is a sandy-bottom lake (chlorine-treated) with water slides and paddleboats. Go-karts and arcade games also are available.

Guthrie

Guthrie Railroad Museum (all ages)

Third and Kendall Streets (across from courthouse); (270) 483–2683. Open by appointment only. Free.

This red caboose is filled with items of interest to train buffs, from photos and lanterns to model trains (not running) relating to the L&N railroad.

Robert Penn Warren Birthplace (ages 8 and up)

Third and Cherry Streets; (270) 483–2683. Open Tuesday to Saturday from 11:30 A.M. to 3:30 P.M. Free; donations accepted.

You can introduce older children to the works of one of America's greatest literary figures at this modest cottage. Robert Penn Warren was born here in 1905 and went on to become one of America's most distinguished writers and the nation's first poet laureate. His most famous work is probably *All the King's Men,* but he wrote many volumes of beautiful poems, as well as a couple of children's books, *Remember the Alamo* and *Gods of Mount Olympus* (you may be able to find them at your local library). Children will enjoy seeing the childhood pictures and other mementos, and if your child likes to read or listen to you read poetry, pick up a volume at the house's gift shop.

Where to Eat

American Cafe, 306 North Ewing Street; (270) 483–2288. Popular local spot for plate lunches and burgers seven days a week. $

Hopkinsville

Pennyroyal Area Museum (ages 4 and up)
217 East Ninth Street; (270) 887–4270. Open Monday to Friday from 8:30 A.M. to 4:30 P.M. $

All kinds of interesting things relating to local history are on display in this former post office building. Adults will enjoy the exhibits about the "Tobacco Wars" of 1914 and clairvoyant Edgar Cayce (who lived in Hopkinsville), while youngsters will be drawn to the antique toys, carriage, and 1924 Ford "Skeeter" automobile that was made in Owensboro.

Trail of Tears Commemorative Park (all ages)
Pembroke Road (US Highway 41); (270) 886–8033, www.trailoftears.org. Park open daily year-round. Free. Museum open Thursday to Saturday from 10:00 A.M. to 4:00 P.M.; closes at 2:00 P.M. and on Monday November through March. Free; donations accepted.

Kentucky has many sites and activities that celebrate pioneer bravery and the settlement of America, but everyone should also learn the rest of the story. This park commemorating the Trail of Tears, the forced removal of the Cherokee people from North Carolina to western reservations, is an informative and moving experience. The site is documented as a real encampment spot along the trail as it passed through Kentucky, and two chiefs, Fly Smith and White Path, are buried here. Large statues commemorate the chiefs, and a log cabin Heritage Center contains exhibits from seven Cherokee clans. Ask at the center about the historic driving tour; this is a national route with many stops in western Kentucky.

Tribal Gathering

In September, Native American clans gather in Hopkinsville for an **Intertribal PowWow.** Some 16,000 people come each year to participate in and watch drum contests, dances, storytelling, crafts, and other activities celebrating Native American heritage. There are many special activities for children. (270) 886–8033.

Round Table Literary Park (all ages)
720 North Drive, Hopkinsville Community College campus; (270) 886–3921. Open daily. Free.

Read the King Arthur legend or watch *The Sword in the Stone,* then bring a picnic and come see a 22,000-pound replica of King Arthur's Round Table. There are a host of other literary-inspired structures in this campus park, including a Greco-Roman-style amphitheater and a statue of the Muse of Tragedy—it's all the legacy of HCC literature professor Frances Thomas and her students.

Ferrell's Snappy Service (all ages)
1001 South Main Street; (270) 886–1445. Open Monday to Saturday, twenty-four hours.

It isn't a visit to Hopkinsville without a stop (or at least driving by to see) this tiny eight-stool diner. Ferrell's has been dishing out burgers and chili since 1936 and is now a Kentucky landmark.

Copper Canyon Ranch (all ages)
14750 Ovil Road (north of Hopkinsville, off Highway 189); (270) 269–2416. Open by appointment. $$, children under 5 free.

Tim Emery loved westerns when he was a kid, and as an adult he has spent nearly two decades building his own Old West town—complete with livery stable, general store, saloon, a Punch-and-Judy puppet show, and something the Old West didn't have, Hillbilly Putt-Putt. The Emerys stage reenactments of gunslinger and action events such as a bank robbery and shootouts for youth groups, but they are also interested in entertaining families and smaller groups. So if your posse is searchin' for Wild West fun, give Tim a call.

Where to Eat

Hickory Smokehouse, 5415 Madisonville Road; (270) 886–0688. Barbecue and fixins'. $

Homestead Restaurant, 627 North Drive; (270) 538–8850. Fried chicken and burgers. $

Horseshoe Steak House, 2112 Fort Campbell Road; (270) 886–7734. Good burgers and steaks. $

Where to Stay

Best Western, 4101 Fort Campbell Boulevard; (270) 886–9000. $$

Fairfield Inn and Suites, 345 Griffin Bell Drive; (270) 886–5151. $$

For More Information

Hopkinsville/Christian County Convention and Visitors Bureau, 2800 Fort Campbell Road; (800) 842–9959, www.visit hopkinsville.com.

Fort Campbell

Don F. Pratt Memorial Museum (ages 4 and up)
Building 5702, Tennessee Avenue, 18 miles southwest of Hopkinsville via US 41; (270) 798–4986. Open Monday to Saturday from 9:30 A.M. to 4:30 P.M. Free.

Fort Campbell Military Reservation, which straddles the Kentucky–Tennessee border south of Hopkinsville, has been home to the "Screaming Eagles" 101st Airborne Division since the base was founded in World War II. The Division was at D-Day and participated in Desert Storm, as well as recent military actions in Afghanistan. Uniforms, World War II memorabilia, photos, and a restored World War II glider plane are among the indoor-outdoor exhibits. Enter the base through Gate 4 off US 41A, where you'll be issued a visitor pass.

Fairview

Jefferson Davis Monument State Historic Site (all ages)
US 68 (10 miles east of Hopkinsville); (270) 889–6100. Open daily from 9:30 A.M. to 4:30 P.M. $

The presidents of both the Union and the Confederacy during the Civil War were born in Kentucky. Jefferson Davis, president of the Confederacy, was born near Fairview in 1808. The monument is a 351-foot-tall obelisk that offers a panoramic view of the surrounding countryside. The visitor center features exhibits about Davis and Kentucky during the Civil War.

A Day **Family Adventure**

While you're traveling in Kentucky, just reading the map can be entertaining—there are so many unusual and funny place names. You may even find a town with your family name. My daughter and I happened upon Daysville during a trip to western Kentucky (on US 68 not far from Elkton). To be honest, there wasn't much to it, but I did enjoy snapping a picture of her in front of the sign to commemorate our day in Daysville. Interesting town names to look for on your map in western Kentucky: Hardmoney, Neosheo, and one of our favorites, Monkey's Eyebrow.

Dawson Springs

Pennyrile Forest State Resort Park (all ages)

20781 Pennyrile Lodge Road; information: (270) 797–3421, reservations: (800) 325–1711. Open year-round. Many activities **free.** Lodge rooms $$–$$$, cottages $$–$$$$, camping $. Dining $.

Surrounded by 15,000 acres of forest, this park offers a lovely setting for a day of picnicking or hiking or a longer stay. Play tennis or miniature golf, rent a pedal boat or rowboat, play regular golf on the nine-hole course, or explore the 5 miles of hiking trails. There are also mountain bike trails outside the park area. The park has a small but lovely wood and stone lodge with a restaurant overlooking the lake. Cottages and a seasonal campground also are available.

Princeton

Adsmore (ages 6 and up)

304 North Jefferson Street; (270) 365–3114. Open Tuesday to Saturday from 11:00 A.M. to 4:00 P.M., Sunday from 1:30 to 4:00 P.M. Adults $$, children $.

Come "meet" a family from the early 1900s and learn about their daily life at this house museum. Engaging tours change eight times a year and relate to real events in the lives of Garrett family members. Katharine Garrett lived here all her life, and before she died in the 1980s, she set up a foundation so the house could be preserved and operated as a museum. Because there are so many well-preserved items—from furniture to clothing to photographs and letters—tours are set up to offer an in-depth, detailed, and changing look at life in the household. Each tour is set up around a different event—a wedding, a wake, holidays, Katharine's birthday in the spring, and so on—with appropriate items displayed. Children will especially enjoy

Katharine's childhood room, with toys and child's clothing and pictures of her dog, Trouble. The Ratliff 1840s Gunshop, housed in a cabin near the mansion, is a tour option that some children will enjoy.

Caldwell County Historical Railroad Museum (all ages)

116 Edwards Street, across from Big Springs Park, downtown; (270) 365–0582. Open May through December, Wednesday to Sunday from 1:00 to 4:00 P.M. Free; donations accepted.

Train enthusiasts will want to stop by to see the model trains, railroad nails, photos, signals, and renovated caboose.

Where to Eat

Jewell's Open Pit Bar-B-Q, 730 US 62E; (270) 365–5415. Pork plates and delicious cornbread. $

Majestic House, 208 U.S. Highway 62; (270) 365–3009. Daily specials, varied menu. $

Where to Stay

Stratton Inn, 534 Marion Road (Western Kentucky Parkway at Highway 91 north); (270) 365–2828. Rooms with refrigerators and microwaves available. $

For More Information

Princeton/Caldwell County Chamber of Commerce, 110 West Washington Street; (270) 365–5393.

Princeton **Picnic**

Pick up a delicious barbecued ham sandwich at **Newsome's Old Mill Store,** 208 East Main Street, Princeton (open Monday to Saturday; 270–365–2482), and head a block over to **Big Springs Park** for an enjoyable lunch. Although the store is famous for its country ham, children will like the barbecued ham better because it's tender and sweet. They'll also like the genuine country store atmosphere, with produce on the sidewalk and baskets of goods sitting and hanging inside. The park was a stopping point on the Trail of Tears march.

Lake Barkley/ Kentucky Lake Area

There are all kinds of marinas, recreation centers, restaurants, campgrounds, and lodging in the area right around Kentucky's two biggest lakes, Lake Barkley and Kentucky Lake. At the center of the lakes is the Land Between the Lakes National Recreation Area. We've combined attractions in Grand Rivers, Cadiz, Benton, Eddyville, and other towns close to the lakes, since any would be within easy access if you're in the area.

Land Between the Lakes National Recreation Area (all ages)

US 68/Highway 80 between Kentucky Lake and Lake Barkley (access off Interstate 24 through Grand Rivers); (800) LBL–7077, www.lbl.org. Open year-round; some attractions seasonal.

Nature activities, an 1850s homestead, and the sheer wilderness feel of it all will make you want to return again and again to this 140,000-acre outdoor playground flanked by Lake Barkley on the east and Kentucky Lake on the west. LBL extends into Tennessee, and it's about 40 miles from one end to the other.

There are over 200 miles of trails for hiking and biking (bike rentals available in summer), as well as sixteen lake access areas along the 300 miles of shoreline. Whether you come for a day or a week, you'll find something interesting to do. If entering from Highway 453, stop at the North Welcome Station (open March through November from 9:00 A.M. to 5:00 P.M. daily); if entering from US 68, stop at the Golden Pond visitor center (open year-round from 9:00 A.M. to 5:00 P.M. daily) to get started. Special attractions include:

Woodlands Nature Station. Northern end of LBL, between Honker and Hematite Lakes. Open March through November. This is a very child-oriented center for viewing animals (the backyard exhibit includes owls, coyotes, and a red wolf). There are also guided nature hikes and numerous special events, from guided owl

Amazing
Kentucky Fact

Kentucky's "big lakes" are actually big and bigger—Lake Barkley is about 58,000 acres, and Kentucky Lake is about 160,000 acres. Kentucky Lake and Lake Barkley have more combined shoreline than Lake Superior.

Amazing
Kentucky Fact

Kentucky is bordered by seven states—more than any other state. Can you name them?

(Tennessee)

(Missouri, Illinois, Indiana, Ohio, West Virginia, Virginia,

walks to a "Howl-o-Ween" celebration. Open daily from 9:00 A.M. to 5:00 P.M. April through October; open Wednesday to Sunday in March and November ($). You can rent canoes here summer through fall ($ per hour). (270) 924–2000.

Elk and Bison Prairie. Near the center of LBL, this is an auto path through a habitat restoration area that's home to buffalo and elk. We didn't see any elk, but we enjoyed looking. Open year-round, dawn to dusk daily. (270) 924–2000. $

Golden Pond Planetarium and Observatory. Just south of the elk and bison area at the Golden Pond Visitor Center. General astronomy shows in an eighty-one-seat planetarium, plus occasional outdoor "Star Parties." Open March through December. Several shows daily in summer. (800) 455–5897. $

The Homeplace. South of Golden Pond (actually, just over the Tennessee line). We walked into the log house just as the family was sitting down to lunch. "Come on in and look around," the mother said (although we weren't invited to eat). Children love seeing the feather beds, the giant Percheron draft horses, and other animals when you drop in on an 1850s family as they go about their daily work and lives. Open March through November. A variety of special events include sheep shearing in the spring and harvest festivities in the fall. $

Hiking and Biking Trails. The trails range from ⁷⁄₁₀ mile to the 69-mile North/South Trail and come in all difficulty levels. Several easy trails start at the Nature Center. Pick up maps and information about where to rent bikes at the welcome centers.

Horseback Riding. If you don't bring your own horse, you can take a guided trail ride (ages six and up) or pony ride at J Bar J Riding Stables at Wranglers Campground ($$$ trail ride; $ pony ride). Open Tuesday to Sunday April through October; November through March by reservation. (270) 832–6513.

Camping. There are several camping areas. Good options for families are the shelters offered at Piney and Wranglers campgrounds. These are one-room buildings with one double bed and one or three bunk beds, plus porch and electricity. Open March through November. (270) 924–2044. $

Lake Barkley State Resort Park (all ages)

3500 State Park Road, off US 68, Cadiz; information: (270) 924–1131, reservations: (800) 325–1708. Open year-round. Many activities free. Lodge rooms $$–$$$, cottages $$–$$$$, camping $. Dining $.

A beautiful post-and-beam lodge overlooks the lake at this popular state resort park. The park features indoor and outdoor pools, an eighteen-hole golf course, miniature golf, and tennis courts. Several trails begin near the lodge; despite the name, Wilderness Trail is probably the easiest. You can rent anything from a fishing boat to a big sightseeing pontoon at the marina. The large lodge dining room overlooks the lake. In addition to the main lodge, accommodations also are available in the ten-room Little River Lodge, in cottages, and in a year-round campground.

Barkley Dam and U.S. Corps of Engineers Visitor Center (all ages)

Dam located off Highway 453 near Grand Rivers; Corps visitor center on US 62, northwest of the dam; (270) 362–4235. Open daily. Free.

It's fascinating to watch barges come through the locks at this 10,180-foot-long and 157-foot-high dam with locks. The U.S. Corps of Engineers visitor center features displays on the dam and on steamboat days on the Cumberland River.

Lake **Break**

Some nonwatery things to do:

- Visit the **Janice Mason Art Museum** in the old post office building at 71 Main Street in Cadiz; (270) 522–9056. Kid-friendly art space with changing local exhibits. Closed Monday. Free.

- Hear some toe-tapping music in a family atmosphere at **Lakeland Jamboree,** 61 Jefferson Street, Cadiz; (270) 522–0086. Friday and Saturday nights at 7:00. $

- A working model of an iron furnace and exhibits relating to "Eddyville Castle" (the medieval-looking Kentucky State Penitentiary) are among the exhibits about local history tended by a volunteer staff at the **Lyon County Museum** (Water Street in Eddyville; 800–355–3883). The museum is open Tuesday to Saturday from 1:00 to 5:00 P.M. and by appointment.

- Visit **Drury's Candyland,** 734 US 62, Lake City; (270) 362–8067. See how they've been making old-fashioned taffy, peanut brittle, and 150 other kinds of sweets for forty years.

Kentucky Dam Village State Resort Park (all ages)

Off US 62/US Highway 641, near Gilbertsville; information: (270) 362–4271, reservations: (800) 325–0146. Open year-round. Many activities **free.** Lodge rooms \$\$–\$\$\$, cottages \$\$–\$\$\$\$, camping \$. Dining \$.

Another waterside playground for day, weekend, and extended visits, Kentucky Dam Village offers picnic areas, marina with boat rental, horseback riding, swimming, trails, and an eighteen-hole golf course. You can stay at the lodge, rent a one- to three-bedroom cottage, or camp. The campground is open year-round and features showers and a laundry. The lodge dining room serves regional specialties.

Kenlake State Resort Park (all ages)

Highway 94, south of US 68, between Aurora and Hardin (mailing address: 542 Kenlake Road, Hardin 42048); information: (270) 474–2211, reservations: (800) 325–0143. Open year-round; some activities seasonal. Many activities **free.** Lodge rooms \$\$–\$\$\$, cottages \$\$–\$\$\$\$, camping \$. Dining \$.

Located on the western shore of Kentucky Lake, this is the only state resort park with indoor tennis courts. The Tennis Center offers temperature-controlled courts and racquet rental for day visitors as well as overnight guests. Other park features are picnic areas, playgrounds, a nine-hole golf course, and boat rentals. The lodge offers garden or lake views. You can rent a cottage with a lake view, in the woods, or adjacent to the golf course. The campground is seasonal.

Patti's 1880s Restaurant and Settlement (all ages)

1793 J. H. O'Bryan Avenue, Grand Rivers; (888) 736–2515, www.pattis-settlement.com. Open daily from 10:30 A.M. to 8:00 P.M.; open until 9:00 P.M. April through December. \$–\$\$\$

If you haven't been here before and think you're just going out to eat, you may wonder where the restaurant is as you follow the path through the settlement, past the miniature golf course, playground, animal area, gardens, and shops. Eventually you get there and join the throngs waiting for a table. Read about the family who turned a twenty-seat burger joint (Hamburger Patti's) into an entertainment empire. Patti's has been featured in many national publications and is a must-see family stop for food and fun in the lake area. (And, hey, the food's even good—try the 2-inch pork chops and "mile-high" meringue pies. My daughter still talks about the flowerpot bread.)

Venture River Water Park (all ages)

280 Park Place, Eddyville (I–24, exit 40); (270) 388–7999. Open in summer Monday to Saturday from 10:00 A.M. to 7:00 P.M., Sunday from 11:00 A.M. to 7:00 P.M. \$\$\$

As if 180,000 acres of lakes weren't enough water! But the big attractions here are the five big slides and the wave pool. There's a kiddie pool and other areas for little ones, plus floating pools for the less adventurous.

Maggie's Jungle Golf and Jungle Run (all ages)

US 641, near Gilbertsville; (270) 362–8933. Open Memorial Day through Labor Day, Monday to Friday from 10:00 A.M. to 9:00 P.M., Saturday and Sunday from 10:00 A.M. to 10:00 P.M. Golf $, animal area $; $$ with cart.

Another lake-area classic, this minigolf course features a large elephant statue and water stream, plus a camel, emu, and other creatures in the Jungle Run. You can walk it or rent an open-air Safari Car that seats two adults and three small children.

Where to Eat

Country Cupboard, US 62 west, Eddyville; (270) 388–5178. Huge home-cooking buffets for three meals daily, with dessert buffet. $

Countryside Family Restaurant, 1842 Canton Road, Cadiz; (270) 522–5859. Order from buffet or sandwiches and specials on regular menu. $

Green Turtle Bay Resort, Barkley Drive, Grand Rivers; (270) 362–5377. Hearty breakfast, grilled and deli sandwiches, homemade pies. $

Miss Scarlett's Restaurant, 708 Complex Drive, Grand Rivers (exit 31 off I–24); (270) 928–3126. Catfish, homemade soups, kids' menu. Nightly specials and all-you-can-eat catfish special on Friday. Lunch $, dinner $$.

Where to Stay

Grand Rivers Inn, 1949 J. H. O'Bryan Avenue, Grand Rivers; (270) 362–4487 or (800) 884–4487. Family-run hotel in downtown Grand Rivers with outdoor pool; rooms have refrigerators and microwaves. $$–$$$

Green Turtle Bay Resort, Barkley Drive, Grand Rivers; (270) 362–8364 or (800) 498–0428. Condominiums with lake or bay view. Two swimming pools, tennis courts, beach, organized kids' activities. $$$$

Lighthouse Landing, Highway 453 off I–24 (exit 31); (270) 362–8201 or (800) 491–7245. Cottages with fully equipped kitchens, campground with laundry and bathhouses. Marina, boat rentals, sailing lessons. Cottages $$$–$$$$, camping $$.

For More Information

Cadiz/Trigg County Visitor Information Center, Main Street (P.O. Box 735), Cadiz 42211; (270) 522–3892.

Lyon County Tourist Commission, P.O. Box 1030, Eddyville 42038; (800) 355–3885, www.lakebarkley.org.

Grand Rivers Chamber of Commerce, P.O. Box 181, Grand Rivers 42045; (888) 493–0152.

Marshall County Tourist Commission, P.O. Box 129, Gilbertsville 42022; (800) 467–7145.

Soapbox **Speeders**

Homemade soapbox race cars take over the streets of Murray in June. The **Mid-America Soapbox Derby** is part of the city's Freedom Fest activities. Area businesses sponsor cars, and there are heats for adults and children. The main action is on Main, Sixteenth, and Chestnut Streets. This is a preliminary to the International Soapbox Derby in Akron, Ohio. (800) 651–1603.

Murray

Wrather–Western Kentucky Museum (ages 5 and up)
University Avenue (off Sixteenth Street), Murray State University Campus; (270) 809–4771. Open Monday to Friday from 8:30 A.M. to 4:00 P.M., Saturday from 10:00 A.M. to 1:00 P.M. Free.

The soapbox derby cars and antique radio exhibit are highlights for children at this regional history museum. There are all kinds of cool things, from Civil War artifacts to old tools, nicely arranged.

Playhouse in the Park (ages 6 and up)
Performances at Murray City Park, Gil Hopson Drive; (270) 759–1752; tickets: (800) 651–1603. Several productions annually; schedule varies. $$

This community theater group performs family-oriented musicals, comedies, and mysteries; call to see what's coming up.

Where to Eat

Log Cabin Restaurant, 505 South Twelfth Street; (270) 753–8080. Country cooking and barbecue. $

Matt B's Pizza, 1411 Main Street; (270) 759–1234. Pizza and Italian favorites. $

Mayfield

Wooldridge Monuments (all ages)
Maplewood Cemetery, US Highway 45 and North Seventh Street. Open daily. Free.

This is just something that children and adults will find curious—eighteen sandstone and marble figures erected in the late 1890s by a man named Henry G. Wooldridge as his grave monument. Known as the "strange procession that never moves," it includes statues of Wooldridge on his famous horse, hounds, a fox, a deer, and various family members. Guess Mr. Wooldridge didn't want to face eternity alone!

Where to Eat

Carr's Barn, 216 West Broadway; (270) 247–8959. A tiny place (just sit on stools at the counter) with great barbecue. $$

Hill's Barbecue, 2001 Cuba Road; (270) 247–9121. Western Kentucky–style barbecue. $$

Hickman

Warren Thomas Black History Museum (ages 8 and up)
603 Moulton Avenue; (270) 236–2423. Open by appointment. **Free.**

Exhibits on local African-American history include a display about the Tuskeegee Airmen (a local man was a member). The museum building itself is the largest artifact; it was a church built in 1890 by former slaves, and pews still remain.

Clinton

Columbus Belmont State Park (all ages)
350 Park Road, off Highway 123, west of Clinton; (270) 677–2327. Open year-round; some activities and museum open daily April through October from 9:00 A.M. to 5:00 P.M.; weekends October to April. Many activities **free;** museum $.

OK, if you were Confederate troops and your job was to stop Union boats from coming up the Mississippi River to Paducah and other cities, how would you do it? Bet nobody in your family came up with the idea of a giant chain across the river. Well, the Confederates did, and you can see part of the chain and its huge anchor, along with cannons and other Civil War artifacts, at this scenic riverside park. There are also earthen-wall fortifications that you can walk among. Your kids will love the anchor even if they aren't interested in Civil War history. And everybody will enjoy the miniature golf, play areas, and great view overlooking the river. There's a small museum of Civil War artifacts in a building used as a hospital during the conflict.

A Day **Family Adventure**

This is a little silly, but we did it accidentally (couldn't get off the highway before the bridge) and got a kick out of it once we realized what was going on. From Wickliffe Mounds, turn right onto US 51/60/62 combined and take the bridge across the river. Once across, bear left onto US 60/62 and cross another bridge. Turn around and come back. Congratulations! You've just visited three states—Kentucky, Illinois, and Missouri—in ten minutes!

Wickliffe

Wickliffe Mounds State Historic Site (ages 6 and up)
94 Green Street (U.S. Highway 51/60/62 west); (270) 335–3681. Open daily March 1 through November 30; closed weekends December through February. Hours are 9:00 A.M. to 4:30 P.M. $

If there are any budding archaeologists in the family, stop by this attraction south-west of Paducah. Not only will they get to see a real excavation site, but they'll also get words of encouragement from the on-site archaeologist. This is a preserved exca-vation of a 3,000-year-old mound village, with pottery and other artifacts on display and information about how early inhabitants lived. (The skeletal remains of adults and infants are replicas, by the way.) The gift shop includes some educational posters and materials as well as inexpensive reproductions of early pottery figures.

Paducah

William Clark Market House Museum (ages 5 and up)
121 Market House Square; (270) 443–7759. Open March through December, Monday to Saturday from noon to 4:00 P.M. Closed January and February, and Monday and major holidays year-round. $, children 5 and under free.

An entire 1870s drugstore, complete with glass counters, old patent medicine bot-tles, and elaborately carved Victorian woodwork, is housed within Paducah's 1905 market house building. Along with the drugstore items, there are all kinds of other curiosities—something for just about every interest, from history to fine glassware to folk art. Children will especially enjoy the 1913 LaFrance Fire Engine, the hand-carved statue of Henry Clay (once they learn it was carved by a twelve-year-old boy), and the Civil War spurs and sabers. (My son was also impressed by the huge punch bowl from the USS *Paducah*—it includes 700 ounces of silver.) The guides are very friendly and knowledgeable about local history. They also gave us a vivid accounting of the exciting annual Battle of Paducah Celebration in the city in late March, which involved lots of civilian Civil War reenactments around downtown as well as a battle reenactment.

Paducah Wall-to-Wall (all ages)
100 Broadway; (800) PADUCAH. Open daily year-round. Free.

Take time to stroll by these large, colorful murals recounting scenes from Paducah history. Paducah is located right on the river, and this is a decorative floodwall. (Plus it's a good stroll: There are more than thirty murals.) The murals were done by artist Robert Dafford (who also did the murals in Maysville in northern Kentucky) and capture scenes ranging from the Civil War Battle of Paducah to scenes from Paducah Summer Fest. One panel re-creates a 1948 Harley-Davidson magazine cover featuring local motorcycle riders posing with the statue of Chief Paduke that stands in the city's Noble Park. Cool.

Yeiser Art Center (ages 4 and up)
200 Broadway; (270) 442–2453, www.theyeiser.org. Open Tuesday through Saturday from 10:00 A.M. to 4:00 P.M. Free; donations accepted.

This fine arts museum, located at the other end of the Market House from the general history museum, features changing exhibits of fiber and other visual arts. It's a kid-friendly place that offers some quality educational programs for schools. Exhibits change and vary from the works of local and regional artists to traveling exhibitions from the Smithsonian Institution. Young artists will also be interested in the annual juried show of work by high school students from the Paducah area (usually January through March). The education section of the Web site has work sheets and other guides, designed for teachers but also useful for parents in helping children get the most out of a trip to an art museum.

And Dot's the Story

The nation's supply of Dippin' Dots, the freeze-dried beads of ice cream sold at malls, amusement parks, and other fun-lovin' locations across America, is made in Paducah. The "Ice Cream of the Future" was invented by Curt Jones in the late 1980s when he was a research microbiologist in Lexington, Kentucky. Cryogenics, a method of flash-freezing using very low temperatures, was one of his specialties. Jones wondered if one of his favorite foods, ice cream, could be produced that way. The Dippin' Dots production plant moved to Paducah in 1990.

After Dinner Fun

Every Saturday evening from early May through mid-October, downtown Paducah features outdoor entertainment (from music to strolling clowns) and activities for all ages. Shops stay open late, too, for After Dinner Downtown. (800) PADUCAH.

Market House Theatre (ages 6 and up)
132 Market House Square; (270) 444–6828 or (888) MHT–PLAY, www.mhtplay.com. Schedule varies; call or check Web site for current offerings. $$

In addition to its mainstage season, this theater company offers several youth theater productions each year.

Paducah Symphony Orchestra (ages 6 and up)
Performances are at Four Rivers Performing Arts Center, 100 Kentucky Avenue; (270) 444–0065 or (800) 738–3727. Concert dates vary. $$

Performances of interest to children include the Children's Chorus performances and annual Christmas concerts. At the March symphony performance, winners of the year's Young Artist Competition perform with the symphony.

River Heritage Museum (ages 5 and up)
117 South Water Street; (270) 575–9958. Open Monday to Saturday from 9:30 A.M. to 5:00 P.M., Sunday from 1:00 to 5:00 P.M. $

This museum shows the importance of the river to area history and commerce. Children will enjoy the steamboat models and the build-a-river exhibit, which lets them explore river formations by manipulating sand and water. Older children will also be interested in the observation area of navigation simulation activities at the Seaman's Center for Maritime Education next door. The center trains riverboat captains.

Noble Park (all ages)
Twenty-eighth Street and Park Avenue; (800) PADUCAH. Open daily year-round. Free.

Take a picnic lunch to this 150-acre park and spend a morning or afternoon walking the nature trail or the pathway around the scenic lake, watching (or joining) the action at the skate park, exploring the Civil War redoubt (small earthen fort), enjoying the playgrounds, or fishing. Your children will probably want to take a picture of the huge statue of Wacinton. This statue of a Chickasaw Indian was carved from a 56,000-pound red oak by Hungarian-born sculptor Peter Toth, who has carved and donated a giant sculpture to each state to honor Native Americans. At Christmastime the park hosts a drive-through holiday lights display and shows free family movies in summer.

Tilghman Heritage Center and Civil War Interpretive Center
(ages 6 and up)

631 Kentucky Avenue; (270) 575–5477. Open Wednesday to Saturday from noon to 4:00 P.M. $; children under 6 free.

Children interested in the Civil War will enjoy seeing the artifacts and learning about the 1864 Battle of Paducah. (Don't be surprised if their favorite part is hearing how Confederate colonel A. P. Thompson was decapitated by a Union cannonball just 2 blocks from his home.) The museum is housed in the former home of Confederate general Lloyd Tilghman, who was killed at Vicksburg.

Paducah Railroad Museum (ages 5 and up)

200 Washington Street; (270) 519–7377 or (270) 559–5253, www.paducahrr.org. Open Friday from 1:00 to 4:00 P.M., Saturday from 10:00 A.M. to 4:00 P.M., or by appointment. Free; donations accepted.

Railroad buffs will want to stop by this downtown museum to see the exhibits and meet some kindred spirits. Among the many items on display are section cars, lanterns, model trains, dispatch and signaling equipment, and lots of photos. The museum is operated by the Paducah chapter of the National Railroad Historical Society and is staffed by volunteers who know a lot about train history and love to share stories and information.

Museum of the American Quilter's Society (ages 6 and up)

215 Jefferson Street; (270) 442–8856, www.quiltmuseum.org. Open year-round Monday to Saturday from 10:00 A.M. to 5:00 P.M. Also open Sunday from 1:00 to 5:00 P.M. April through October. $; under 12 free.

Is there a quilter in your family? Everyone who has snuggled under a quilt knows that these multilayered coverlets provide warmth; at this museum you can see why quilts truly are an art form. The collection focuses on contemporary quilts—some of which are so detailed and amazingly beautiful that they look more like paintings than textile works (and many actually incorporate paint and other nontraditional materials). Youngsters can learn how to make a "fabric sandwich" and will enjoy the wide variety of themes reflected in the collection—everything from Lewis and Clark and the Beatles to aviation and farm animals. There's also a collection of miniature quilts. Every year the museum participates in Moda Fabrics' School Block Challenge competition. Students in grades K–12 receive fabric and work in groups to create 16-inch quilt squares. An exhibition of entries and winners runs from January through March each year. The museum also sponsors a summer quilt camp for students in grades 1–12.

Younger students make quilt blocks and older students create multiblock quilts. Look under the education section of the Web site for some activity ideas; they're geared to school groups but you can adapt many for use at home.

Where to Eat

C.C. Cohen, 103 Broadway, near Market House Square; (270) 442–6391. Steaks, burgers, and sandwiches. Lunch $, dinner $$. Ask about the resident ghost!

Kirchhoff's Bakery and Deli, 118 South Second Street; (270) 442–7117. Deli sandwiches and calzones. $

Max's Brick Oven Cafe, 112 Market House Square; (270) 575–3473. Casual dining in a restored building; outdoor dining area seasonally. Brick-oven pizza and pasta. $

The Pork Peddler, Park Avenue at Eighth Street; (270) 442–7414. Terrific barbecue and homemade desserts. $

Whaler's Catch, 123 North Second Street; (270) 444–7701. Indoor-outdoor dining. Seafood is the specialty. $$

Where to Stay

Executive Inn Riverfront, 1 Executive Boulevard; (800) 866–3636 or (270) 443–8000, www.jrsexecutiveinn.com. Huge hotel complex (434 rooms) with its own shopping arcade, plus indoor pool and game room. Get a river view for a little extra, and watch boats and barges from your balcony. $–$$

Pear Tree Inn by Drury, 5002 Hinkleville Road; (270) 444–7200. Spacious rooms, outdoor pool, free continental breakfast. $$

For More Information

Paducah/McCracken County Convention and Visitors Bureau, 128 Broadway, P. O. Box 890, Paducah 42002; (800) PADUCAH, www.paducah-tourism.org.

Marion

Ben E. Clement Mineral Museum (ages 4 and up)
205 North Walker Street; (270) 965–4263. At press time, open Friday and Saturday from 10:00 A.M. to 3:00 P.M. Days and hours may vary, so call ahead. $

Some 30,000 colorful fluorite crystals large and small are housed in the former Crittenden County Elementary School annex. The specimens represent the private collection of Ben E. Clement, a scientist and educator who came to Kentucky after World War I because of interest in the then-fledgling fluorspar mining industry centered in Crittenden County. From 1920 until his death in 1980, Clement accumulated one of the largest collections of fluorite specimens in the world. The collection also includes fossils and mineral carvings.

Mantle Rock Native Education and Cultural Center (all ages)
110 South Main Street; (270) 965–5882. Hours and activities vary; call or stop by.

Stop by this small center, which shares space with a community barber shop, to buy reasonably priced Native American crafts and to learn about a remarkable part of local history. This is the headquarters of an effort to re-establish a Cherokee presence in the area of Mantle Rock, a natural rock formation west of Marion, off Highway 133. During the forced removal of the Cherokee peoples west—an event known as the Trail of Tears—some 3,000 Cherokees sought shelter at Mantle Rock while the river was frozen and impassable in the winter of 1838–1839. Many died and were buried in rock-covered graves. Mantle Rock is now a Native American Historical Landmark and a site of pilgrimage for many people of native descent.

The education center was founded by Marti "Momfeather" Erickson, a Native American born in eastern Kentucky who moved to Nebraska before returning to Marion in December 2002. The center sponsors workshops and classes relating to Native American culture, along with other special events, and can arrange guided tours of the Mantle Rock area.

Amish Ways

The Marion-area Amish community offers baked goods and other products for sale at shops and stands in the Highway 91, US 60, and Ford's Ferry Road area. Detailed maps of the Amish area are available at the Mantle Rock Native Education and Cultural Center.

Where to Eat

The Front Porch, 914 South Main Street; (270) 965–3035. Catfish, steaks, beans, and hush puppies in a homey setting. $

Marion Pit Bar-B-Q, 728 South Main Street; (270) 965–3318. Delicious barbecue with homemade sauce. Carry food out or eat in a screened-in area. $

Thom's Sweet Shoppe & Cafe, 102 South Main Street; (270) 965–2211. Sandwiches, soups, and salads, plus soda fountain items in a charming old-fashioned drugstore building with a marble ice-cream fountain. $

For More Information

City of Marion Tourism Commission, 113 Carlisle Street; (270) 965–5015, www.marionkentucky.us.

Morganfield

James D. Veatch Camp Breckinridge Museum and Arts Center

(ages 7 and up)

1116 North Village Road; (270) 389–4420. Open Tuesday to Friday from 10:00 A.M. to 3:00 P.M., Saturday from 10:00 A.M. to 4:00 P.M., and Sunday from noon to 4:00 P.M. $

In addition to uniforms, medals, pictures, and other World War II artifacts, this former military camp officer's club building features some unusual sights that put a human face on the complex issues of war. Painted on the walls are beautiful murals of the Black Forest and other German scenes created by a German prisoner of war, Daniel Mayer, who was imprisoned here from 1943 until 1945. He painted the scenes from memory and from postcards sent by his wife. Mayer's own story has a sad ending: He died at Camp Breckinridge in 1945 and is one of four German prisoners of war buried at Fort Knox. The building also houses Unicorn Players, a community theater group that does several productions a year, some of which may be of interest to older children. (270) 389–9121.

Where to Eat

Brandon's Restaurant, 531 US 60 east; (270) 389–0500. Home cooking. $

Feed Mill, 3541 US 60 east; (270) 389–0047. Cajun food. $

Henderson

John James Audubon State Park (all ages)

3100 US 41 north; (270) 826–2247. Open year-round; museum open 10:00 A.M. to 5:00 P.M. daily March through November, 8:30 A.M. to 4:30 P.M. Wednesday to Sunday December through February. Many activities **free.** Museum admission $. Cottages $$–$$$$, camping $.

Children can climb into a giant bird's nest, learn how birds are able to fly, and see a red-tailed hawk up close at this nature center and art museum. Older visitors will enjoy the extensive collection of huge folio nature prints by the famous artist and exhibits about his work and his time in the Henderson area. From the viewing area you and your children can look through binoculars to spot live birds. More birds and wildflowers are among the things you'll see along the park's easy nature trails. You can rent a pedal boat or fish from the shore at the small fishing lake (it's quiet—no motorized boats allowed). The park also includes tennis courts, a nine-hole golf course, picnic areas, and playgrounds. For a peaceful getaway, stay in one of the park's five one-bedroom cottages (each has a fireplace). There's also a handicapped-accessible two-bedroom cottage and a seasonal campground.

Audubon Mill Park (all ages)

Second and Water Street; (800) 648–3128. Open daily. **Free.**

Watch the boats dock, play or have a picnic, and see the millstone used when John James Audubon operated a gristmill at this site. Check the local calendar for special concerts and events.

Audubon Bird Sculptures (all ages)

Second, First, Elm, and Main Streets, downtown Henderson; (270) 826–3128. **Free.**

After you see the original bird paintings at the John James Audubon State Park museum, come into Henderson and see life-size sculptures based on Audubon's works. Murray, Kentucky, native Raymond Graf created these eight cast-bronze sculptures as a special public art project for the city, and seeing them makes a nice walk through the downtown area. Begin at Audubon Mill Park, head down Second Street, turn right on Elm, and right again on First Street to return to the park.

Henderson Fine Arts Center

Henderson Community College campus, 2660 South Green Street; (270) 850–5324. Various performances and ticket prices.

This 1,000-seat auditorium boasts a 4,000-square-foot stage with state-of-the-art light and sound systems. It's host to a variety of concerts and drama performances, some of which are appropriate for children.

Hot Event

Henderson's biggest event is the annual **W. C. Handy Blues and Barbe-cue Festival,** held mid-June in downtown Henderson. Honoring the "Father of the Blues," William Christopher Handy—who lived in Henderson around the turn of the twentieth century—this festival sponsored by the Henderson Music Preservation Society brings in great regional and national blues, zydeco, and gospel acts for **free** concerts. In addition to the official Kentucky State Barbecue Championship, there are barbecue dinners and bake sales sponsored by local churches, plus an array of children's games and activities. (800) 648–3128, www.handyblues.org.

Where to Eat

Downtown Diner, 122 First Street; (270) 827–9671. Breakfast and lunch, daily specials. $

Ralph's Hickory Pit, 739 North Green Street; (270) 826–5656. Barbecue and daily specials. $

Wolf's, 31 North Green Street; (270) 826–5221. Famous for its bean soup and open-faced Hot Brown sandwich. $

Where to Stay

Holiday Inn Express, 2826 US 41 north; (270) 869–0533. Indoor pool, free breakfast bar. $$

For More Information

Henderson County Tourist Commission, 101 North Water Street; (800) 648–3128 or (270) 826–3128, www.henderson ky.org.

Owensboro

International Bluegrass Music Museum (all ages)

114 Daviess Street; (270) 926–7891. Open Tuesday to Saturday from 10:00 A.M. to 5:00 P.M., Saturday and Sunday from 1:00 to 5:00 P.M. Closed major holidays. $, children 6 and under **free.**

Bluegrass music originated in Kentucky, and western Kentucky was the home of "the Father of Bluegrass Music," Bill Monroe. This museum features exhibits on bluegrass, its roots, and its stars. Kids will love the oversize instruments.

Owensboro **in Bloom**

Late April and May are scenic times to visit Owensboro. A 25-block area around Griffith Avenue is called the "Dogwood Azalea Trail" for its beautiful spring blooms.

Owensboro Museum of Science and History (all ages)

220 Daviess Street; (270) 687–2732. Open Monday to Saturday from 10:00 A.M. to 5:00 P.M. and Sunday from 1:00 to 5:00 P.M. $, entire family admission $$.

From giant mammoth bones to real birds and reptiles, this museum lets children explore science and natural history. There's a special area for toddlers, plus an Encounter interactive area on the second floor. One of the most popular areas with the ten and under set is the **PlayZeum,** a colorful indoor playground with crawl tubes, bridges, a "riverboat," "train," and "tree houses." Children can use up a lot of energy (and imagination) as they play here. NASCAR fans will want to see the **SpeedZeum,** with race cars, motorcycles, and other items relating to NASCAR and motorcycle drivers from the area, including NASCAR's Jeff Green, Darrell Waltrip, Michael Waltrip, Jeremy Mayfield, David Green, Mark Green, and legend G. C. Spencer, and motorcycle racers Tommy, Nicky, and Roger Lee Hayden. The museum also includes the **Wendell H. Ford Government Education Center.** Exhibits trace the career of longtime U.S. senator from Kentucky and former governor Wendell Ford, a western Kentucky native, as well as other Kentucky political figures such as Abraham Lincoln and Alben Barkley, and relate to civics lessons, such as how a bill becomes a law.

Natural **Attractions**

Two good nature areas in the Owensboro area are

- **Panther Creek Park,** 5160 Wayne Bridge Road, off Highway 81, about 5 miles southwest of Owensboro. Picnic areas, six-acre lake, nature center, paved pathways with activities. Trail of Dreams leads to lookout tower. Interesting solar fountain. Facilities available. Nature center closes at dusk. (270) 926–6481.

- **Yellow Creek Park,** 5710 Highway 144, east of Owensboro. Easy to moderate hiking trails, playgrounds, picnic areas, and ball fields. Open daily year-round. (270) 281–0436.

Sassafras Tree (all ages)

Corner of Frederica Street and Maple Avenue. Free.

This isn't just any old tree. According to the American Forestry Association, it's the *world's largest* sassafras tree—about 100 feet tall and 21 feet in diameter. And it is old—about 300 years.

Moonlite Bar-B-Q Inn (all ages)

2840 West Parrish Avenue; (270) 684–8143. Lunch and dinner buffets daily. $$, under 3 free.

In much the same way that the sassafras tree is not just any old tree, this is not just any old restaurant. Moonlite is an internationally known institution of smoked meats, and as you dine at the buffet, you may find yourself elbow to elbow with visitors from around the world. It's also a great family success story. Several generations of the Bosley family work here, and since the 1960s, they have turned a little barbecue joint into a world-famous restaurant. (They've also made about eighteen additions to the building—this place is huge!) You can order off the menu, but most people go for the lavish buffet. A separate roomful of food, the buffet features ribs, beef, pork, chicken, and lamb, plus veggies and a salad bar.

RiverPark Center (ages 6 and up)

101 Daviess Street, next to the Bluegrass Music Museum; information: (270) 687–2770, tickets: (270) 687–ARTS, www.riverparkcenter.org. Schedule and ticket prices vary.

This modern complex on the river reminds you that you're in Kentucky's third largest city. Check the schedules of concerts and theater for performances appropriate for families. The center hosts children's theater performances and sponsors a summer arts camp for kids.

Owensboro Symphony Orchestra (ages 6 and up)

Performances at RiverPark Center; office at 122 East Eighteenth Street; (270) 684–0661, www.owensborosymphony.org. Schedule and ticket prices vary.

This professional orchestra's season usually includes at least one family concert. Older children may also enjoy the pops concerts and occasional special concerts combining bluegrass and classical music. The Youth Orchestra, made up of local student musicians, gives concerts in November and April. The OSO has a great section on its Web site, OSO for Kids, that features information about instruments and music and includes puzzles and activities.

AnnualEvents in Western Kentucky

- **Last Chance Eagle Viewing,** late March, Land Between the Lakes; (800) LBL–7077

- **Benton Tater Days,** early April, Benton; (270) 527–3128

- **Dogwood Trail Celebration,** mid-April, Paducah; (800) PADUCAH

- **Kite Festival,** April, John James Audubon State Park; (270) 826–2247

- **American Quilter's Society Annual Show,** late April, Paducah; (800) PADUCAH

- **International Bar-B-Que Festival,** early May, Owensboro; (800) 489–1131

- **W. C. Handy Blues and Barbecue Festival,** mid-June, Henderson; (800) 648–3128

- **McCracken County Fair,** late June, Paducah; (800) PADUCAH

- **Freedom Fest,** late June or early July, Murray; (800) 651–1603

- **Henderson County Fair,** mid-July, Henderson; (800) 648–3128

- **Paducah Summer Festival,** late July, Paducah; (800) PADUCAH

- **Hummingbird Festival,** early August, Land Between the Lakes; (800) LBL–7077

- **Bluegrass in the Park,** mid-August, Henderson; (800) 648–3128

- **Kenlake Hot August Blues Festival,** late August, Aurora; (800) 325–0143

- **Labor Day Celebration,** Labor Day weekend, Paducah; (800) PADUCAH

- **Trail of Tears Intertribal PowWow,** September, Hopkinsville; (270) 886–8033

- **Hopkinsville Salutes Fort Campbell Week,** September, Hopkinsville; (800) 842–9959

- **Western Kentucky Highland Festival,** mid-September, Murray; (270) 443–2064

- **Corn Festival,** September, Morganfield; (877) 459–1593

- **Barbecue on the River and Old Market Days,** late September, Paducah; (800) PADUCAH

- **Shaker Farm Day,** early October, South Union; (800) 811–8379

- **Trigg County Ham Festival,** early October, Cadiz; (270) 522–3892

Owensboro Museum of Fine Art (ages 6 and up)

901 Frederica Street; (270) 685–3181. Open Tuesday to Friday from 10:00 A.M. to 4:00 P.M., Saturday and Sunday from 1:00 to 4:00 P.M. **Free.**

This museum's diverse collection includes European and American art, an Atrium Sculpture Court, a collection of beautiful German stained glass, and even children's art (in the Young at Art gallery).

Goldie's Best Little Opryhouse in Kentucky (ages 6 and up)

418 Frederica Street; (270) 926–0254, www.goldiesopryhouse.com. Open Friday and Saturday at 8 P.M. year-round. Reservations recommended. $$

This place has been crankin' out good old bluegrass, country, and gospel sounds for family audiences for two decades. Its annual talent contest (eight weeks beginning in early September) offers a $1,000 prize (ages thirteen and older can enter, so start the kids practicing now so they'll be ready).

Western Kentucky Botanical Garden (all ages)

Thompson-Berry Complex, US 60 north near Owensboro; (270) 993–1234. Open year-round from dawn to dusk; visitor center open Monday to Friday 9:00 A.M to 3:00 P.M. **Free.**

This ever-growing (literally!) botanical garden is a good place for an educational walk. Nine of twenty-three planned gardens are complete, including the Fruit and Berry Garden, Herb Garden, Rose Garden, Daylily and Iris Garden, and the family favorite, the Children's Butterfly Garden. Numerous events and demonstrations are offered for children, from learning to ID trees to making a "pizza garden."

Where to Eat

Briarpatch Restaurant, 2750 Veach Road; (270) 685–3329. Home cooking and daily specials. $

Old Hickory Bar-B-Q, 338 Washington Avenue (Twenty-fifth and Frederica); (270) 926–9000. Moonlite gets all the fame, but many locals think this restaurant also serves world-class barbecue. $

Where to Stay

Executive Inn Rivermont, One Executive Boulevard; (270) 926–8000. High-rise near the RiverPark Center. Indoor and outdoor swimming pools, game room. $$–$$$$

Hampton Inn, 615 Salem Drive; (270) 926–2006. Hot breakfast, convenient to attractions. $$$–$$$$

Sleep Inn, 51 Bon Harbor Hills Drive; (270) 691–6200. Newer hotel with indoor pool and complimentary continental breakfast. $$

Windy Hollow Campground and Recreation Center, 5141 Windy Hollow Road; (270) 785–4150. Open April through October. Tent and hookup camping, with fishing, beach, miniature golf, picnic areas (many area residents come here as a day destination). $

For More Information

Owensboro Visitor Information Center, 215 East Second Street; (800) 489–1131 or (270) 926–1100, www.visit owensboro.com.

Index

Q

Quiet Trails Nature Preserve, 100

R

Rabbit Hash General Store, 53
Race World, 176
Radcliff/Fort Knox Convention and Tourism
    Commission, 32
Railway Museum of Greater Cincinnati, 59
Raven Run Nature Sanctuary, 90
Rebecca-Ruth Candy, 106
Red Mile Harness Track, The, 83
Red River Gorge, 132
Renaissance Fun Park, 20
Renfro Valley, 160
Renfro Valley Visitors Center, 161
Richmond, 121–23, 126
Richmond Visitor Center, 126
Ringo's Mill Bridge, 75
River Heritage Museum, 199
RiverPark Center, 207
Riverside, The Farnsley-Moremen
    Landing, 19
Riverview at Hobson's Bend, 176
Robert Penn Warren Birthplace, 184–85
Roebling Suspension Bridge, 58
Rosemary Clooney House, 69
Rough River Dam State Resort Park, 33
Round Table Literary Park, 186
Royal Spring Park, 102
Russell Sims Aquatic Center, 177
Russell Springs, 165–66
Russellville area, 184
Ruth Hunt Candies, 135

S

Salato Wildlife Education Center and Game
    Farm, 107
Salt Festival, 54
Sara Bush Johnston Lincoln Memorial, 30
sassafras tree, 207

Sawyer, E. P. "Tom," 19
Schmidt Museum of Coca-Cola
    Memorabilia, The, 29
Schneider's Sweet Shop, 65
Science Hill, 43
Shadow of the Buffalo Powwow, 50
Shaker Village of Pleasant Hill, 112
Shawnee Park, 14
Shelby County Flea Market, 43
Shelbyville, 43–44
Shelbyville/Shelby County Tourism
    Commission, 44
Sheltowee Trace National Recreation
    Trail, 136
Sheltowee Trace Outfitters, 157
Shepherdsville area, 27, 28
Shepherdsville Music Show, 28
Shepherdsville/Bullitt County Tourism, 28
Simon Kenton Harvest Festival, 71
Simon Kenton Shrine, 71
Singletary Center for the Arts, 87
Six Flags Kentucky Kingdom, 15
Skatepark in Woodland Park, 91
Slade, 131, 133
Slowpoke Farm, 27
Somerset/Monticello area, 161
Somer Splash Water Park, 161
South Union, 183
South Union Shaker Village, 183
Southern Kentucky Festival of Books, 177
Southern Lights, 81
Sparta, 52–53
Speed Art Museum and Art Sparks,
    The, 10–11
Speed, John and Lucy, 16
Springfield, 40–41
Springfield/Washington County Chamber
    of Commerce, 41
St. Joseph Proto Cathedral, 39
Stage One Children's Theatre, 5
Stained Glass Theater, 64
Standardbred Horse Farms, 43
Stanford, 118
State Capitol, 105
Stearns, 162–64

About the Author

A nearly lifelong Kentuckian, Teresa Day writes scripts for educational television programs and documentary videos. She began her writing career as a feature writer and newspaper editor. She currently manages an arts education project for Kentucky Educational Television. Previous travel credits include editing three editions of the Globe Pequot guidebook *Kentucky Off the Beaten Path.* Teresa lives near Georgetown, Kentucky, with her husband, Charlie, and their three children, Michael, Anthony, and Esta.